ADVERSE EVENTS

Adverse Events

Race, Inequality, and the Testing of
New Pharmaceuticals

Jill A. Fisher

NEW YORK UNIVERSITY PRESS

New York

NEW YORK UNIVERSITY PRESS
New York
www.nyupress.org

References to Internet websites (URLs) were accurate at the time of writing. Neither the author nor New York University Press is responsible for URLs that may have expired or changed since the manuscript was prepared.

Library of Congress Cataloging-in-Publication Data
Names: Fisher, Jill A., 1976–   author.
Title: Adverse events : race, inequality, and the testing of new pharmaceuticals /
Jill A. Fisher.
Description: New York : New York University Press, [2020] |
Includes bibliographical references and index.
Identifiers: LCCN 2019039473 | ISBN 9781479877997 (cloth) |
ISBN 9781479862160 (paperback) | ISBN 9781479861439 (ebook) |
ISBN 9781479850518 (ebook)
Subjects: LCSH: Drugs—Testing—Social aspects—United States. | Human experimentation in medicine—Moral and ethical aspects—United States. | Racism in medicine—United States. | Equality—Health aspects—United States.
Classification: LCC RM301.27 .F56 2020 | DDC 615.10973—dc23
LC record available at https://lccn.loc.gov/2019039473

New York University Press books are printed on acid-free paper, and their binding materials are chosen for strength and durability. We strive to use environmentally responsible suppliers and materials to the greatest extent possible in publishing our books.

Manufactured in the United States of America

10 9 8 7 6 5 4 3 2 1

Also available as an ebook

CONTENTS

LIST OF TABLES AND FIGURES

Introduction

"Your Health Is Your Wealth"

Imagine you've been asked to test the safety and tolerability of an experimental drug. To do so, you will consume either the drug or a placebo—an inert sugar pill—in a Phase I clinical trial.[1] You've been informed about the risks of the drug, and you've also been told there are no medical benefits of taking it. The only direct benefit to you of participating is that you will receive up to $5,175 for completing the study.[2] If you choose to enroll in the clinical trial, you must spend 20 consecutive nights literally locked in a research facility and then return for a final outpatient study visit. You won't be able to leave the facility once you check in unless you withdraw from the study. No one can visit you at the facility, and you will share a bedroom with several strangers. You will be told what to eat, when to eat, and when to sleep. You must submit to over 50 blood draws and other less invasive medical procedures and physical exams.

The reason you've been asked to participate in this clinical trial is that you've been deemed healthy. You're under 55 years of age, have a body mass index (BMI) categorizing you as healthy, have normal blood pressure, kidneys and a liver that are functioning well, and you do not use nicotine products or illicit drugs. You might think of the clinical trial as an opportunity to leverage your health as a type of commodity—income for you in exchange for data for a pharmaceutical company. But before you decide if you will participate, perhaps you need to know more.

What Are Phase I Trials?

Pharmaceutical research and development (R&D) progresses through multiple stages before a product is released to national markets.[3] Beginning with so-called bench science in laboratories and proceeding to safety and efficacy testing on nonhuman animals, the earliest stages of R&D aim to identify molecular entities that have the potential to treat or cure disease. Only when researchers deem those investigational compounds to be promising and reasonably safe can clinical testing—studies that enroll human subjects—begin. According to current industry norms (and regulated by national agencies such as the US Food and Drug Administration [FDA]), the testing of new pharmaceuticals in humans must begin with Phase I clinical trials to help establish the safety profiles of investigational drugs and set dose levels for future studies. Most, but not all, Phase I trials use healthy volunteers as research participants. Phase II studies enroll a small number of patients to gather additional safety data and provide preliminary evidence about the investigational drug's efficacy. In a sense, Phase II studies are like a proof-of-concept trial, allowing companies to assess whether the product is worth a larger-scale investment of time and resources. For those drugs that show sufficient promise, Phase III studies are designed to provide evidence of the product's efficacy by enrolling hundreds or thousands of patients as research participants.[4] With results from all three clinical trial phases, pharmaceutical companies can then seek approval to market their drugs. If approved, the FDA—or other countries' regulatory bodies—might also require post-marketing surveillance studies, called Phase IV trials, in order to have more safety or efficacy data about the product even as it is widely prescribed to patients. Given the complexity of the drug development process, a clinical trials industry consisting of companies that assist in the design, management, and analysis of these trials now exists and profits from pharmaceutical companies' efforts to get new drugs to market as quickly as possible (Fisher 2009; Mirowski 2011; Petryna 2009).[5]

This book focuses exclusively on Phase I clinical trials conducted on healthy volunteers.[6] In most therapeutic areas, healthy volunteers are the preferred research participants for these safety studies; however, terminally ill or disease-affected patients are also sometimes used. In lay terms, Phase I trials measure the bodily changes, or "adverse events" (AEs), that occur when research participants are given an investigational drug. Starting with small doses and increasing the number of milligrams over the course of a trial, investigators assess the tolerability of the drug as they seek to find a therapeutic dose without burdensome side effects. After administering an investigational drug to participants, researchers document all physiological changes that are captured by medical procedures as well as participants' self-reported symptoms. These changes can and do include a range of experiences that researchers suspect are not caused by the investigational drug, which is why the preferred term is "adverse event" rather than "adverse effect." AEs such as headaches or stomach upset are common occurrences, and they prove ambiguous with regard to causation. Researchers must then adjudicate, along with the pharmaceutical company sponsoring the trial, which adverse *events* are or could be actual adverse drug *effects*.

Given the goals of Phase I trials, the advantage of enrolling healthy participants over patients is three-fold. First, there is less ambiguity in the interpretation of AEs when there are no underlying illnesses that create symptoms in participants. Second, the risk of serious complications is diminished when participants have normal kidney and liver function and can withstand temporary impairment to these organs. Finally, and arguably most important, the recruitment of healthy volunteers tends to be very rapid, especially compared to studies requiring ill or diseased participants (e.g., Battelle 2015; Fisher 2007), and efficient recruitment helps to speed successful products through the development pipeline and onto the market.

Phase I trials are distinct from later-phase studies (i.e., Phase II, III, and IV trials) not only in the enrollment of healthy volunteers but also in the design of the study protocols. Phase I studies tend to be conducted in residential clinics that specialize in this type of research.[7] These studies are also shorter in length, lasting only several days or weeks compared to several months or years for later-phase trials, and they generally require participants to consent to a clinic confinement for some part of, if not the entire, study. The confinement period enables control of participants' diet and frequent collection of data about the investigational drugs, primarily through electrocardiograms (referred to as ECGs or EKGs) and blood and urine collection. For example, on the day a drug is administered, it is not unusual for the protocol to require ten or more blood draws during a 24-hour period. The confinement also helps to ensure that participants are reasonably safe during the study because the research staff can monitor them and intervene should any serious adverse event occur.

Will You Participate in the Trial?

As you consider whether to enroll, you might turn to the informed consent form for specific information about the study. You likely want to know what drug is being tested, what medical condition the drug is being developed to treat, and whether it is currently available on the market in any other form. You are probably also curious about the risks, notably what the drug's side effects are expected to be. The study you are considering includes in its consent form a list of potential risks that you might recognize as fairly typical for Phase I trials. They range from mild to severe: headaches, diarrhea, constipation, nausea, dizziness, skin reactions, allergic reactions, anemia, depression, liver problems, impaired kidney function, seizures, severe arrhythmias, and death. If you ask, the research staff will be quick to reassure you that no one in previous groups of the trial has experienced any severe or life-threatening reactions.

To make your decision, you might want to know more about the logistics of the study: what the specific dates of the confinement period are, what amenities the facility has, and what clinical personnel will be available to you. Most facilities are impeccably clean (though sometimes drab) and have professional and friendly research staff (though sometimes not equally skilled in venipuncture). The food may leave something to be desired, but all your meals will be prepared for you while you're there. There are also large-screen TVs, movies, video game consoles, computers, pool tables, books, and Wi-Fi to help occupy you during the downtime, which will be considerable during those 20 days in the clinic. Think of it as a vacation, albeit a strange one. Or if you'd prefer, think of it as a job because the countless restrictions—no caffeine, no exercise, no recreational eating—and the detailed regimen—especially the personalized daily schedule that specifies to the minute your "events" such as drug dosing, blood draws, and meals—will certainly remind you that your body is not completely your own while you are there.

You could be hesitant to enroll based on your assumptions about who else might be participating as healthy volunteers. You might wonder how similar to you the other participants will be. Perhaps you expect that Phase I trials are filled with students. You imagine they are young people transitioning to adulthood who need the financial boost that the study compensation provides, but this assumption would be incorrect. While students were historically the primary source of research participants at universities (Prescott 2002), they are not the usual pool of Phase I healthy volunteers.

Who Participates in Phase I Trials?

Men and racial minorities are the predominant Phase I trial participants. Study protocols frequently place restrictions on the participation of women of "childbearing potential," often excluding those who take hormonal contraceptives or requiring them to be surgically sterile (Corrigan 2002). Thus, the percentage of men is typically around 65–70 percent overall and can be 100 percent for particular studies (Chen et al. 2018). Phase I safety protocols provide an explanation for women's underrepresentation in these studies, but there is no parallel scientific reason for the *over*representation of minorities. Nonetheless, relative to the US population as a whole, blacks and Hispanics make up a disproportionate number of healthy volunteers, with roughly 60 percent coming from these two groups (Fisher and Kalbaugh 2011). This trend runs counter to national concerns about the underrepresentation of these groups in later-phase research (see Epstein 2007) and makes Phase I trials a key place to study minorities' participation in medical research.

To recruit healthy volunteers, clinics advertise by highlighting the financial compensation for participation. In general, the amount a study pays is tied to the length of the confinement, with an average rate of $200 to $250 per night dictating the total payment. Because all research participants have the right to withdraw from a study at any point for any reason, clinics incentivize healthy volunteers through so-called completion bonuses to finish the study. This means that participants who withdraw from a Phase I trial receive a pro-rated amount of $100 to $125 per night instead of the full $200 to $250, and the difference in total compensation is reserved for those who finish the trial. In other words, the compensation is used as both a recruitment and a retention tool.

Because the monetary compensation is the primary, if not sole, motivator to enroll as a healthy volunteer, the catalyst for Phase I participation is often financial need. Such need can be singular and related to a specific bill or purchase, or it can be the product of persistent economic insecurity. Just as adverse events occur within studies, so, too, they occur in participants' everyday lives and affect their financial status. Unemployment, bad credit, debt, and incarceration are adverse events that many in the US experience but that disproportionally affect men of color. In this context, clinical trials can be an attractive option for counteracting any temporary or sustained challenges to one's financial situation. Moreover, healthy individuals can enroll repeatedly in Phase I trials and gain a revenue stream to combat or hold at bay adverse life events when they are triggered.

As a result, the vast majority of healthy volunteers participate *serially* in clinical trials (Elliott 2008; Tishler and Bartholomae 2003), and those who enroll frequently can even be thought of as "professional" participants who earn their living in this way (Abadie 2010). Although these individuals depend financially on such studies, their ability to participate cannot be taken for granted. Some first-time participants underestimate the difficulty of getting into these studies, but the "veterans" know that qualifying for Phase I trials is not always easy. First, the availability of studies ebbs and flows, with some clinics seemingly having very few trials for weeks or months on end, followed by a wave of new studies. Second, ensuring that one's body chemistry and vital signs meet the inclusion-exclusion criteria for each study means that, at a minimum, healthy volunteers must maintain their weight, avoid taxing their bodies through exercise or stress, and try to be relaxed during blood pressure readings. Third, even if they match the protocol requirements, they must still be selected for the study. Participants might be invited to enroll based on who has the "best" lab values—such as measures of their blood levels or organ functioning—or on the order in which they screened or called in for their results. Finally, even if selected for a study, participation is not guaranteed. Clinics always overenroll healthy volunteers in each Phase I trial. If, for example, a study requires 12 participants, the clinic often brings in 16 with the expectation that it will dismiss four. The extra participants are referred to as "alternates," "backups," or "reserves." The clinics do this because they want to fill all their study spots for each group of healthy volunteers, and they have to ensure, first, that everyone who is selected to participate will actually check in on the day of the study and, second, that all those individuals will again pass all the required screening tests and remain eligible for the study. Healthy volunteers cannot rest easy that they are in the study until after they have "dosed" (i.e., taken the investigational drug or placebo). Together, these obstacles to participation mean that Phase I trials are a precarious source of income.

So-called professional participants try to improve their study chances through various tricks of the trade. They often develop relationships with recruiters and other research staff in the hopes that their good rapport will result in favoritism. Preferential treatment can manifest in terms of being selected for a specific trial or even being given information about upcoming studies so they can know when to call for a screening appointment. Professionals also frequent numerous clinics to increase their opportunities for studies. Indeed, some travel extensively around the country and are thus able to expound upon the virtues or drawbacks of clinics in Austin (Texas), Baltimore (Maryland), Los Angeles (California), Madison (Wisconsin), Daytona (Florida), Neptune (New Jersey), New Haven (Connecticut), and so on.

By enrolling at multiple clinics, serial participants can also choose to disregard the stipulated washout period between studies and maximize the amount of money they earn from Phase I trials. The washout period is the window of time—usually no shorter than 30 days—during which participants are not allowed to join a new study. Established as part of study protocols both for the safety of healthy volunteers and for the validity of clinical trial data, washout periods are difficult to enforce because there is no centralized registry of trial participants. Clinics keep track of their own study participants, but beyond that, they rely primarily on an honor system in which they ask healthy volunteers about the timing of their last clinical trial.[8] Because of the high density of Phase I facilities in some regions of the United States, even individuals who do not travel far for studies can ignore the washout period by rotating their participation between two or more clinics and providing false information about their trial history (Edelblute and Fisher 2015).

By disregarding the washout period between studies, healthy volunteers can enroll in a greater number of studies, but they might also be increasing their risk of harm. To counterbalance this danger as well as to enhance their health more generally, serial participants alter their health behaviors. Many quit smoking, stop using recreational illicit drugs, and abstain from alcohol. They also increase their consumption of vitamins and minerals, and they drink copious amounts of water to flush the investigational drugs out of their bodies. Health is not just something healthy volunteers have, but a precarious state that is affected by their behaviors and actions leading up to when they screen for studies. In short, *health is a commodity that must be produced* if serial participants want to continue to qualify for clinical trials. As one participant asserted, "Your health is your wealth," when you want to enroll in Phase I trials. Thus, for serial participants, a lot of time, energy, and even money must be invested to succeed at earning an income this way.

Serial participants' orientation to Phase I trials coupled with the confinement structure of the studies contribute to a community of healthy volunteers. Serial participants tend to be generous with information and inform new participants about their experiences. They also share information within their networks by sending text message tips about available studies, warning others about AEs to expect, and swapping advice about preparing one's body for the next study. At the same time, however, they can jealously guard information about studies to minimize competition. The mode is generally to take care of themselves first—secure that coveted spot in a screening lineup—and then help out fellow participants when they can.

Solidarity among healthy volunteers can also be understood in terms of the stigma associated with participation. Rather than talking about their participation in Phase I trials with family, friends, co-workers, or acquaintances in their everyday lives, many healthy volunteers keep their involvement in research a secret. This means that the primary people with whom healthy volunteers talk about clinical trials are other participants. By doing so, they simultaneously deepen their networks and their identities as Phase I participants.

Whom Would You Tell about Your Phase I Experiences?

If you did consent to participate in a clinical trial, how would you make sense of that activity? How would you feel about having tested an investigational drug? What would determine if it was a one-time occurrence or the start of a long-term career? Would it become a shameful part of what you had to do in order to make ends meet financially? Or, would it instead be a story that you told at parties to shock or amuse your friends or colleagues?

Most of us will never enroll in a Phase I trial. While many of us could use some extra money and some of us might even want to contribute to the development of safe and effective pharmaceuticals, we probably will not sign up for such a study. Perhaps our lives will not accommodate checking into a residential research clinic for a lengthy period of time; our jobs and families might be obstacles to participating even if we wanted to enroll. Perhaps we fear that we will be injured or harmed, that the risks of the experimental drug cannot be justified. Perhaps we simply cannot qualify for a study—we may be too sick, too old, too fat, or too female.

Framework for Analyzing Phase I Clinical Trials

The fact that Phase I participation is rare among us means that it remains an unknown yet stigmatized world, with healthy volunteers often derided as being human "guinea pigs" or "lab rats." This book explores that hidden world by going into six Phase I research facilities in the United States—two on the East Coast, two in the Midwest, and two on the West Coast—to make visible healthy volunteers' experiences of adverse events within and outside the research clinic. Drawing upon my ethnographic work, I describe my observations of Phase I clinical trials, giving voice to healthy volunteers' and clinic staff's perceptions of the research enterprise.[9]

At the same time, to demystify Phase I research requires analyses of healthy volunteers' social context *and* the social construction of the science undergirding these clinical trials. On one hand, individuals' decisions to enroll in trials as healthy volunteers are predominantly motivated by adverse life events that often accrue for those at the bottom of the social and economic hierarchy. On the other hand, the Phase I industry's reliance on serial participants to generate data on drug adverse events undermines the validity and generalizability of these critical safety trials. This is because serial participants' focus on qualifying for studies makes them more and more suitable for the controlled nature of Phase I trials and less and less representative of the general population.

This book argues that US Phase I trials are fundamentally built upon and shaped by social inequalities and that the resulting system exploits participants to make pharmaceutical products appear safer than they really are. To explicate each part of this broader argument, I develop two concepts: *imbricated stigma* and *the healthy volunteer as a model organism*. These two organizing concepts anchor this book's discussion of Phase I trials in micro- and macro-level phenomena because both focus on the individuals who enroll in Phase I trials as well as on the broader political and economic context for their participation. Additionally, both engage the human-guinea-pig label in different ways. The concept of imbricated stigma acknowledges the multiple forms of stigma to which healthy volunteers are subjected, including but not limited to the stigma of research participation, whereas the concept of the healthy volunteer as a model organism, with its reference to nonhuman animal research, elucidates how serial participation is a deliberate and indispensable part of Phase I science. This latter concept shifts the focus from healthy volunteers' personal motivations in order to query the norms of the profit-driven Phase I industry and the practices of research staff. While each concept performs important analytic work on its own, the book's argument can be rearticulated through their dual lenses: profound social inequalities manifesting in imbricated stigmas create the structure for healthy individuals to become human model organisms, restructuring their lives and behaviors in the service of the Phase I industry. While it may seem intuitive that Phase I trials' highly controlled environment bears little resemblance to real-world conditions, it is also the case that everyone involved—from the pharmaceutical companies sponsoring the studies, to the clinics conducting them and the healthy volunteers paid to participate—is incentivized to game the system in ways that ultimately generate validity concerns and may threaten public health. Developing these concepts below, I further define each of them and illustrate their value in analyzing healthy volunteers' participation in Phase I trials.

Locating and Theorizing Stigma in Phase I Participation

Medical research is deeply associated with images of guinea pigs and lab rats. These creatures are not only conjured to describe nonhuman animal research, but they are also used pejoratively to depict the role of human subjects in the research enterprise. The connotation of such terms is that participants are dehumanized by researchers: they are used like laboratory animals, cannot benefit, and will likely be harmed or even killed by the experiment. Moreover, there is often the implication that human subjects are being duped by researchers who do not tell them full and truthful information. Some may protest that this view of research does not share much in common with the majority of contemporary clinical trials, in which detailed (if not overwhelming) information is always provided about studies through the informed consent process and in which the possibility for therapeutic benefit is often present. Yet, the image of human lab animals still prevails and can be witnessed in the assertions of those who reject research participation by saying they do not want to be "guinea pigs."

The prevalence of this human-guinea-pig trope underscores the stigma associated with clinical trial participation. Medical research has long been associated with mad scientists, body snatchers, and other frightening scenarios (e.g., Kirby 2002; Lederer 1995; O'Neill 2006). The documented historical abuse of black participants in the US Public Health Service's infamous Tuskegee Syphilis Study fueled distrust of researchers, which has created a barrier to recruiting minority participants to therapeutic clinical trials and thereby denies these groups the prospect of gaining direct medical benefits (Corbie-Smith et al. 1999; Corbie-Smith, Thomas, and St. George 2002; Reverby 2000; Shavers-Hornaday et al. 1997).

While this stigma does not seem to prevent minorities from enrolling in Phase I trials, it nonetheless affects how healthy volunteers *experience* their participation, especially in how others perceive their involvement in research. This is all the truer for Phase I trials because healthy volunteers seek the financial reward of enrolling, not the potential for a cure for or the amelioration of a disease (motivations that have some credibility in explaining participation in later-phase clinical trials). Enrolling in research solely for money can signal to others that one's financial situation is dire—and dire enough to disregard one's health or personal welfare. Thus, within this frame, clinical trial participation as a healthy volunteer becomes a shameful act because only desperation would encourage someone to do it.

However, stigma surrounding Phase I participation is much more complex than what is suggested by its association with laboratory animals. Individual healthy volunteers are subject to multiple types of broader social stigmas that form the backdrop of their participation. In other words, healthy volunteers are typically already stigmatized in some capacity and face resulting forms of discrimination before they ever come to clinical trials. For some, it could be the stigma of being poor, being a racial minority, being an undocumented immigrant, and/or having been incarcerated. For others, it could be the stigma of being young, having limited education, being unemployed, and/or even being a political activist. These forms of stigma can be compounded, neutralized, or even mitigated by the stigma of being a research participant.

In his pivotal work on stigma, Erving Goffman (2009 [1963]) underscores that stigma is produced by social relationships in which some individuals are cast as "normals" whereas others are seen as tainted or discounted, having a "spoiled identity." The power of stigma is that it is a form of discrimination that reduces some individuals' life chances based on essentially arbitrary factors that mark those individuals as less than normal. Discrimination, however, requires recognition of the stigmatized other. Goffman illustrates that there are two forms of stigma: discredited and discreditable. *Discredited stigma* is that which is visible and observable. It could include visible markers of race, such as the color of someone's skin, or disability, such as use of a wheelchair. In contrast, *discreditable stigma* is not readily observable and relies on the transmission of information about an individual's identity, behaviors, or other characteristics. Because of the material effects of being stigmatized, individuals can attempt to "pass" by concealing discreditable stigmas from others. Goffman gives the examples of mental illness and homosexuality as forms of discreditable stigma that can be hidden so that the individual can pass as normal in society. Phase I trial participation would be another form of discreditable stigma. The challenge for those with such stigmas is to manage information about themselves so that they will not be subject to discrimination or loss of personal relationships. In some instances, Goffman argues, individuals might choose to reveal a less stigmatized part of their identities to mask the "real" stigma and pass as nearly normal.

To understand the multiple forms of stigma that healthy volunteers encounter as part of their lives within and outside the Phase I clinic, I propose the concept noted earlier of *imbricated stigma*.[10] "Imbrication" typically refers to the overlapping pattern dictating how tiles or shingles are laid to create a surface that is stronger, more impenetrable, and more durable for its staggered structure.[11] Thus, I define "imbricated stigma" as the myriad combined stigmas that individuals face by virtue of how they look, the activities in which they engage, or the identities they inhabit. When imbricated, the component stigmas retain their own ignominy or social disadvantage for the individual, but taken together, they reveal the broader pattern of profound, tenacious inequalities through which material resources are distributed unevenly throughout society. Individuals are subject to different patterns of imbrication based on their social address and life experiences. Some individuals are subject to numerous stigmas, whereas others are relatively privileged, being white or educated even if unemployed or poor. Thus, healthy volunteers as a group experience a range of stigmatized identities, with some of the component imbricated parts being more intractable and others more malleable.

Importantly, the effects of imbricated stigma are not solely repressive. While individuals themselves might face greater obstacles when fettered with multiple stigmas, they are not necessarily captive to these imposed stigmatized identities. Indeed, the more deeply imbricated the stigma, the more emboldened individuals might become to attempt creative solutions to combat their social disadvantage. This could include the decision to engage in another stigmatized activity, such as Phase I trial participation. For example, a young black man who is unemployed, never finished high school, and has a history of incarceration experiences imbricated stigma in the sense that each of these types of stigma can operate singly or in combination as he navigates his world. Like imbricated materials, the imbricated stigmas he experiences are obdurate, with race relations and economic opportunities highly resistant to change. In this context, the stigma of research participation can add one more form of judgment for him to face (perhaps from his family or friends), but a clinical trial can also relieve the stress of his other forms of stigma by providing an unparalleled economic opportunity that his history of incarceration, educational background, and skin color might routinely foreclose.[12]

Analyzing Phase I clinical trials through the lens of imbricated stigma helps to contextualize why individuals become involved in medical research and how, once enrolled, they perceive their study participation. Rather than seeing clinical trial participation as random and equally open to anyone in society, imbricated stigma focuses attention on the specific pattern of how and why certain segments of the US population are the most likely to enroll.[13] Groups with the most social disadvantages are the most likely to prioritize the benefits of participation over the risks. Participation rates bear this out, with minority men not only being overrepresented in Phase I trials more generally but also being more likely than non-Hispanic whites to become *long-term* serial participants. Specifically, of the 235 healthy volunteers in my sample, the six people who had participated in more than 50 clinical trials were black men, and more than a third of black healthy volunteers had participated in more than ten studies (29 out of 84 participants), a rate twice that of whites (15 out of 88).[14] Hispanic healthy volunteers were also typically serial participants, but they generally did not have the same long-term pattern of study enrollment. Indeed, nearly two-thirds were in their third through tenth study (30 out of 50 participants), and only two Hispanic participants had enrolled in more than ten studies. In contrast, the whites in my sample were in the majority only when it came to being *first-time* healthy volunteers—a circumstance that suggests that perhaps with no racial source of stigma, they were more likely to participate in clinical trials as a single-time event rather than a recurring activity.[15]

Beyond the numbers, I illustrate throughout this book how these patterns of participation are inflected *qualitatively* by different imbrications of stigma. In particular, healthy volunteers variously adopt or reject the identity of a research participant (or professional lab rat) based on how they see themselves and feel perceived by others in nonresearch contexts. Additionally, immigration politics play out in how healthy volunteers perceive each other on the West Coast, with non-Hispanic participants accusing Spanish-speaking immigrants of stealing study opportunities from "Americans." Imbricated stigma also affects healthy volunteers' and research staff's perceptions of how individuals engage information about the risk of clinical trials and their decisions to enroll in studies. Imbricated stigma thus creates a basis for judgment about who is well informed about and well suited to Phase I trials.

Analyzing Healthy Volunteers as Model Organisms

Returning to the image of the human guinea pig or lab rat, the metaphor might be especially apt for healthy volunteer clinical trials compared to later-phase trials on affected patients. The typical confinement structure of Phase I trials can be seen as simulating the laboratory conditions used for nonhuman animal research. Once inside the clinic, participants are subjected to a controlled environment and the specific trial protocol. Notably, these conditions are quite artificial compared to the so-called real world in which people can exercise and consume whatever foods and beverages they desire. Frequent medical procedures, such as collection of blood, urine, feces, and even cerebrospinal fluid, are performed

Additionally, the seriality of their Phase I participation positions the majority of healthy volunteers as a type of model organism. Having a pool of participants who are willing and able to adapt to the structure of Phase I trials is a critical element of the science. Healthy volunteers who enroll repeatedly in clinical trials might differ from the general population in their ability to tolerate investigational drugs or, more practically, the confinement period (Sibille et al. 1998). Serial healthy volunteers are self-selecting based on their prior experiences in trials, which are typically positive, otherwise they might choose not to enroll in subsequent trials. Just as laboratory-based researchers rely on a constant supply of nonhuman animals to continue their work, the Phase I industry as a whole depends on serial participants to fill the thousands of Phase I studies conducted each year. Without individuals who continue to enroll—regardless of how often each person actually participates—recruiting healthy volunteers would likely take much longer and trials would be more difficult to conduct.

Another way in which healthy volunteers become model organisms is a result of Phase I clinics' selection of individuals who have done prior studies with them. While I have referred to healthy volunteers with a history of enrolling in Phase I trials as "serial" participants, this moniker does not make distinctions based on which clinics those participants frequent. Whether someone participates solely at one clinic or travels to clinics all over the country, it is the regularity of their enrollment in trials that makes them serial participants. In contrast, the clinics describe healthy volunteers who have already completed studies with them as "repeat" participants. Research staff have strong preferences to enroll repeat participants because those healthy volunteers have already been vetted.[23] Repeat participants typically have a lower screen failure rate than the general public, are accustomed to the clinic and its rules, and are expected to complete the studies. In this way, repeat participants are known quantities from the point of view of the research staff, whereas prospective healthy volunteers with whom the staff have no direct personal experience are rogue variables and raise the question of how well suited to Phase I trials they might be. This privileging of repeat participants affirms their status as model organisms because clinics' supply of healthy volunteers is actively curated and relatively circumscribed.

An important benefit of analyzing the healthy volunteer as a type of model organism is that it places individuals' decisions about their participation in Phase I trials within the larger system of science. There has been much attention within the field of bioethics to the "subversive" character of serial participants,[24] but there is also a perverse tendency to blame the individuals who engage in deceptive practices, such as ignoring the washout period between studies. This position fails to question how the Phase I industry itself enables, and at times encourages, some serial participants' rule-breaking. I train my focus instead on how the research enterprise creates incentives and disincentives that structure the practices of everyone involved. The model organism framework places emphasis on the practices both of healthy volunteers *and* research staff.

Book Overview

By placing these two concepts—imbricated stigma and the healthy volunteer as a model organism—at the center of my analysis, my goal is to underscore both the social inequalities on which the research enterprise is built and the agency of individuals as they navigate their study participation within the structure of Phase I science. This is not a story about Big Bad Pharma, although it could be.[25] It is about how experiences of being a healthy volunteer are embedded in a larger social context, which is often characterized by discrimination and economic insecurity. The scientific context is also important because it necessitates that healthy volunteers submit to the controlled conditions dictated by the study protocols, and it rewards those who are best suited to the environment by selecting them for additional trials. While Phase I trials are not necessarily transformative experiences for healthy volunteers, participation in these studies can nonetheless disrupt traditional responses to stigmatizing conditions by offering a new, but potentially risky, mechanism to get ahead. Of course, Phase I trials do not guarantee healthy volunteers' success in reshaping their lives, but they do create an alternative economic pathway that, as the following chapters illustrate, includes not only risks but also important nonfinancial rewards.

To begin our journey into the world of Phase I research, chapter 1 provides ethnographic detail about entering and being confined to a clinic. It aims to create a sense of place by examining what one such clinic looks like and how it operates as well as the clinic's social world, including the camaraderie and conflicts among healthy volunteers. I also describe my methods, including how I gained access to the clinics, how much time I spent conducting this research, and demographic information about the research staff and healthy volunteers I interviewed.

Chapter 2 turns our attention to the economic motivations of healthy volunteers. Drawing upon the concept of imbricated stigma, I describe how individuals' social positions shape their view of Phase I trials. I examine not only the catalysts in their lives that lead to study enrollment but also how economic need, employment opportunities, and consumer culture influence how participants view the value of study compensation. There are, however, differences in the cultures of Phase I participation based on the region of the country. Chapter 3 focuses on this theme to further unpack variations in how patterns of imbricated stigma influence healthy volunteers' perceptions of Phase I trials, particularly with respect to the longevity of their study involvement.

Chapter 4 examines the Phase I clinics. I provide a brief history of the Phase I industry to contextualize the opportunistic nature of many of the clinics that are currently operating in the United States. Clinics' concerns about profitability and/or reputation lead to different investments in their facilities and staffing, which in turn result in a wide variation in experiences for healthy volunteers depending on where they enroll.

Turning attention to study protocols in chapter 5, I describe the highly controlled nature of Phase I trials and how research staff actively cultivate healthy volunteers as model organisms by conditioning them to the demands of the trials. These practices by research staff also raise important validity concerns about Phase I trials, which are analyzed in chapter 6, focusing particularly on how healthy volunteers, clinics, and the pharmaceutical industry are all incentivized to make investigational drugs appear safe.

A book on clinical trials would be incomplete without a discussion of risks. In chapter 7, I draw on secondary data about the safety of Phase I trials to discuss how research staff and healthy volunteers alike struggle to make sense of the omnipresent hypothetical risks of studies outlined in consent forms in the face of tangible evidence of the trials' relative safety. Healthy volunteers' construction of trials as safe is further enabled by their categorization of some studies as riskier than others. In chapter 8, I describe these risk constructions as a type of model organism epistemology, illustrating how this knowledge comes from personal experiences as well as stories and rumors they hear from other participants. Regardless of the veracity of their claims about risk, healthy volunteers mobilize this information about Phase I trials when deciding which studies to join and which to avoid.

Next, chapter 9 takes a different tack on the discussion of risk. While healthy volunteers are concerned about Phase I trial risks, they are often much more vocal about the economic risk of *not qualifying* for studies. This chapter examines how being disqualified from studies heightens their sense of risk as they attempt to earn income through clinical trials, which profoundly influences their health behaviors even outside of their study participation. These actions on the part of healthy volunteers indicate that Phase I participation could improve their general health even as they expose themselves to the unknown risks of investigational drugs.

Finally, the book's conclusion reflects on the political and economic context of US Phase I trials. A society characterized by deeply imbricated stigmas ensures that there will always be healthy volunteers willing to enroll in Phase I trials, whether these are the same or new participants who need the financial compensation. Ultimately, attending to the underlying social inequalities animating the Phase I industry is critical to understanding what is at stake when healthy volunteers are used in drug development.

1

Entering the Clinic

As I sat in the waiting room of Pharma Phase I, a pharmaceutical company's clinical pharmacology unit, my excitement turned to nervousness.[1] It was the first day of my field work, and I had no idea what to expect once I passed through the locked doors separating me from the clinic. It was late November 2009, and I was not the only one waiting to be admitted. When I arrived, there were already six other people there. Two African American men, two African American women, and two white men were grouped in those pairs around the room. They all wore visitor badges and had suitcases at their feet. The room was incredibly quiet, and when I caught one African American man's eye, he smiled anxiously. In that moment, I realized there was tension in the room; the others waiting were nervous too.

The director of operations had warned me by email that Pharma Phase I was a high-security building and my access would be restricted. A security guard searched my bag on arrival, and he confiscated my cellphone because of its built-in camera. Fortunately, my digital audio recorders raised no concern. It was not long before the director's assistant came for me, but as in other medical facilities, I was merely being moved to another place to wait. We quickly passed through the clinic's screening area, where research staff were setting up their workstations, and through another locked door into the administrative suite, where I was given a cubicle near the director's office. It was apparent how limited my movement through the building would be because everywhere was another set of locked doors that required a badge swipe to unlock. I looked around, curious to see something that would give me insight into the clinic's operation. Instead, I found only detailed instructions on what to do if someone phoned in a bomb threat. The security focus—especially the company's logoed "threat awareness" information for employees—brought home for me that a clinic owned and operated by a major pharmaceutical company had different concerns than a university or academic medical center.

It was another long 45 minutes before Gail, the director of operations, became available. A white woman in her forties, she introduced herself and greeted me warmly. Apologizing for my wait, she told me that the research staff were excited about my visit and that everyone would undoubtedly welcome me to shadow them as they worked. She added, "Our company values transparency, and opening our facility to a university researcher is a fun thing for us to do."[2] Gail had coordinated my two-week visit to occur when the clinic was conducting multiple trials, and she had a full house of healthy volunteers.

We set out on a tour of the building so I could see the space's layout and get an overview of the clinic's standard operating procedures (SOPs). The screening area had become a bustle of activity. Gail explained that the research staff were conducting check-in procedures for a new clinical trial. She named each staff member as she related how the screening area was divided into stations so that multiple healthy volunteers could be examined at once: an area for measuring height and weight, a phlebotomy station, beds for blood pressure and ECG readings, restrooms for urine samples to be collected, private rooms for any additional physical exams, and another waiting area. Gail suggested that I remain there to watch the intake procedures and to follow the participants to the study clinic afterward. She pointed out that my introduction to the residential part of the clinic could then be through the eyes of the healthy volunteers and the orientation they receive. Then she laughed, "Don't be surprised though if you're the only one who hasn't been here before!"

Surrounded by movement and activity, I momentarily had difficulty focusing on any one workstation. The ECG area eventually won my attention. Oddly, it was not being used in that moment to measure prospective participants' heartbeats. One of the African American women from the waiting room earlier that morning stood with Stephanie, a white staff member in her thirties, who emptied all the woman's personal belongings from her suitcase and placed them on one of the beds. When the bag was empty, Stephanie began picking each item up to inspect and return to the suitcase. There was also a large plastic bin to the side. The process was rapid for the woman's clothing, but when Stephanie got to the other items, she scrutinized them more carefully. Stephanie opened the woman's laptop and shook her books before putting them in the bag. Next, Stephanie grabbed a bottle of lotion; she turned to the woman and said, "You know you can't have this." The woman responded, "Well, I hoped I could. It's winter, and my skin is so ashy." Wordlessly, Stephanie took a large zip-top bag from the plastic bin. After writing the woman's study number on the bag, she placed the lotion in it and set it to the side. Finally, she told the woman, "You'll get it back when you check out. Make sure you ask for it. We probably have something in the clinic you can use for dry skin." The woman didn't respond, and Stephanie went back to inspecting the remaining items on the bed. Soon everything else was back in the suitcase. The plastic bag was zipped and placed in the bin. Stephanie instructed the woman to go to the waiting area until everyone was checked in. Stephanie put the repacked suitcase to the side with a few other bags that I then realized must have already been cleared.

As I watched Stephanie start to inspect the next participant's belongings, another staff member, a white woman in her early forties, came and stood next to me. She introduced herself as Erica and told me that as the recruiter, she was there to make sure check-in proceeded smoothly. I learned that, unlike many other research clinics, Pharma Phase I assigned recruiters to specific studies, making them responsible for managing all the participants from screening through check-in, to processing the study compensation. This role was more like a research coordinator at other clinics. Until Erica came over to me, she had been standing at a desk at the room's entrance, filing massive amounts of paper into different binders.

Although Erica was friendly, she was also clearly wary of me. She had approached me, it turned out, because she felt defensive about the bag checks and wanted to justify the process. She expounded on how critical these inspections were to the study's integrity and participants' safety by ensuring that only authorized items made it into the clinic. I asked how the participants knew what they were allowed to bring with them, and Erica went to get a copy of the "House Rules" document everyone received during their screening visit. It included a detailed list of acceptable and prohibited items. Evidently, the list had expanded dramatically over the years from items that were proscribed primarily for scientific reasons to sundry other types of things. For instance, participants were not allowed to bring any food, gum, or beverages. Of course, illicit drugs were banned, but prescription drugs and over-the-counter (OTC) medications were also prohibited (and participants would have already attested that they did not use any). More surprising, however, was that most cosmetic products were also banned because many contain alcohol and vitamins. Erica indicated that unless an item was in its original packaging and listed all its ingredients, it also would not make it into the study clinic. Over time, Pharma Phase I barred additional items for other participants' and research staff's safety and comfort. This included obvious prohibitions on weapons to an unexpected ban on CDs and DVDs that were not the original media. Pornography had been added to the list when a man had brought magazines that made the research staff uncomfortable. The primary—and most contentious—ban was on any devices with built-in cameras, most commonly cellphones and laptop computers.

Erica confessed that many prohibited items generated complaints from participants. The women, in particular, perceived the restrictions on beauty products as harsh and inconvenient. Yet, nothing compared to the protests staff received about camera phones. The rule existed mostly to protect participants' privacy, Erica explained, but it also safeguarded confidential corporate information. Erica could, however, relate to participants' frustration because the rule had also applied to research staff until just several months prior when senior administrators successfully argued that smartphones would increase the clinic's efficiency and improve communication. Given the prevalence of cellphones with built-in cameras, Erica noted that many participants felt persecuted by the rule and saw the clinic's ban on these devices as an injustice. Some of the regular participants had adapted to it, putting their current SIM card into an old cellphone when confined to Pharma Phase I and signaling their level of commitment to enrolling in clinical trials.

With the bag-search procedure justified, Erica returned to her workstation. The screening procedures had winded down; one participant was at the phlebotomy station and another was getting an ECG, but otherwise the rest of the clinic workspaces were empty. I joined seven participants in the waiting area. One woman talked to another about her anxiety about passing all the screening tests. One of the guys chimed in, "I *need* this study. I've already spent the money it pays!" Someone else made a joke, but remembering the tension I had felt in the first waiting room, I realized that the participants were nervous not because of any study risks but because of *the risk of being disqualified* from the clinical trial.

One of the white men introduced himself as Bob and bluntly asked, "Who are you? What's your story?" I detailed who I was and why I was there, emphasizing that I did not work for the clinic or pharmaceutical company and that I was a university professor. I then affably warned them I would hit them up for interviews in the coming days. They politely murmured acquiescence, and I added that they would receive a $20 Visa gift card for participating. A few of them then looked at me with more interest. At that moment, the participant who had been at the phlebotomy station arrived in the waiting room. Bob immediately turned to him and proclaimed, "James, this lady is here to interview us, and she's going to give us 20 bucks." The new arrival, an African American man in his twenties, paused to consider me, then came over and sat in the chair next to mine: "Okay, I'll go first."

Before I could respond, Erica showed up to announce that orientation would begin soon. She asked the participants to remind her if anyone had not done a study at Pharma Phase I before. Everyone was silent. After a moment, someone asked, "When are we getting lunch?" Erica's expression did not change a bit, "We'll get you guys into your rooms, then we'll do most of the orientation in the cafeteria while you eat." Another participant came into the waiting area, and Erica looked around as if to assess who else might be missing. James whispered to me, "Go ahead, ask me the questions." I told him it would be better to do the interview later when we had more time and privacy. He looked worried, so I let him know I would be around for two weeks, then asked how long he would be there. He laughed and replied, "I've got time. We're here 'til Christmas Eve eve." One of the women made an affirming sound and stressed, "We're here more than *three weeks*." At some point in this exchange, the final participant had slipped into the waiting room, making a total of ten healthy volunteers in this study group. Erica inquired again whether anyone was new to Pharma Phase I, but everyone had been there at least once before. Erica thanked them for being on time that morning and for making it easy to get through all the pre-study screening procedures quickly. It was now time to go to the clinic's residential space.

Erica guided us all down the hallway and through two more locked doors. Another staff member, Denise, had been waiting for the group. Denise, a white woman in her forties, was the nurse manager, and she had been charged with the study orientation. After welcoming the group, she informed them that lunch would begin in five minutes in the cafeteria. The participants' luggage was somehow in front of us, and Denise gestured to it and told the participants to take their bags to their assigned rooms, which were labeled with their study numbers. As the participants started to wander away, she announced that the women were in the three rooms closest to us and the men were on the opposite hallway. After they were gone, Denise turned to me, and as I opened my mouth to introduce myself, she stated, "You must be Jill." Clearly, the staff were well aware of my visit. With that, Erica took the opportunity to scan her badge at the locked door behind her and left us.

Several minutes later, the group had reassembled in the cafeteria. The room had a long wall of windows and was bright and airy. Dining tables reminiscent of a middle school, with their single attached stools, filled the room. Some counter-style seating lined the windows. Denise sat there on a high stool, with a stack of folded chocolate-brown t-shirts next to her. The participants were seated at the tables where plastic lunch trays had been set out. They had a sandwich, chips, apple, and one of a variety of different diet sodas. A few participants traded soda cans. I sat down on a stool a bit off to the side. Bob, the guy who had spoken to me first in the screening waiting room, yelled out to me, "Hey, why aren't you eating?" Before I could respond, Denise snapped, "Just eat your lunch. Worry about yourself, not Jill." At this, the participants all bowed their heads, looking down at the food on their trays.

Denise told them she would go over the study information while they ate. She emphasized that they should interrupt with questions because if they waited until the end, they would forget what they wanted to know. She picked up a consent form that had yellow highlighting marked sporadically throughout. The participants were enrolled in a drug-interaction trial that would investigate the effects of taking two drugs daily for 21 days. Both drugs were already on the market: one had been FDA approved for use in the United States; the other was available only in Europe. The study's scientific goal was to measure the drugs' pharmacokinetic interaction, or how the combined use of the drugs changed how they were absorbed, metabolized, and excreted. All participants would receive one dose of the FDA-approved drug each day. Half of the participants would receive three daily doses of the other drug while the other half would receive three daily doses of a placebo. The study was double-blind, so neither the research staff nor the participants would know who received the active drug or placebo. Denise also reviewed the number of blood draws and ECGs and read the schedule of physical exams and other medical evaluations.

Denise inquired whether the information sounded familiar, and most of the participants nodded in response. She stood up and distributed a t-shirt to each person, telling the group, "Your study color is brown. You must wear your t-shirt at all times. If you are cold and you want to put on a sweatshirt, you have to put your t-shirt on over it, on the outside. No exceptions. Clean t-shirts can be picked up at the nurses' station. If you want to get scrubs, you can pick those up there too. I want to see everyone in their t-shirts as soon as you are done with lunch." Stuart, a white participant in his early fifties, raised his hand, and Denise called on him by name. He wondered whether he had to finish his lunch because he did not want the chips. Denise replied that this meal was "not a procedure," so they could leave the chips on their tray but they could not have them later. She quickly added, "Starting tomorrow at breakfast, everything on your meal tray needs to be consumed, every pat of butter or drop of juice we give you. No exceptions."

Denise invited more questions before they dispersed. One of the African American women, Malia, asked when they would find out whether they were definitely in the study. Denise anticipated all the labs would be ready in a few hours and a physician would look at them before going home, meaning they should know by dinner who was "cleared to dose." Only eight of the participants would be admitted to the study, and two were alternates. The last two people to arrive at the clinic that morning were the alternates, which explained why so many had shown up well in advance of check-in and were in the first waiting room when I got there. Everyone was to stay overnight in the clinic, and the alternates would be discharged only after eight participants received their first dose of the study drugs. Wayne, an African American man in his late thirties, identified himself as an alternate and asked whether there would be other clinical trials they could do and still get paid by Christmas. Denise instructed him to check with Erica or another recruiter before he left if the study did not "use" him.

By that point, everyone had finished eating, and Denise gave them permission to leave the cafeteria. They got up, carrying their trays to the return window, and Denise hastily reminded them to put on their t-shirts. Turning to me, Denise offered to show me around the residential part of the clinic. The cafeteria was located at one end of the large clinic space. It had entrances on opposite sides of the room that led to two long parallel hallways. We walked down one of these corridors, and Denise pointed out that the building's exterior side was lined with bedrooms. Pharma Phase I could house fifty participants, and even though the occupancy varied considerably, that night all the beds would be full. Most of the doors were open, and I observed that the women's rooms contained two beds whereas the men's rooms mostly had four. The rooms were spartan and, much like hospital rooms, contained medical beds with monitoring equipment, a rolling table that hovered over each bed, and small nightstands. There were also televisions hanging from the ceiling in front of each bed. Some rooms had an armchair as well. Several participants had brought their own blankets and personalized their space with items from home.

On the other side of the hallway were the participant bathrooms and laundry facility. Denise pushed open the door to the women's bathroom and we entered. It was a large space with toilet stalls on one side, mirrors and sinks in the middle, and shower stalls on the third side. There were blow dryers set out on the counter and large hampers for towels, scrubs, and t-shirts. Denise requested I use only the staff restroom located in the nurses' station to maintain participants' privacy. The nurses' station was on the same side of the hallway and had large plate glass windows separating it from the rest of the clinic. There were doors into the nurses' station from both corridors, and I counted half a dozen staff sitting at computer terminals or talking with each other. There were binders and stacks of paper everywhere in the room. In the hallway under the plate glass window to the nurses' station, there was a small desk with a single telephone. Pharma Phase I had installed the landline for participants' use, enabling them to make free long-distance calls to anywhere in the United States, but it did not accept incoming calls.

As we continued walking down the corridor, I saw that the nurses' station was completely open on a third side. On this end were four phlebotomy stations. Three participants in chartreuse t-shirts sat in three of the stations, and a staff member drew blood from one. Facing this area and occupying the rest of the clinic's center space was the "procedure area" with rows of armchairs that reminded me somewhat of a movie theater. That impression was reinforced by the two massive televisions—one on either side of the entrance to the nurses' station—facing the chairs. Of course, unlike a movie theater, the armchairs had flip-up tabletops, and there were wheeled carts with monitors and other medical equipment between every other chair. Beds with ECG equipment, rather than armchairs, were lined up in the last row. The parallel hallways also met there, and one could quickly cross through the space to get to bedrooms on the other corridor. Participants were scattered throughout the room, some watching the televisions, some talking together, and others sleeping. I saw a rainbow of t-shirt colors: orange, green, pink, chartreuse, teal, and brown.

Denise ushered me to the very end of the hallway to the recreation room. It was a spacious corner room, lined with windows on two sides. It had another large television, a pool table, computer stations, and a smaller television connected to a video game console. There were cozy (nonmedical) armchairs lined up in front of the two televisions. When we entered, the room was full of activity. The large-screen television blasted *Jackass*, the reality show in which people engage in dangerous, gross, and largely stupid stunts and pranks. Participants slouched in the armchairs, talking and giving a running commentary on what was happening in the show.[3] A smaller group played Madden football on the game console. All the computers were occupied, with participants checking email, watching YouTube, and playing games such as FarmVille. The t-shirt colors varied, but it was striking to see that between the two rooms, almost every participant was a man and African American. The exceptions were an African American woman on a computer and a white man asleep in the procedure area.

The final stops on my clinic tour were the two medical examination rooms and the small library, which included books, magazines, and several comfortable chairs. The library was designated a quiet zone, but Denise admitted it was rarely used. She offered that I could conduct interviews in any of these last few rooms as long as I could relocate if someone else needed the space. She also invited me to the daily shift-change meetings at 2:00 PM when the morning staff provided the evening staff with study updates, such as adverse events that had occurred.

Denise glanced at her watch and noted that I still had plenty of time before that day's meeting, so I could get started with interviewing. She said, "I'll leave you to it" and walked briskly to the nurses' station. Suddenly alone, I slowly walked through the procedure area, debating whether to approach some participants at random to tell them about my study. Before I had firmed up my resolve, Bob—wearing his brown t-shirt—comically raced toward me bellowing, "I'm ready for my interview!"

Project Methods

The most difficult part of this project was obtaining access to field sites. Phase I facilities can be thought of as guarded organizations (see Monahan and Fisher 2015b). Many places I contacted were concerned about the possibility of an outsider coming in to write an exposé about their practices, especially given how ethically fraught human-subject research can be.[4] Adding to the challenge of gaining entry to these clinics was my intention to vary my sample by geographic location and organization type. At the project's outset, I did not yet know that the majority of healthy volunteers were racial and ethnic minorities, but I wanted to include clinics across the country to see what demographic differences might emerge. Additionally, my previous research on the clinical trials industry (Fisher 2009) alerted me to the different players involved in Phase I research. I knew that academic medical centers, pharmaceutical companies, contract research organizations, and independent, for-profit research clinics all conducted healthy volunteer trials, and it seemed important to appraise how these organizations might operate differently. To gain access to Phase I clinics, I had to make a lot of cold calls, send emails, and remain persistent. I explained to each contact not only what I wanted to do and why but also what my research was not trying to do. Many were open to participating in this project, but there were also personnel whose suspicion about my intentions was unassuageable.

In the end, I selected six clinics in which to do field work in 2009 and 2010, with two on the East Coast, two in the Midwest, and two on the West Coast.[5] All facilities were dedicated to Phase I research, but some conducted trials that enrolled both healthy volunteers and affected patients, such as people with diabetes or hypertension. These clinics included one pharmaceutical company ("Pharma Phase I"), one academic medical center ("Academic Phase I"), two international contract research organizations ("CRO Phase I" and "Mega Phase I"), and two local, for-profit research clinics ("Cottage Phase I" and "Local Phase I"). The clinics' capacity ranged from 16 to 300 beds (mean = 94; median = 58), and they were situated in a variety of buildings, including a hospital, in a corporate office park, or freestanding. I keep the identities of the clinics and their research staff confidential, and all healthy volunteers participated in my study anonymously, meaning I neither collected nor recorded their names.[6] To maintain confidentiality, I have masked some details about the clinics' exact size, configuration, and location. Notably, industry changes, such as closures and corporate restructuring, affected some of these and other Phase I clinics since my field work.

My time at each clinic varied based on its schedule of active Phase I trials, but it was also affected by research staff's openness to being observed as well as their misperceptions about how long qualitative research should take. In sum, I spent 38 days and clocked about 450 hours in the six clinics, with my shortest visit lasting two days and the longest 14 days (mean = 6; median = 4.5). My typical research day began at 8:00 AM and concluded around 7:00 PM. On mornings with important dosing protocols or study procedures, I arrived at the clinic by 6:00 AM. Likewise, some evenings were also busy, and I stayed until after 9:00 PM to observe all the day's events or use the quieter clinic time to conduct interviews. As is typical with ethnographic methods, I simply made myself available while I was in the field, and I adapted to the clinics' schedules.

I used both formal and informal strategies for my clinic observations. Formal observations occurred during structured activities, such as sitting in on consent and screening processes, watching healthy volunteers receive drug doses and medical procedures, listening to the staff hand off information at shift changes, and participating in clinics' "client tours" when administrative staff pitched their services to prospective pharmaceutical company clients. The informal portion of my observations usually occurred during clinic downtime, when there were few procedures or other study-related activities taking place. During these times, I often simply hung out with healthy volunteers while they ate meals, played games, and watched television. In other cases, I focused on the research staff by spending time in the nurses' stations or in break rooms. During all my observations, I had countless conversations with staff and healthy volunteers in which they candidly told me about their Phase I trial experiences. For better or worse (Monahan and Fisher 2010), I was quite visible within the clinics, and staff and healthy volunteers were often aware of my presence and interacted with me as an outside observer.

Additionally, I conducted a total of 268 semistructured interviews with research staff and healthy volunteers across the six clinics. Thirty-three interviews were with research staff and included administrators, physicians (investigators), nurses, phlebotomists, project managers, and recruiters.[7] I followed a general interview guide about clinical trial work, but I adapted questions to tap into each staff member's expertise and job responsibilities. In addition, I asked staff about their perceptions of the healthy volunteers, including questions about how well informed they thought participants were about Phase I trial risks. Staff interviews ranged from ten to 105 minutes, with an average of 44 minutes per interview.

I also interviewed 235 healthy volunteers who were either enrolled in or screening for a Phase I trial.[8] I designed the interview guide to solicit information about participants' Phase I experiences; their motivations to enroll in studies; their perceptions of the risks and benefits; their perceptions of the clinics, research staff, and other volunteers; and their families' and friends' perceptions of their clinical trial involvement. These interviews serendipitously gave me "indirect access" to other Phase I clinics (see Monahan and Fisher 2015b). Even though not all the clinics I contacted granted me access, nor could I visit all those that did, healthy volunteers routinely circulated among different clinics, including all of those that refused my request. As a result, the healthy volunteers themselves elucidated how the clinics differed and provided insights into why certain clinics might have been more reticent to have an ethnographer in their midst. Based on healthy volunteers' stories, I gather that I was denied access to some of the "worst" Phase I clinics, but I was also barred from some reputed to be exceptionally good.

I invited all healthy volunteers I met in the clinics to participate in an interview, and approximately 95 percent consented. I attribute the high response rate to the combination of interest in my project that most volunteers expressed, boredom while they were in the clinics, and the $20 Visa gift card they received for participating. The interviews ranged from five to 100 minutes, with an average of 17 minutes per interview. Interview lengths varied in part because the duration was controlled by the participant,[9] but also because healthy volunteers who were relatively new to clinical trials had fewer examples and experiences to report. Additionally, there were regional differences in the interview lengths, with the average interview with East Coast participants lasting 25 minutes compared to 12.5 minutes and 15 minutes with Midwestern and West Coast participants, respectively. These regional differences reflect the fact that the most experienced healthy volunteers participated in the Northeast and the most inexperienced lived in the Midwest.

My sample of healthy volunteers was quite diverse and broadly representative of the population of people who participate in US Phase I trials (Fisher and Kalbaugh 2011; Grady et al. 2017). Healthy volunteers are predominantly men, and 73 percent of my sample were men. Although participants' racial and ethnic backgrounds varied by clinic and region of the United States (tables 1.1a, 1.1b, 1.1c), my overall sample included 37 percent non-Hispanic white, 35 percent African American or black, 22 percent Hispanic, 4 percent Asian, and 1 percent Native American participants. Individuals ranged in age from 18 to 74, but the majority were in their twenties (29 percent), thirties (31 percent), or forties (20 percent).[10] Their Phase I trial experience also varied widely, with some enrolled in their first study and one participant estimating he had completed 100 studies (mean = 7; median = 3). As noted earlier, African Americans were the most likely to be long-term serial participants, and non-Hispanic whites were overrepresented among first-time participants—a difference that indicates a more profound disparity in which groups of healthy volunteers are the most likely to rely on Phase I trials for income (see figures 1.1a, 1.1b, and 1.2).

TABLE 1.1A: Demographics of All Healthy Volunteers and by
East Coast Clinics

Clinic Pseudonym	All Clinics	Pharma Phase I	Academic Phase I
Location	US	East Coast	East Coast
Total Participants	235	42	29
Sex			
Male (n)	73.2% (172)	88.1% (37)	79.3% (23)
Female (n)	26.8% (63)	11.9% (5)	20.7% (6)
Race/Ethnicity			
White, non-Hispanic (n)	37.4% (88)	19.0% (8)	17.2% (5)
White, Hispanic (n)	20.9% (49)	4.8% (2)	0% (0)
Black (n)	35.7% (84)	61.9% (26)	82.8% (24)
Asian (n)	3.8% (9)	11.9% (5)	0% (0)
Native American (n)	0.9% (2)	0% (0)	0% (0)
Multiracial (n)	1.3% (3)	2.4% (1)	0% (0)
Immigrants	23.4% (55)	21.4% (9)	0% (0)
Age			
18–19 (n)	0.4% (1)	0% (0)	0% (0)
20s (n)	28.9% (68)	33.3% (14)	27.6% (8)
30s (n)	31.1% (73)	38.1% (16)	34.5% (10)
40s (n)	20.4% (48)	21.4% (9)	37.9% (11)
50s (n)	9.8% (23)	7.1% (3)	0% (0)
60s (n)	8.5% (20)	0% (0)	0% (0)
70s (n)	0.9% (2)	0% (0)	0% (0)
First-time participants (n)	30.6% (72)	11.9% (5)	17.2% (5)

TABLE 1.1B: Demographics of Healthy Volunteers by Midwest Clinics

Clinic Pseudonym	CRO Phase I	Cottage Phase I
Location	Midwest	Midwest
Total Participants	36	46
Sex		
Male (n)	75.0% (27)	52.2% (24)
Female (n)	25.0% (9)	47.8% (22)

TABLE 1.1B: (cont.)

Race/Ethnicity		
White, non-Hispanic (n)	44.4% (16)	78.3% (36)
White, Hispanic (n)	0% (0)	0% (0)
Black (n)	52.8% (19)	17.4% (8)
Asian (n)	0% (0)	4.3% (2)
Native American (n)	0% (0)	0% (0)
Multiracial (n)	2.8% (1)	0% (0)
Immigrants	0% (0)	2.2 (1)
Age		
18–19 (n)	2.8% (1)	0% (0)
20s (n)	30.6% (11)	37.0% (17)
30s (n)	27.8% (10)	17.4% (8)
40s (n)	13.9% (5)	23.9% (11)
50s (n)	0% (0)	19.6% (9)
60s (n)	25.0% (9)	2.2% (1)
70s (n)	0% (0)	0% (0)
First-time participants (n)	72.2% (26)	32.6% (15)

TABLE 1.1C: Demographics of Healthy Volunteers by West Coast Clinics

Clinic Pseudonym	Local Phase I	Mega Phase I
Location	West Coast	West Coast
Total Participants	47	35
Sex		
Male (n)	74.5% (35)	74.3% (26)
Female (n)	25.5% (12)	25.7% (9)
Race/Ethnicity		
White, non-Hispanic (n)	38.3% (18)	14.3% (5)
White, Hispanic (n)	44.9% (21)	74.3% (26)
Black (n)	10.6% (5)	5.7% (2)
Asian (n)	2.1% (1)	2.9% (1)
Native American (n)	2.1% (1)	2.9% (1)
Multiracial (n)	2.1% (1)	0% (0)
Immigrants	40.4% (19)	74.3% (26)

Age		
18–19 (n)	0% (0)	0% (0)
20s (n)	25.5% (12)	17.1% (6)
30s (n)	19.1% (9)	57.1% (20)
40s (n)	10.6% (5)	20.0% (7)
50s (n)	19.1% (9)	5.7% (2)
60s (n)	21.3% (10)	0% (0)
70s (n)	4.3% (2)	0% (0)
First-time participants (n)	38.3% (18)	8.6% (3)

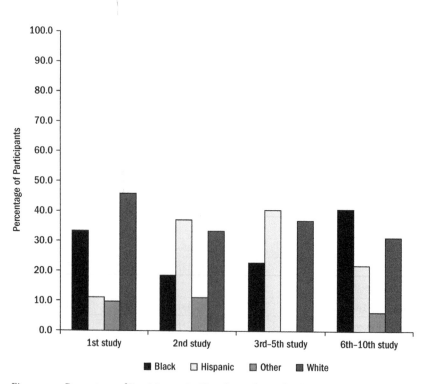

Figure 1.1a: Percentage of Participants in First through Tenth Clinical Trial by Race/Ethnicity

This information about my sample of healthy volunteers provides insight into whom I met while visiting the six research clinics. However, it conveys little about what it might be like to be locked into a research facility with strangers. Due to the confinement structure, Phase I trials create their own social world. This is an important aspect of healthy volunteers' clinical trial experiences, and it shapes both their perceptions of each other and their interest in enrolling in subsequent trials.

The Social World of the Clinic

At all the clinics I visited, I observed groups of healthy volunteers hanging out together, playing video games, and watching television. For

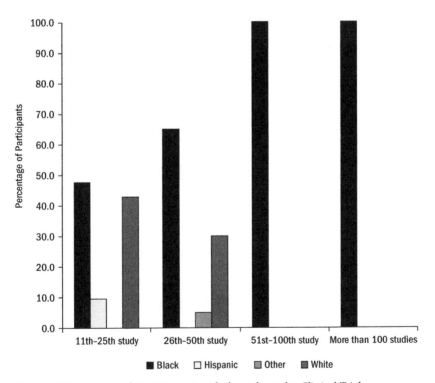

Figure 1.1b: Percentage of Participants in 11th through 100th+ Clinical Trial by Race/Ethnicity

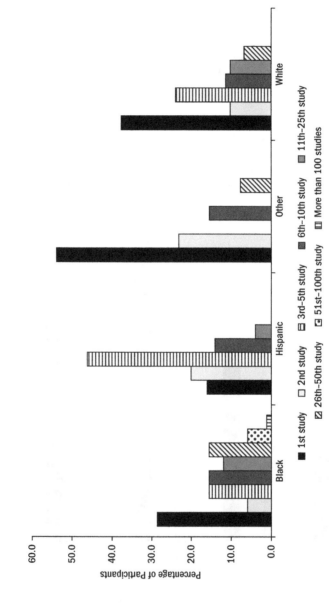

Figure 1.2: Percentage of Clinical Trial Experience by Race/Ethnicity

many, the time they spent with other participants was an unexpected pleasure. Studies' confinement structure has scientific goals, but it also creates a world within which strangers are brought together for 24 hours a day for days or weeks at a time to share a common space. Like other intensive group experiences, such as prison or military service (Lerman 2013; Ward 2016), this time together, even for short studies, can quickly bond participants or put them at odds.[11] Healthy volunteers share the extraordinary experience of being dosed with investigational drugs, poked and prodded over the course of the study, and sometimes stricken by the same adverse medical events. Indeed, suffering together—even if it is simply through blood draws and bad food—and the limited privacy in the clinics encourage fellowship among healthy volunteers.[12] Not only do relationships form within a single clinical trial, but participants might also meet the same study friends in subsequent trials.

Healthy volunteers often described these relationships as meaningful to them, even though they were largely temporally and spatially bound to specific clinical trials. Many men, especially those older than 35, noted the difficulty of making friends as an adult,[13] and they enjoyed the Phase I clinics' social atmosphere because they could hang out with and get to know other men. This was certainly true for Brian, a white serial participant in his mid-fifties. He declared, "The thing I like about 'em [clinical trials] is it's almost like being back in college at the frat house. It's that camaraderie, 'cause I don't know a lot of people [outside of studies]. . . . I had my business, and then when that went away, then all of a sudden you're sitting there finding that you don't really have any friends. . . . So I actually enjoy it when I go to these [study] places." Like many other participants, Brian felt as though close relationships were absent in his "real" life and the camaraderie of studies provided the opportunity for earnest, even if fleeting, friendships.

Most of these relationships never crossed over into healthy volunteers' outside lives, but there were the occasional exceptions to the rule. One of the more common relationships that carried on past the study was when participants found they had a romantic interest in one another. Several described dating someone from a Phase I trial. For instance, Tia, an African American woman in her early thirties who had participated in more than 35 studies, was in a committed relationship with a man she had met in a study. She related how initially their friendship had consisted of watching movies or playing cards together when they were at the same clinic. After several such experiences, they started to see each other outside of the clinic and embarked on a "real" relationship. Similarly, for a few long-term serial participants, friendships they had made in studies became their central social network. Ken, an African American man in his late thirties, had started enrolling in studies in 1990 and regularly participated throughout the country. Thinking about the extent to which his life revolved around studies, he asserted, "I've met my best friends in here [study clinics], compared to people I know back at home, because we [participants] have things in common and we share some of the same interests."

Thus, a typical day in the clinic is characterized by healthy volunteers' camaraderie, and most participants get along well with each other. However, the length of the confinement plays an important role in the social dynamics, with tensions more likely to foment in longer clinical trials as a type of study fatigue—missing home and losing patience with the environment's artificiality—sets in. When this happens, even minor annoyances can cause heated disputes. Sharing the Phase I clinic space certainly provides healthy volunteers with many opportunities to act egocentrically and show disregard for other participants. This can occur in myriad ways, ranging from monopolizing the television to not using headphones to listen to music or videos, turning on bedroom lights at night, or talking too loudly on the phone at all hours of the day and night. Other times, it is participants' religious or political views that raise consternation in their fellow volunteers. Specifically, some complained that during studies Christian missionaries wanted to convert them or save their souls, anti-Semitic individuals made offensive remarks, people on both sides of the political spectrum made unwelcome comments about Republicans and Democrats, and East Coast clinical trial "activists" tried to organize participants for collective action.

In order to minimize conflict, the clinics I visited had instituted rules to structure healthy volunteers' interactions and incentivize good behavior. Fighting, both verbal and physical, was generally considered an actionable offense that could result in participants' removal from a clinical trial, which would then reduce their compensation to a prorated amount and make them ineligible for the study completion bonus. The clinics also had other rules to help participants coexist, such as prohibitions on offensive language, television sign-up sheets, limitations on computer or game console time, and mandatory "quiet" hours in the evening. Although these rules could never guarantee a peaceful atmosphere, they minimized some behaviors that could trigger disputes. The potential loss of the stipend—the primary, if not sole, reason they had enrolled in a clinical trial—certainly structured participants' interactions.

Trouble at Pharma Phase I

One day during my visit to Pharma Phase I was exceptionally quiet. There were fewer healthy volunteers in the clinic because participants had been discharged from a few of the studies that had been in-house when I first arrived. It was also a slower day; there were few procedures scheduled, so there was generally less activity in the clinic. I joined the dozen participants gathered in the recreation room. Most were watching television, which was broadcasting Fox News' coverage of golfer Tiger Woods' marital infidelity.

The news commentators announced that some of Tiger's sponsors had canceled his promotional contracts. The assembled participants—all of whom were men—began to discuss whether the companies should have dropped Tiger. James asserted that the morals clause in Tiger's contracts was bullshit because nobody cared that he cheated on his wife. However, Bennett, an African American in his late twenties, protested that the sponsors were right. Bennett stood behind the cluster of armchairs, and it would have been impossible to deny the mischievous look on his face. He dramatically pronounced, "My heart is broken that Tiger is not the man I thought he was!" Amid the other participants' vociferous protests, Bennett just laid it on thicker and thicker, seemingly enjoying his contrary position. He professed that as an African American man, he was disappointed in Tiger because he wanted a black role model who would show him how to be successful and rich *and* moral. To put his unpopular defense of Tiger's sponsors over the top, he declared he would buy some Gatorade as soon as he got out of Pharma Phase I to show his appreciation for the company's principled stance.

It suddenly felt like the temperature in the room had heated up a few degrees. Many of the other participants were truly angry that Bennett had taken the corporations' side over Tiger Woods', a minority man who had taken the world by storm when he became one of the highest-paid athletes of his time and revitalized public interest in golf as a sport (Badenhausen 2009). Some participants debated Bennett, and a few left the room, perhaps believing the situation could lead only to trouble and not wanting to be there when it happened. Bob tried to defuse the situation: "Look at him, he doesn't believe what he's saying! He thinks it's funny that you're all getting so upset." That prompted Bennett to protest more, insisting he was entitled to his opinion, especially since he was right.

The tension was palpable. Voices were raised, and some participants had stood up combatively. Responding to the audible chaos, Josh, a white research tech and former paramedic, appeared in the doorway and whistled to get everyone's attention. Silence fell over the room immediately. Reminding them that Pharma Phase I prohibited fighting, Josh asked if everyone really wanted their study payments docked by $150. Bennett innocently left the recreation room while Bob changed the television channel, declaring, voice thick with irony, "This is now a Tiger-free zone." Some of the other men laughed, and everyone settled back down in his chair. James wondered out loud what was wrong with Bennett, and Bob quickly shut the comment down. It took another ten minutes or so for the agitation in the room to fully dissipate.

Despite how well groups of healthy volunteers typically get along, clinic stays can generate friction. The incident with Tiger Woods demonstrates how a difference of opinion—especially when coupled with a little bit of mischief—has the potential to spark arguments and frustration. Minor annoyances certainly add up for anyone, especially in lengthy studies, but some groups of participants get marked as those who strain normal levels of tolerance through patterns of unwelcome behavior. Beyond individuals who might instigate conflict, healthy volunteers' assumptions about each other also mediate their social interactions.

Stigmatized Social Relations

Beneath the surface of bonding and friendship, healthy volunteers confront a host of mainstream racial, ethnic, and gender biases that must be managed in the Phase I clinic. On one hand, this includes the experience of non-Hispanic white participants who might find themselves in the unaccustomed position of being in the numerical minority. The interactions they have with other participants often illustrate how they stigmatize non-white groups or use offensive labels. On the other hand, there are more conventional instances of gender- and sexuality-based vulnerabilities that occur as a result of the confined clinic space. Participants' recounted experiences of these stigmatized social relations were not always because of biased individuals, but rather because societal norms and values structured how different groups could interact within the clinic.

Ironically, white healthy volunteers' prejudices often manifested through their surprise that racially and ethnically different participants *could* get along so well. For example, when I met Hank, a white man in his late thirties, he was at CRO Phase I in his first clinical trial. The friendships he had made during the study amazed him because "for the different type of the ethnics that are here, everybody gelled. . . . 'Cause you would think with the people that we have here, you wouldn't think they'd gel as well as we did." White participants often reflected explicitly on how being in a clinical trial with other groups proved some of their assumptions about those groups had been wrong. Herbert, a white man in his seventies, remarked that the "coloreds" and "illegals" he had met in studies at Local Phase I impressed him; to see that the right people were rewarded for their hard work compared to the "awful lot of lazy people here [in this country]" made him "feel good about America." While oftentimes offensive, comments like these were well-meaning. Either way, what they primarily revealed was white participants' relief that the experience of different racial and ethnic groups had defied their initial apprehensions.

In contrast, minority participants from marginalized groups did not wax poetic about these positive interactions. For the sake of the group, they also had to abide any microaggressions to which they were subjected, just as they might in everyday life. Moreover, negative comments directed at minority participants further demonstrated how social stigmas can be attached to them by other demographic groups. This manifested in how young black men, in particular, were widely perceived as unruly participants. Older participants (i.e., typically those who were 30 and above) used words such as "restless," "active," and "loud" to describe these younger men, and some argued that they should be spared sharing a space with young participants who act discourteously. Mikhail, a white man in his forties who had emigrated from Russia, articulated this more explicitly than others. Mikhail insisted that to get through a clinical trial, healthy volunteers must be capable of interacting with people from groups they do not like:

> I mean if you're a certain person that only feels comfortable to be around prescribed and defined social atmospheres, you have to suspend those criteria and be more open toward just about, you know, any type of person that can be. Because there are just a tremendous variety of people [in the clinic] and not always to the benefit of your *choice* of the type of people you want to be around. Quite, quite often people come from marginal segments of society, and . . . you have to socially interact here because you'll come into moments of sharing the same resources, you'll have to shower in the same facility. . . . So, you have to also be withstanding of things [i.e., tolerant] and have manners, you know, etiquette, and that can be trying on a long-term basis if you have to stick around for 20 days.

In other words, from Mikhail's perspective, white people like him must have high levels of tolerance because these racially and ethnically coded "marginal" participants fail to behave the way more civilized society would expect or desire. Problematic as it is, Mikhail's framing is also noteworthy because it places the burden of responsibility on him to get along in the face of these challenges (as well as giving him the credit for doing so).

Most criticisms of other participants are cast as annoyances, but some healthy volunteers are also perceived as threatening. Or, perhaps more aptly, participants who are in the numerical minority often identify individuals who make them feel unsafe during confinement. This is especially the case for women and sexual minorities who feel as though they are the target of unwanted attention from heterosexual men. These concerns about other participants also shape the social world of the clinic.

Because Phase I studies are filled predominantly by men, it is not uncommon for only a handful of women to be present in the clinic at the same time. When the space can accommodate it, most clinics make bed assignments based on biological sex. Women largely preferred this and expressed dismay when clinics did not do so. For example, Michelle, an African American woman in her thirties, had just come from a clinic where all participants shared a single dormitory-style bedroom. Michelle had been surprised by this arrangement, remarking, "It was like twenty guys and it was only like four or five girls. So, you know, you just try to—, I just stayed closer to them [that is, the other girls], even if it is just a few of them."

Being in the numerical minority does not necessarily constitute a threat. Women, however, might feel vulnerable when they are marked as potential romantic or sexual objects. Younger women were more likely to be viewed in this light by heterosexual men of all ages. Consequently, many women feel unsafe, especially when men go too far with their interest in them. This was one of Sarah's complaints about the clinic confinement. Sarah, a white woman in her early twenties, noted that there are typically a few men who seem determined to hook up with the women in studies. She had been the target of persistent, unwanted flirting, but another participant had a worse experience. She remembered, "The last study I was in [at Cottage Phase I], there was this one guy who wouldn't leave my roommate alone. . . . He was way older than her, and it was just creepy to the point where he'd like be outside our door." These experiences can have a chilling effect on women, making them feel as though it is their responsibility to send men the "right" signals or to remove themselves entirely from larger co-ed groups.

Importantly, women's actual behavior rarely triggers these problematic gender dynamics.[14] Instead, men's interactions with women can be infused with bold displays of heterosexual masculinity. This was the case with a group of men hanging out together at Pharma Phase I. To my astonishment—though also true to cliché—much of their conversation consisted of sexist jokes, discussions about women's bodies, and debates about the pros and cons of different high-end cars. One of the men was Dwayne, an African American man in his late thirties who had participated in roughly 25 studies. His primary work was as a personal trainer, and he looked the part. Throughout my interview with Dwayne, he performed his masculinity by underscoring his avoidance of any investigational drugs that could negatively affect his sexual drive. He also insisted that healthy volunteers' value to science is so high that "I should have hors d'oeuvres coming to me, lap dances, you know, stuff like that." For women, this masculine environment might be experienced as hostile—a feeling further compounded by the fact that they cannot leave and must sleep in the clinic.

If women feel vulnerable in Phase I clinics due to their small numbers, then gender and sexual minorities might feel even more at risk. Bedroom assignments by biological sex are appropriate for many participants. However, some participants' safety might actually be compromised by classifying them based on their genitalia or chromosomes. One compelling example of this is when transgendered healthy volunteers enroll in Phase I trials. I met Alexandra, a white transwoman in her forties who had participated in about a dozen studies, at Pharma Phase I. She had long hair and presented as a woman, but from the clinic perspective, Alexandra was male and always assigned to a room with male participants. She accepted that she could not fully claim her identity in these spaces, but she indicated that she had to adhere to a certain comportment during studies: "Keep your business to yourself and not to be kind of, you know, in, in-, you know, like not to be in people's faces and kind of try to get on with everyone."

Additionally, homophobic remarks were not altogether uncommon in the clinic, indicating the extent to which homosexuality continues to be stigmatized. For example, in the interview I conducted with Bennett before the Tiger Woods incident, he mentioned he tried to conceal his homosexuality from other participants. He felt the stakes were high, saying, "I've been persecuted. I've been attacked. I've been verbally attacked. . . . Anything that you could possibly think of that you could do in a social setting has pretty much happened to me in here, and it's just like, you are in a closed quarters with these people." Bennett likely did not fully succeed at hiding his sexual identity. During my interview with Bob, who later tried to defuse the Tiger Woods situation with humor, Bob got so distracted mid-interview when he saw Bennett that he called Bennett over to discuss his outfit. Bennett wore plaid boxer shorts, his required clinic t-shirt over a hoodie, and bright purple Converse sneakers. When Bob criticized his outfit, Bennett snottily retorted that he should mind his own business. Bob rejoined, "Well, the style took me off. I had to, man. I had to comment." To which, Bennett exclaimed, "My mother always told me that if someone's talking about you, you must be doing something right. I just came from *my* world, which was eating lunch, not affecting yours—kinda in two different parallel universes—and you stopped your entire world to comment on something that I'm doing. I gotta be doing something right!" Bob looked a bit unnerved at that and said, "It's definitely—, it's a unique fashion statement." Preventing Bennett from having the last word, Bob turned back to me, "Okay, where were we?" When Bennett walked away, Bob whispered contemptuously under his breath, "Fruit."

Although women, transgendered people, and sexual minorities might not literally be targets of harassment or violence in studies, they often feel more vulnerable in the Phase I clinic space. As a result, they exercise some degree of caution in their interactions with heterosexual men. Social dynamics might nevertheless vary from clinic to clinic or even from study to study, depending on the enforcement of the clinic's rules or the actual group of healthy volunteers brought together. Participants in the numerical minority might have positive experiences in studies—and indeed many do—but they are less able to set or control the social tone of the clinic.

Contextualizing Healthy Volunteers' Phase I Participation

Entering the Phase I clinic is not limited to participating in or witnessing how a certain type of science is conducted; it is also about joining a social world. That world is particularly interesting because it is populated by healthy volunteers who serially enroll in studies and find camaraderie in the experience. The intensity of the confinement engenders meaningful relationships among participants, even if their bonds are temporally and spatially bound to the clinic and a specific Phase I study. Many healthy volunteers truly enjoy their time together and even find the social aspects of the experience motivation to continue enrolling, which, in turn, can further encourage some to become a type of model organism for drug development.

Still, there are tensions that brew during studies, at times remaining below the surface and at others boiling over. While much of the antagonism simply results from banal differences among participants, such as preferences about what television shows to watch or how loudly to speak on the phone, certain groups do tend to have difficulty interacting with others. Women and sexual minorities might feel vulnerable in an environment in which they are in the numerical minority, especially when there is an aggressive performance of heterosexual masculinity. Moreover, notwithstanding most healthy volunteers' proclamations about how well everyone gets along regardless of race and ethnicity, demographic differences like these fuel tensions that reflect the assumptions participants bring with them to a clinical trial and color their experiences with others during confinement. These tensions reveal aspects of how imbricated stigma operates: not all healthy volunteers are subject to the same pernicious patterns of social inequality; some can assert their superiority or dominance over others even within what perhaps should be the equalizing space of the Phase I clinic.

The clinics' social dynamics also provide the context for healthy volunteers' perceptions of the benefits of the financial compensation, their identities as research participants, and their conceptions of Phase I risks—of which perhaps the most important to them is the risk of not qualifying or being selected for a study. Unlike other types of clinical trials, Phase I science occurs in one place in which participants temporarily live in the controlled confines of the experiment, interacting with other healthy volunteers, research staff, and sometimes pharmaceutical company representatives. This serves as a potent reminder of the materiality of the scientific enterprise, and Phase I trials' context profoundly shapes the kinds of truth-claims that can be made about investigational drugs (Gieryn 2018). As the remainder of this book illustrates, healthy volunteers are in it together—literally, in that they are in the same clinic space undergoing the same trial procedures and risking the same adverse study events, and more generally, in that they experience adverse life events that make Phase I trials such an appealing financial option.

2

"Doing the Lab Rat Thing"

From my first interaction with Bob at Pharma Phase I, I knew he was a funny and interesting character. As with other healthy volunteers, I started out our interview by asking how many studies he had done. He simply laughed and started counting on his fingers. Realizing an answer might be a long time coming, I interrupted his counting to infer, "So this is not your first study?" He guffawed good-naturedly, "No, as you can tell by my—." Instead of finishing his sentence, he held out his left arm for me to see the scar tissue on his inner elbow, including what appeared to be a hole. Rubbing the spot, he explained, "You can see I got, you know, a cavern there. Been stuck many times. That's my golden vein."

A white man in his early forties, Bob had participated in dozens of research studies. For the previous two years, he had lived out of his car and traveled throughout the United States to earn income through Phase I trials and poker tournaments. Fifteen years earlier, his brother had done a healthy volunteer study and told Bob how lucrative medical research could be. Bob was unemployed, living in St. Louis, and needed cash at the time, so he tried it out and found he enjoyed the experience. He subsequently enrolled serially in what he referred to as "small" studies at Washington University over the next few years. The studies paid a couple hundred dollars for a few hours of his time, but some were grueling, such as the one in which researchers had him ride a stationary bicycle with an endoscopy tube down his throat and the sleep study during which he was woken up throughout the night each time he fell asleep. His favorite one in those first few years was a positron-emission tomography (PET scan) study that mapped his brain in different colors, and the researchers gave him a copy of the images to take home.

I asked Bob how he had gone from enrolling in local studies to traveling the country. He hesitated while considering the question for a moment. Cautious about providing the details, he admitted he was stuck in St. Louis after a run-in with the law. When his five-year probation ended, he wondered whether he could leave town and still participate in studies. He recalled, "I started doing some research on my own . . . 'cause I was always trying to figure out, 'Well, gosh, where can I go do these? [Where can I] do a study at, besides local?' [I was looking for] something that was out of town or wherever, or, you know, maybe one that pays a decent amount of money. So then I stumbled across a couple of websites, and then I realized, 'Wow, there's a list, and there's people doing 'em! There's all these different places, and [they're] all over the country.'" Ultimately, Bob decided to pursue two financially risky avenues for earning income: screening for Phase I trials and poker tournaments. Combining the two activities, he explained, justified going to distant cities. Even though study participation was far from guaranteed, traveling to screen was worth it because, when he got in, the compensation lasted him for a few months. Plus, without studies, poker could generally keep him afloat for a few weeks. That said, he remembered a three-month losing streak he suffered in Austin when he did not qualify for any clinical trials and lost money on poker. He used his last $75 to drive from Texas to screen successfully in Kansas. Running out of money, he sanguinely claimed, helped him learn how to live frugally.

Reflecting on all the clinics he had visited since leaving St. Louis, Bob commented, "I'm probably unique from most of these guys in here because most people don't do what I do." Bob was indeed exceptional in how he participated in clinical trials. He had traveled the entire length of the United States for studies, checking into Phase I clinics in at least 17 states: Washington, California, Nevada, Arizona, Texas, Kansas, Nebraska, Missouri, Wisconsin, Illinois, Indiana, Tennessee, Maryland, Pennsylvania, New Jersey, New York, and Connecticut. He traveled anywhere, but to maximize his chances of qualifying, he prioritized the parts of the Midwest and Northeast with a higher density of Phase I clinics. Further, he even used Craigslist to subsidize his travel through ride-shares, picking up passengers who paid for gas en route to their destination. He slept in his car, in university libraries, or on the couches of people he met on his travels. Importantly, getting into a clinical trial meant not only income but a free place to sleep, three meals a day, hot showers, and a place to do laundry. He recognized that this lifestyle had its downsides and summed up his participation by saying, "That's what I've been doing with my life [the] last couple of years. . . . It's been okay, you know, it's been a lot of traveling. You know, a lot of times I'm lonely." Bob was also not naive about the stigma attached to medical research: his mother thought he was crazy for enrolling in trials, and he had difficulty establishing romantic relationships with women. Explaining others' views, he asserted, "Everybody has this preconceived notion about testing stuff [drugs] on people, and usually it's not good. It's usually, you know, negative."

Bob's story about how and why he got involved in clinical trials also shares common features with those of many other healthy volunteers. Bob's life was characterized by imbricated stigma. He was unemployed and homeless and had a criminal record. Given that stigmatizing social factors such as these stacked the deck against him, gambling on clinical trials and poker was a reasonable, if not shrewd, way to earn a living, regardless of the additional stigma attached to enrolling in medical research and gambling—and to himself as a healthy volunteer and gambler. The scholarly literature on Phase I participation emphasizes healthy volunteers' financial motivations to enroll (e.g., Almeida et al. 2007; Grady et al. 2017; Tishler and Bartholomae 2002; Tolich 2010), but this framework often oversimplifies their decision-making. In particular, it obscures the adverse life events that bring people to clinical trials initially and why some become serial participants. Clinical trial participation *is* a stigmatized activity, but it offers healthy volunteers a unique resource for the management of *other* stigmatized aspects of their identities. By providing substantial lump-sum compensation, Phase I trials allow participants to offset and mask otherwise intractable material disadvantages they experience in their lives. Importantly, the more imbricated the stigmas they face, the more they position themselves to become model organisms and shape their lives to clinical trials to make money.

Stigma, Insecurity, and Material Inequalities

Imbricated stigma is tied to the profound social and economic inequalities structuring US society. Since the 1980s and exacerbated in the late 2000s by the Great Recession, the United States has experienced massive job loss, especially of high-wage, benefits-bearing jobs in manufacturing. The rise of the service sector cannot compensate for these employment losses, especially considering that service-sector jobs pay low wages, offer few if any benefits, and often provide insufficient hours or are temporary (Pugh 2015). Additionally, state and federal governments have scaled back social services to needy families and instituted injurious immigration policies. As a result of these changes, many people have found themselves in financially precarious situations (Katz 2013; Standing 2011).

Whereas much attention has been spent examining the growing gap between the rich and poor, scholars have increasingly focused on the toll that employment insecurity now takes on people of all social classes. For example, Jacob Hacker (2006) details how income volatility currently threatens more people with poverty, even if only temporarily. Hacker further demonstrates how the risk of downward mobility has outpaced the possibility of getting ahead even for the previously affluent and middle classes. With neoliberal policies systematically dismantling the social safety net, fewer opportunities exist for maintaining, let alone enhancing, one's standard of living. Consequently, more people face the material risk of losing their home or car and thus the social stigma attached to being unemployed, impoverished, and/or homeless.

A weak economy has different effects based on how class, gender, and race—and especially their intersections—structure social positions for individuals and groups. Changes in the employment market have created challenges for men, especially for African Americans and Latinos, in lower-income and service-sector jobs (Holder 2016; Ribas 2015; Wilson 2010). Men are also more likely than women to obtain only seasonal or contingent work, and many such positions have higher than average risk of injury or harm (Paap 2006). Moreover, people of color encounter more impediments to securing steady employment than their white counterparts (Kalleberg 2011). Immigrants, regardless of how well they speak English, are also subject to discrimination, and available employment is often limited to just a few sectors. For instance, regardless of the training or employment history they might have had in their countries of origin, immigrant Latino men might find that their primary job options are in construction, lawn care, or other trades, while immigrant Latina women are funneled into child care and house cleaning (Redstone Akresh 2006; Salami and Nelson 2014). African Americans also face racism in employment, with black men experiencing the most difficulty of any group securing good jobs and steady work (Thernstrom and Thernstrom 2009). Finally, for individuals who have a criminal record, work options are severely restricted, and African Americans are, again, at an even greater disadvantage and have the worst employment rates post-incarceration (Pager 2008).

Work profoundly mediates identity, including how we are seen by others and how we see ourselves (Kwon and Lane 2016). Importantly, being unemployed and collecting public assistance are both stigmatized as stemming from individual deficiencies, such as irresponsibility and laziness (Halpern-Meekin et al. 2015). Rather than perceiving these as unjust *structural* problems, many individuals instead understand their desperate circumstances as *individual* challenges requiring them to prove their self-worth through their determination and/or ingenuity (Silva 2013). Public policy has even leveraged these cultural beliefs as part of neoliberal welfare reforms, such as welfare-to-work programs (Marchevsky and Theoharis 2006).

The complementary myth that hard work is ultimately rewarded by upward mobility also contributes to families struggling harder for less (Iversen and Armstrong 2006). For example, when more traditional employment paths toward financial security are unavailable, the working poor and lower middle classes often hold multiple jobs and/or seek alternative income sources in the gig and informal economies (Arnold 2007; Friedman 2014). Companies such as Uber and TaskRabbit promise individuals flexible opportunities to make money, but in the process, they also crowd out others more traditionally employed in these sectors (Schor 2017). Immigrants, in particular, have crafted identities as what Zulema Valdez (2011) calls "survival-strategy entrepreneurs" because of their cultivation of self-employment opportunities.[1] Such immigrants often perform diverse forms of day labor based on opportunity, not their skill sets per se. While these activities can support a family, they are notoriously insecure as income sources wax and wane. They also require individuals to cultivate new clients and avoid attention from the authorities. Yet, they are often pursued with the hope that economic success— and all its material trappings—can and will follow.

In addition to our work, what we buy as consumers becomes part of our identities. Failure to consume the right products and brands can cause social exclusion and stigma for all social classes (Sandıkcı and Ger 2013). Consumer culture makes particularly strong demands on individuals and families struggling to make ends meet by requiring them to participate in and consent to the planned obsolescence and upgradability of products (Slade 2006). The fashionable life of technology, such as cell phones, has also shortened dramatically, and the newest devices have additional hidden costs to maintain music, apps, and various add-ons. Clothing may be cheaper than ever before, but with low cost comes a short lifespan. Ironically, the harder one works to keep up, the more entitled one feels to a new car, new TV, and so on to make the effort seem worthwhile (Rosen 2006; Twitchell 2012). Nor does poverty exclude people from consumer culture. Conspicuous consumption occurs at all income levels, and it may even compel those with fewer economic resources to purchase more expensive products to demonstrate that they can (Gilroy 2010; Lury 2011). Such spending engenders debt and additional financial hardship, and that is a difficult cycle to break (Schor 1999).

Consumer culture might even prompt a particular kind of engagement in the informal economy. Those who are involved in illicit activities, including selling drugs or other illegal goods, might stylize themselves as "hustlers."[2] As a type of economic resourcefulness, hustling is aimed not only at economic survival but also at getting ahead, especially in finding ways to obtain material markers of prosperity through consumption. In his ethnography of two California communities of Mexican Americans, Daniel Dohan (2003) writes, "Residents with experience in the illicit economy knew that profits, even if short-lived, could be spectacular. Moreover, these profits could quickly be converted into visible signs of prosperity—a sign of prosperity that could outlive in memories and bragging rights whatever fleeting material success the person may have actually enjoyed in the illicit economy" (74). In this context, even with all its instability, the hustle promises—if not actually delivers—more than a low-wage job could provide, which can subsequently reshape individuals' views of those jobs. When seen as dead-end jobs, low-wage work such as in fast-food restaurants also becomes stigmatized to the point that many individuals eschew that form of labor, believing it to be better not to have a job at all (Newman 2009).[3] Philippe Bourgois (1995) interprets involvement in the illicit economy as "a personal search for dignity and a rejection of racism and subjugation" (9), but he notes that it is nonetheless destructive for those individuals involved and their communities. Illegal activities are further stigmatizing because they risk incarceration, injury, and ostracism. Thus, individuals in the lowest income brackets are placed both economically and culturally in an impossible position, particularly for those who are minorities and/or immigrants (Lamont et al. 2016). They must be able to thrive economically despite the odds, and their work and consumption are metrics of their success.

Stigma management is a key feature in navigating social inequalities. As I described earlier, Erving Goffman (2009 [1963]) categorized stigma into two types: discredited and discreditable. Whereas the former has visible markers and cannot easily be hidden from others, the latter type can be concealed by managing what information is known about one's identity. Both discredited and discreditable stigmas operate against those who are the most economically insecure—people of color, the poor, the unemployed, those with criminal records, those on public assistance, and so on. In order to improve one's financial situation, individuals must then manage the stigmatized aspects of their identities by selectively disclosing information or by distinguishing themselves from stigmatized others. For example, an individual might fail to disclose information about a felony conviction and hope that a prospective employer will not do a background check (Harding 2003). Another might spend scarce resources on personal consumption, dressing in a particular way, driving a certain type of car, or having the newest gadgets, in order to deflect attention from a stigmatized aspect of his or her identity (Lamont and Molnár 2001). And some may resort to within-group stigmatizing, such as when middle-class blacks stereotype poor blacks as "ghetto" to position themselves as morally superior (Lacy 2007; Matory 2015). In the context of managing imbricated stigma, engagement in the informal economy, illegal hustles, or alternate forms of employment are not necessarily risks; rather, these activities can be important strategies for subsisting, supplementing household incomes, and projecting a particular self to the world. For some healthy individuals, Phase I trials are an important avenue both to earn income and manage imbricated stigma.

Stigma and Economic Incentives for Phase I Participation

In its recruitment of healthy volunteers, the Phase I industry is structured to harness individuals' financial instability and their experiences
of imbricated stigma. US clinics incentivize enrollment through the
material and symbolic value of lump-sum financial compensation,
highlighting how it can go farther or be used for different purposes
than a typical paycheck issued to wage-earners.[4] Additionally, far from
discriminating against stigmatized groups, clinics actively recruit the
unemployed and people of color. Study recruiters set up booths at job
fairs and develop targeted recruitment campaigns for people of color,
tailoring the advertisement content and buying print or air time in local
media markets. Some clinics also actively recruit immigrants, especially those who speak Spanish, by hiring bilingual staff and providing
informed consent forms in participants' native languages. Moreover, the
clinics neither confirm participants' legal status nor do they run background checks. This means that being an undocumented immigrant
or having a criminal record—two factors that make stable, fair-wage
employment difficult to obtain—does not bar individuals from enrolling
in clinical trials. Finally, most Phase I clinics are located in urban areas
on public transit lines, reducing barriers to participation by making
them more accessible to low-income and minority groups. These clinic
tactics signify a concerted, and very successful, effort to exploit social
inequalities and tap particular populations.[5] They also set the conditions for vulnerable groups to enroll serially regardless of the associated
stigma.

Most healthy volunteers do perceive Phase I trials to be stigmatizing.
Some participants articulated this quite directly. For example, Russell,
an African American in his mid-forties who had participated in over
two dozen studies, said clinical trials are "taboo." He asserted, "Everybody else think, well, that you're a low life. . . . It's a stigma that you're
a bum on the corner . . . [who] messed up, you know?" In this way, the
discreditable stigma does not apply only to the trial itself; it is also inti-
mately connected to the broader belief that anyone who *needs* to enroll
is compensating for some individual deficiency, just as people who are
unemployed or receiving public assistance are thought to be deficient.
Despite awareness that they could be tainted by clinical trial stigma,

many participants enroll, oftentimes serially, because of the other already stigmatized aspects of their identities.

Take, for example, Bennett, the African American participant who instigated the Tiger Woods incident recounted above. Bennett had enrolled in more than two dozen studies in three years, but prior to that, Bennett was living with his mother and had an $8.00-per-hour retail job. His mother's financial situation deteriorated but instead of contributing to the household, Bennett bought a new car, got an expensive cell phone plan, and signed up for classes at a local community college. Sadly, Bennett described how his life unraveled: the family lost their home, he dropped out of school, his car got repossessed, and he got fired from his job when his lack of transportation made him an unreliable worker. Embarrassed by the sudden change in his material circumstances, these financial adversities set him on the path to enrolling in clinical trials, and he continued down it and became a self-proclaimed "lab rat" because of the unprecedented money he could earn. As he explained,

> Probably the biggest personal gain I've ever had is [that] the money comes in a large lump sum. . . . I've made more in a month than most people make in half a year. Longest study I ever did was like 36 days. It was like $7,300. . . . Never have I had that much money in my possession at one time. . . . It's not a lot of money, but it's enough to really do something, you know? It's enough to have somewhat of a free life, you know? . . . I don't consider this a career, but at the same time, busting my hump at McDonald's for $8 or $9 an hour and bringing home $900 to $1,000 in a month when I can make that in a week, just doesn't seem feasible to me, you know? Like doing the lab rat thing, I've grown accustomed to a certain kind of lifestyle, having lump sums of money whenever I need it, you know, and being able to do whatever I want.

Bennett's framing of his participation is not unusual. It celebrates the financial windfalls clinical trials provide while also emphasizing how studies enable a more appealing lifestyle. When job options are undesirable, Phase I trials become an even more attractive alternative to the grind of low-end service-sector jobs.[6]

Bennett's case reveals the importance of how clinical trial participation is structured. Enrollment is flexible, making the "work" autonomous and providing the freedom to earn money as needed. This places the money front and center in participants' decision-making. Louis, a multiracial man in his late fifties who had participated in about 40 studies, baldly depicted his motivation: "I wanted to make some money. . . . It's definitely not because I want to save the world. . . . Let's get that on the record right now. No, I don't want to save the world. No, I need to make money." At the same time, the considerable lump sum also creates misperceptions of the financial advantages of enrolling. Although each clinical trial appears to pay handsomely, it is difficult to earn much more annually participating full time than one would in a minimum-wage job. This does not stop participants from trading apocryphal stories about healthy volunteers who earn $100,000 per year and can afford to buy expensive cars and travel to exotic vacation spots. Yet, few even reach $20,000 annually unless they consistently find and qualify for the best-paying studies.[7] Although Phase I trials are rarely as lucrative as healthy volunteers hope, the money nonetheless serves a critical symbolic function in managing their experiences of imbricated stigma through the material gains—however fleeting—from each study.

Trends in Healthy Volunteers' Financial Motivations

Delving into the specifics of why people enroll in Phase I trials, I find that their explanations typically have two layers. First, there is the explicit reason to join a particular study at a certain moment. For instance, the compensation is earmarked for an overdue bill or to help get ahead on rent. In late November and December 2009, most healthy volunteers at Pharma Phase I were focused on making money for Christmas. The second layer to healthy volunteers' decision to participate is their larger financial need, often exacerbated by their stigmatized social position. As detailed below, healthy volunteers' narratives indicate that they might not want to be "guinea pigs" in medical research, but they also do not want to be unemployed, homeless, and/or broke. By participating, they experience the economic benefit (and typically no harm) that propels them to enroll in additional studies (McManus et al. 2019), and they use clinical trials as a means to manage the imbricated stigma they face in their everyday lives. This was clearly the case for Bob, who lacked better job prospects or income sources.

Most healthy volunteers, however, do not participate in clinical trials full time. Instead, their precarious economic situations motivate them to "supplement" their incomes with these studies. Supplementing has a wide range of meanings, but most notably includes gaining essential revenue to make ends meet, money to be used as investments in the future, and disposable income for consumption. Individual healthy volunteers use their clinical trial income in multiple ways across time, but it is helpful analytically to examine each one discretely. An interesting narrative feature is how the stigma of clinical trials emerges in contradictory ways in relation to participants' financial needs and consumption modes. In their descriptions of how they use their study compensation, participants also reveal the "identity work"[8] they do as they confront their broader stigmatized social positions to narratively justify or diminish clinical trial stigma.

RECREATING THE (STIGMATIZED) SAFETY NET

Without stable employment options and sufficient financial resources, many healthy volunteers credit desperate financial times for their Phase I participation. Rather than perceiving studies as a solution to these problems, healthy volunteers see clinical trials as a type of safety net that could stave off more severe problems. Trials are particularly valuable in counterbalancing seasonal underemployment that occurs in trade jobs, such as construction, roofing, lawn care, and moving. As participants were quick to point out, they do not get a break from their bills when their income dips, and studies help them maintain a steady income year-round. In addition, clinical trials can fill a need when unanticipated or intermittent expenses arise. Medical bills, car repairs, taxes, funerals, and countless other obligations might strain a monthly budget beyond its limits, especially when individual and family incomes limit one's ability to contribute to a savings account that could serve as a personal safety net.

With the combined effects of changes in the economy and cutbacks in social services, clinical trials provide a flexible way to stay afloat and *feel* financially secure. First-time participants' narratives often offered striking examples of this. For instance, Devon, an African American in his late twenties, had recently been laid off after working for seven years in a well-paid union job doing construction. Fortunately, his long-term partner had a stable job that provided benefits, including health insurance for their three children. However, their household income was more than halved by Devon's job loss, and instead of being the larger contributor, his unemployment benefits constituted only a fraction of his partner's salary. Devon was clearly uncomfortable with the situation, divulging, "I'm a mess with all the responsibility still being on me, you know?" He repeatedly mentioned his "responsibility," asserting that he was the one who needed to keep a roof over his children's head and that it was his duty to support his "girl." While the couple obviously needed additional income to stay afloat, Devon's distress was also symptomatic of the stigma he felt as an unemployed man who was receiving government benefits and was also financially supported by a woman. As an African American man, Devon must have also been aware of and responding to the acute stigma associated with black "dead-beat dads" who fail to provide for their children, however sterotypical or mythical such men might be (Edin and Nelson 2013).

To fight this emasculating economic situation, Devon turned to clinical trials, saying, "So I'm just using this as an avenue. . . . This is free money." His eleven-day study paid $3,300, and he mapped out his plans for the money: $1,600 for bills, $1,200 for Christmas presents, and $500 for his savings account. Notably, he had allocated more than a third of the study compensation to gifts, which was likely indicative of both his generosity and his desire to perform his (short-lived) prosperity. Devon's view of the lump sum as "free money" also likely contributed to his plans for it. Although many other participants could see this in a positive light, for Devon, the idea of "free money" seemed to add to his shame about his situation. He justified his participation by comparing himself to other healthy volunteers: "I don't know. There's just some people that's got difference in the ways and why they actually do it. . . . If my [next] job comes along, it's over. Other than that, some people just want to make a career out of it." For Devon, study compensation was a stigmatized source of income, as he perceived free money to be less legitimate than money earned through regular employment. Regardless, gaining short-term income in this way combatted the stigma he felt from being unemployed and allowed him to meaningfully contribute to his household and materially care for his family while searching for work.

The vision of clinical trials as a safety net is a powerful trope even for those with more resources. For example, Benjamin, a white man in his early twenties who was a recent college graduate, enrolled in his first clinical trial because he was jobless and living on his own for the first time. His parents had wanted him to stay with them while he looked for work, but expecting success (which he had not yet found), he moved to a brand-new city. He explained, "Unfortunately, I haven't been able to find a job. . . . I figured, oh, . . . just come out here and be able to find a job in, you know, two months. Wasn't able to. This is a good way to supplement my income and let me continue my job search. . . . So it's, at the end of the day, this is a safety net and good option. I mean it was a decent option. I mean it's not ideal, but it's going to buy me a little time." Even while acknowledging the financial benefit, Benjamin's ambivalence about needing to participate in a clinical trial comes across through his vacillating representation of it as a "good," "decent," and "not ideal" financial option.

Like Devon, Benjamin made unprompted references to the stigma of study participation: "There are general stigmas that go along with [it]. I've been apprehensive to tell people that I was going to a clinical trial. . . . Unfortunately, I didn't have that many options right now, so this was—, this is what happened." Unlike many other healthy volunteers, Benjamin felt more shame about the clinical trial than he did about his joblessness or lack of income. Given his relative privilege as a young, college-educated, white man, the bigger, unarticulated stigma would be for Benjamin to return to his parents' house defeated in his attempt at independence. Trial enrollment effectively bought him time to secure the job and future he was seeking, which is a different kind of safety net compared to that of many other participants.

In this way, rather than adding to their stigma, clinical trials can instead cover healthy volunteers' financial struggles by supplying resources when they are needed. For example, Marcus, an African American in his forties with nearly 20 years of trial participation, explained the important role of studies for him during this time:

> I'm a catering chef, and it's just seasons: you have wedding season, you
> have holiday season. A lot of times, half of the year you're not working,
> so you gotta do what you gotta do. . . . Like at one point I would never

tell nobody what I did [i.e., enrolling in studies], and it's like, hold on, it helped me get a better car, helped me stay afloat to take care of my kids. . . . When you have kids and stuff like that, . . . you have to do what you have to do to maintain. Anybody can sit around and criticize somebody [for participating in clinical trials], but the true soldiers get out there and do what they gotta do to take care of their families.

Like Benjamin, Marcus indicated he was reticent to tell others about his involvement in clinical trials. In contrast, Marcus positioned his study participation as a brave choice, justified by how he has helped himself and especially his children. The safety net—or life-preserver in Marcus's case—is a fraught metaphor. Having a safety net certainly saves people from harm, but *needing* one reveals the precarity of their positions. By portraying clinical trials as a potentially stigmatizing way of staying financially afloat, Marcus affirmed his deeply imbricated stigma that included a long history of economic struggle.

LEVERAGING FUNDS FOR THE FUTURE

In a different vein, some healthy volunteers describe enrolling in Phase I trials not for daily living expenses but to invest those funds toward a better future. Specifically, they are motivated to reduce their debt, invest in their children's education, or accrue capital for small businesses. In each instance, participants want to improve their own or their family's material circumstances beyond what they can accomplish with income from their jobs alone. Here, clinical trials can also serve to minimize or eliminate stigma experienced in their current social positions.

Many participants described being in severe debt. Some had taken on student loans for college, oftentimes for degrees they had never finished, and others owed significant sums on their credit cards. Debt can be particularly stigmatizing when it puts individuals on the path to personal bankruptcy (Thorne and Anderson 2006). Beyond alleviating the psychic toll that owing money can take, some healthy volunteers saw clinical trials as enabling their regular incomes to go farther by eliminating debt. This was why Casey, a white man in his late twenties, had enrolled in his first study. Casey was a bartender, which he joked was not a "real" full-time job, so he had flexibility to get the time off for a study. He explained, "[It's] just for extra money [to] pay for student loans and stuff. So [it's a] pretty nice chunk of change to get rid of a lot of student loans. 'Cause it sucks to pay student loans. It's not fun." Recognizing clinical trials as stigmatized, Casey added, "It's not terrible, but I don't think—. I mean, I'm not like what's-his-face [another participant]. . . . I'm not doing this for a job. . . . I make good money bartending." Casey's self-comparison to another participant provided a means to manage any shame he felt. While his joke that bartending is not a real job suggests it had its own stigma for him, he nevertheless constructed it as legitimate work compared to clinical trials. Indeed, his emphasis on how well bartending paid affirmed that he did not *need* to pursue studies, that it was merely a useful but nonessential tactic to relieve his debt faster. Despite this rhetorical strategy, however, Casey, like other healthy volunteers, ultimately wanted a future with more disposable income if not different work, and he saw clinical trials as a means to that end.

Other healthy volunteers focus on materially improving their children's lives, as seen in Devon's desire to keep a roof over his children's heads, as well as other parents' discussions of how expensive braces, clothes, shoes, and school supplies could be. However, the parents who invested in their children's futures typically did so by using clinical trials to generate money for their education. For instance, Sidney, an African American in his late forties, worked full time as custodial staff in a public school. His observations on the job had worried him about the quality of public education in his district, so he placed his five children in private Catholic school. In eight years, he had enrolled in more than twenty clinical trials, and his strategy was to participate each time their tuition bills were due. With his work schedule providing ample vacation time, including much of the summer off, he had been successful at integrating studies into his schedule. Sidney was unequivocal about the financial benefit of participation: "My children really have been allowed to stay in Catholic school because I do this two or three times a year. So, it has been a blessing for me."

Sidney knew, however, that his Phase I trial involvement was stigmatizing. To combat this, he, too, criticized other healthy volunteers. Casting his own use of the compensation as more virtuous, Sidney bitingly asserted, "I see people buyin' the most ridiculous things. They're on eBay biddin' on some jewelry or a watch or some rims on a car. Now don't get me wrong, that's their business. I really don't care, but I see it. . . .

My [kids'] tuition payment is their watch. . . . I'm like, wow! You really can take $3,000 and get a watch?! Must be the life!" Nonetheless, Sidney kept his study participation a well-guarded secret. He said he had told his wife only to explain his absence each time he checked in for a clinical trial. As far as everyone else was concerned, he declared, "Like my friends? Like my closest friends, my sisters, brother? . . . They don't have a clue! But they do say, 'I don't know how y'all do it. How do y'all keep them kids in Catholic school? How do you pay?' And this is how I do it. I just can't tell 'em. . . . If they ridiculed me, I would really be offended, so I wouldn't put myself in—. Like I'm not ashamed of it; it's just something that's very private to me. It's not something that I share." Although Sidney claimed he was not ashamed, he actively avoided others' judgment. More importantly, however, his silence about his participation could diminish other stigmas he might experience as a black man living in an urban setting. By using studies to pay for his children's education, he could actually appear to be either better off financially or a more skilled money manager than his family and friends.

Another future-oriented purpose that clinical trials serve is to start or bolster small businesses. Participants' investments included a new vehicle for a delivery-based business, advertising for a local moving company, software and online services for an e-commerce company, and property or land for real estate ventures. In each case, clinical trial participation was essentially a decision spurred by the desire to trade their stigmatized position as un(der)employed for an entrepreneurial identity and the possibility of a more prosperous future. For example, Javier, a Latino in his mid-forties, started enrolling in studies two years prior when he lost his job. He initially did it for his family to subsist, but he changed his rationale for participating: "So the idea was I seen that there was a lot of money . . . so I started doing [more] studies, saving my money, and then I just opened up a cleaning service." Although Javier did not tell me how many clinical trials he had done, he had been to at least seven clinics and used to go straight from one study to another until he launched his business a few months prior. Clinical trials, however, remained a necessary source of household income: "Well, once my business gets going really, really good, I won't do studies no more. Like right now, I'm slow, so I decided to do this one. What am I doing home in December and I don't have no work? Why not make a couple of dollars?

My kids could use it. You know?" Despite a lack of material change in his financial situation, Javier's identity as a business-owner was critically important to his self-worth. Unlike Sidney, Javier was not secretive about his study participation, even though he readily acknowledged that "a lot of people think that we're pieces of shits because we do this. They look down at us." Javier explicitly used his business as a shield to deflect both the stigma of trial participation and characterizations of himself as unemployed.

SPLURGING

A third type of financial motivation that healthy volunteers have for enrolling in Phase I trials is to earn truly disposable income, or "fun money" as some participants referred to it. While seemingly frivolous, splurging offers its own mechanism to mitigate stigmatized social positions. This was particularly the case for participants who used their money to travel. Tyler, a white man in his twenties, worked in a restaurant, and while his limited salary was enough to live on, he could not leverage it for the travel he wanted to do. As a result, over the past three years, Tyler had enrolled in fourteen studies to fund his vacations. He recognized trial participation was stigmatized, but he rejected that viewpoint, arguing, "It's like they [friends and family] have an immediate response that's negative, but . . . I've been able to travel. That's all I've done with the money. . . . I've been to Europe three summers in a row. I pretty much travel to all the states just based on this income I had from these studies." As with the participants described above, Tyler's attitude was that his use of the study compensation more than justified, if not negated, its stigma. At the same time, his ability to travel with those funds also attenuated some of the stigma associated with restaurant work. As a college-educated white man, Travis was hounded by friends and family for not pursuing a career, but he could justify his continued service-sector employment by arguing that it gave him the flexibility to explore new places and have new experiences.

White participants, in particular, had a rhetorical strategy of framing their intended travel as virtuous spending: their splurging was part of a self-improvement project of exposing themselves to other cultures. In contrast, non-white participants typically described their travel in more hedonistic terms. For example, Robert, an African American in his twenties who had enrolled in a dozen studies, detailed his plans for the $3,300 he was making at Pharma Phase I: "The reason why [I wanted to do this study] is because I'm going to Vegas. I don't want to spend my job money, 'cause I work as well. I work in the airport, and I get paid $17 an hour there. . . . I'm going to Vegas, so I wanted to have a little money to play with. So that's what I was thinking about. I was like, 'You know what? Get rich or die trying.' Like, [the rapper] 50 Cent's motto, 'Get rich or die tryin'.' You know, I'm like, 'I'm just gonna do it.'" Perhaps Robert was being more responsible by not gambling away his wages, but it is easy to imagine Sidney lumping this into the "ridiculous" ways other participants spend their study money. Yet, it allowed Robert to reject the typical limits his salary placed on his lifestyle and instead party in the unrestrained way of a rich idol.

Clinical trial compensation is easily exchanged for consumer goods, and gratification is delayed only for the study's length—during which, incidentally, healthy volunteers have time to consider and reconsider what they might purchase. Conspicuous consumption allows them to present as being better off than they actually are and translates into markers of material success within their social networks. Participants recounted using study funds to buy expensive items, such as large-screen televisions and portable electronics. At least two—Arthur and Garrett, both of whom were white men in their late twenties—enrolled in their first clinical trials to buy their fiancées more expensive diamond engagement rings than they could have otherwise afforded. In these instances, clinical trial participation generated the resources that would otherwise be unavailable while suggesting to others that expensive items and experiences were always within reach.

The large lump-sum payment from clinical trials encourages splurging because when the compensation is seen as "easy money," it promises more can be made with little effort. Kevin, an African American in his early forties who participated in studies full time, espoused this view: "When you've been doing this stuff for a couple of years, to me, chump change is $2,500. That's the way I feel about it because it goes quick. 'Cause my first check I got for $3,000. And $2,500 [of it], I went bananas with it. . . . I went shopping. I think I was top of the world." Kevin's spending made his family and friends admire his success. Rather than being honest, he told them he worked in hotel renovation, a job that required frequent travel. Speculating on how they would react to the truth, Kevin argued, "People downsize you. They'll, they'll, they'll tear you up and tear your head off: 'What?! You're doing that? . . . You're a lab rat.' . . . Once they call you a lab rat, you're done. You're like a roasted duck. [Laughs.] It's over. You gonna walk into people's house plucking your feathers, 'Kevin, look at him. He's crazy.'" Kevin described his family as being a diverse group, including some who worked in law enforcement and some who sold illegal drugs, but either way, he could keep his trial participation a secret because no one could even fathom what he was doing. Instead, he assumed that "people actually like for you to splurge that money. To them, like friends and family, relatives, when you pull the money out, they're just like, it's an honest dollar, it's a check."

Sometimes participants made consumer purchases against their better judgment. Joseph, an African American in his thirties, was about to begin his fourth study when we met. He talked about how his motivation was always to pay down his loans, but he repeatedly failed to use his study compensation as intended. He related:

> I have student loans calling, beating down my door, stuff like that. So I'm trying to keep them at bay. . . . But then when money comes easy, it goes easy too. You don't give as much as you wanna give back to Sallie Mae. [Laughs hysterically.] You know? 'Cause once you've got the cash in your hand, "I don't have to give it *all* to Sallie Mae. . . . I don't have to give them what I was *gonna* give 'em. I'll just give 'em a small [portion]." And the next thing you know, yeah, . . . I'm in danger of default, and now I've *gotta* do another study.

Joseph's situation is not uncommon, but for many participants, living beyond their typical means is thrilling.[9] They have fun, purchase items they want, and manage to earn the respect of others through splurging.

Covering and Deflecting Trial Stigma

As we have seen, healthy volunteers use Phase I trial compensation in diverse ways depending on their personal situations and their predilection for spending. For many, clinical trial participation is simultaneously liberating and shameful. The money earned in studies is unprecedented for people who have worked minimum wage jobs or have struggled to secure any work, but the stigma of being a human guinea pig or lab rat leads most healthy volunteers to be guarded, if not dishonest, about how they earn this income. At times, however, their trial participation itself makes it impossible to keep the activity a secret. As a result, many healthy volunteers have developed additional strategies for covering or deflecting stigma.

Not only do serial participants develop scar tissue over time from venipuncture, such as the one marking Bob's "golden vein," but all healthy volunteers typically leave clinical trials with some evidence of the study on their bodies. This might include fresh venipuncture marks and temporary bruising, rashes, or irritated skin from study procedures. Longer-term skin discoloration also occurs. For example, Sarah, a white woman in her early twenties, complained about having a "ring" on her arm from a patch study she had done six months earlier. Similarly, Ross, an African American in his forties, learned in his twelve years of participating that he ought to avoid studies requiring him to wear a Holter heart monitor for 24 or more hours. Besides the inconvenience, he explained, "They leave scarring, and for me, I think more than most people, it takes about—, I observed once [it took] 13 months for it to vanish. Yeah. I'm sporting one [now] that [has been there] about 6 months." He then pulled up his shirt to show me the quite visible, circular spots on his chest formed from the adhesive that had held the monitor leads in place.

For people like Ross who are highly secretive about their clinical trial participation, these marks on the body raise unwelcome questions from family or friends. Reynaldo, a Latino in his late thirties, had not told anyone except his wife about the six studies he had done. Nonetheless, he felt that his secret was visible, which made him fret: "My arm has a mark on it, and I don't like that the people watch me." I asked him what people thought of this scar, and he replied anxiously, "I don't know. I don't know what they would think, but I don't like that they looking at my arm. Maybe [they think] that I'm on drugs, [a] dealer or something like that. I don't know. I don't know, and I don't want to find out what they think." Many participants consciously wore clothes that would cover such marks to avoid others' scrutiny.

As a single man, Marshall found himself in some more difficult situations keeping his study participation a secret. An African American in his thirties, he had quit his job teaching in an inner-city public school to participate in clinical trials full time. A drawback to this career decision was how difficult it made dating when he avoided disclosing how he earned his income. He recounted one incident in which he felt forced to come clean:

> I was in bed with a girl one time, [and] she saw the bruise on my arm. . . . She was like, "What is that [mark]?" . . . I paused. Nobody ever asked me, so I was like—I'm thinking of what to say, I'm not a good liar—I was like, "Do you really wanna know?" . . . I told her, [and] she ain't believe me. I explain it to her and was like, "What do you think I do?" She said, "I just assumed you sold drugs . . . 'cause you don't ever work."

Marshall was unflustered that this girlfriend and others had presumed he was a drug user and/or dealer. For him, these identities provided cover, substituting what he saw as a less stigmatized activity for his study participation.

Comparisons with dealing drugs also serve a different purpose for healthy volunteers. As some people struggle with the economic necessity of clinical trial participation or even perhaps the guilty pleasure of enjoying the "easy" money, they deflect the stigma they feel about studies by highlighting its legality. Robert, the participant who was planning his trip to Vegas, asserted, "At first, I used to be embarrassed [about participating in studies], but not paying my bills? . . . So it's better for me [to] do this than I come rob you. 'Cause I will rob you." Robert was looking me directly in the eyes with a serious expression as he said this, and I laughed a little nervously and told him, "Well, good thing I live in Nashville; I don't have to worry about it." He immediately backpedaled, saying, "No, I'm sorry. I was just joking. No, I'm joking. My parents didn't raise me like that. But most kids from the 'hood—like friends that I know—they would do that, they would rob you. Like if it really comes down to like having nothing, they'd do that."

As he continued, Robert created another distinction between clinical trials and illegal activities: "This is something that you can do and fall back on. So that's why I think this is like a real good thing for people. . . . I feel like I don't have to sell drugs or [be] doing any illegal activity." Robert made these assertions as though he did not hold a full-time job, so I was struck by his choice to defend his study enrollment this way. Even more striking, though, is that this was a common rhetorical move, but only among black participants; that is, it was only black men and women who deflected the stigma of participating in clinical trials by emphasizing that what they received was "legal money." In so doing, they drew problematically upon cultural stereotypes about black, inner-city life. Regardless of one's background, however, it is much harder to deflect stigma by contrasting participation to a "regular" job, so over and over again, they mobilized the binary of studies or crime.

Certainly, some participants had sold drugs or engaged in other illegal activities. Participants with a criminal record who legitimately had major obstacles to finding employment were particularly keen to underscore clinical trials' legality. For example, Nelson, an African American in his thirties, had a criminal record and struggled to find work. He proclaimed, "[Participating in studies] it's legal. I'm not hurting anybody. If anything, I'm doing more to help, and it beats the alternative, selling drugs or doing something you're not supposed to do." Whereas Nelson sounded defensive about his study enrollment, Manny, a Native American in his late twenties, seemed desperate. He discovered clinical trials at his parole hearing when someone showed him an advertisement in a free weekly newspaper. He felt the pressure to make money immediately, confiding, "Where else am I gonna get it [income]? Car's broke down, you know. What are we gonna do? If I don't pay my parole, I'm gonna go back to prison."[10] His girlfriend, who was also unemployed, insisted that rather than miss paying his parole fees, he should return to crime by getting "back into what you were doing [before]." Manny, however, wanted a fresh start and planned to seek out more studies, adding, "That's pretty much how I see it, is [as] income. That's for real. And anything else is maybe helping out, you know, seeing what the medicine does too." Both men positioned clinical trials as a better option than breaking the law, but interestingly, each noted a societal benefit of their participation as well.

Despite the financial motivations that bring them to Phase I studies, healthy volunteers' efforts to deflect stigma often combine assertions about clinical trials' legality with claims about their contribution to science and society.[11] Eddie, an African American in his early forties who had participated in more than 50 studies, became particularly animated as he recalled a conversation he had with his mother:

> I said, "What I'm doing is legal! . . . I'm making legal money right here." I said, "Actually, I'm like a medical soldier for you. I'm the guy who goes out in the field and I take the first hit. I make sure that you can live your life—you know what I'm saying?—with these medications. They test 'em on us [healthy volunteers] first, then they test 'em on Phase II or Phase III, make sure they're safe for people that are sick, and then they come to you." I said, "So I'm doing a great thing for you. 'Cause without me, . . . you'll be the experiment."

Eddie mobilized a masculine trope of war, positioning himself on the frontline to directly protect his mother and anyone else who might disapprove. Eddie's comment also echoes Marcus's assertion that "true soldiers" protect their families, but Eddie's military metaphor goes further in that his contributions as a participant are heroic on a much grander scale: his sacrifice not only brings in needed income but also saves others' lives. Javier, the serial participant who started a cleaning business, became similarly impassioned as he contrasted clinical trial stigma with the societal benefit. Thinking of others' reactions to the news that he was a "pharmaceutical tester," he protested, "If it wasn't for guinea pigs like us, we wouldn't have no medicines. . . . People should look at us not like as guinea pigs but as angels. . . . The judge, the President of the United States, everybody somewhere along the line has to take some kind of medication. And like I keep stressing, if it wasn't for guys like us, you wouldn't have the medication out here." Thus, Javier appealed to the pervasiveness of medication use to argue, essentially, that contributions like his directly helped the most important or powerful people in society. This line of reasoning might not persuade Javier's friends or family members who judge him, but it is nonetheless a powerful rhetorical strategy to challenge the stigma he experienced.

Yet another way that participants deflect clinical trial stigma is through upward and downward self-comparisons with other healthy volunteers.[12] Upward social comparisons abate stigma by averring that people of higher social positions also enroll in clinical trials. For example, David, a white man in his forties, provided a textbook example of this strategy when he told me, "This is nothing to be ashamed of. . . . It has no boundaries. . . . I met bankers here, lawyers, I'm telling you, smart ass people that you be like, 'Damn, you doing the study?!'" In other words, if intelligent and successful people could be found in Phase I trials, then it must be a respectable thing to do. This might make the need for money less disgraceful as well. If people in elite professions are also occasionally wanting for cash and join clinical trials to earn it, then someone without the same social and economic advantages should not be ashamed to have financial needs.

At the same time, there are limits to what makes clinical trial participation "normal," and this is where downward social comparison comes in. These types of comparison include the examples above of Sidney looking down on other participants' splurges or Devon and Casey claiming that as first-time participants they were better than people who made clinical trials their career. A more pronounced downward self-comparison was many of my informants' fervent belief that clinical trials were most stigmatized for older healthy volunteers who had enrolled for decades. Despite pursuing studies full time, Bennett described the horror he felt at the thought of becoming one of those older participants:

> There're people out there who have been doing it for a while. I was in this study with this guy who was 55, 54 years old. . . . With the guidelines for most studies, you have to be between 18 and 55, so he only had like six months left before he was not going to be able to do a good majority of the situations [i.e., studies]. And we were talking about what we were gonna do when we got out, and he just was speaking some foolishness with his money. And I said, "Please, God, don't ever let that be me. Please, God, don't let me be 55 doing this and doing exactly what I was doing when I was 25, 26. Please, God. Please let me have the mental stability to grow and be productive and just move somewhere else, forward and up, forward and up, forward and up."

Bennett's negative appraisal of this older participant combines judgment of his age with his use of the study compensation. This is particularly interesting when Bennett himself admitted to spending his money on "designer shopping sprees," dispatching with his entire study check within days of receiving it, but in Bennett's eyes, whereas his youth excused this behavior, the participant who would soon be too old to enroll was pathetic. This type of downward social comparison effectively shifts the stigma away from younger healthy volunteers. Relying on clinical trial income, thus, is an acceptable part of youth; the shame comes when someone cannot prove their social worth outside of clinical trials as he or she ages. Both upward and downward social comparisons illustrate the power of deflecting stigma to insulate oneself from self-criticism.

Clinical Trials and Imbricated Stigma

Clinical trial participation is stigmatized, but its opprobrium must be assessed in relation to the larger constellation of stigmatized positions that motivate individuals' involvement in Phase I studies. As with most discreditable stigmas, management of those "spoiled" identities is a crucial way to influence how others perceive one's social position (Goffman 2009 [1963]). In an era of economic instability, clinical trials are one of many options for individuals to pursue short-term income. What is particularly important about Phase I participation is how it can mitigate other stigmas that individuals experience. The substantial lump-sum compensation from trials provides a safety net, investment for the future, or the material comfort of consumer goods. Participants can appear to others as much more financially secure than they really are, including giving the impression they have regular employment when they do not and/or they earn more income than do many others in similar positions. All this is made possible by the structure of Phase I trials, which actively recruit healthy volunteers who bear the material effects of social inequalities, particularly minorities, the unemployed, people with a criminal record, and undocumented immigrants. While continued participation is not required of healthy volunteers, the financial incentives encourage serial enrollment from some participants, who for lack of better economic options might become the model organisms the industry needs to test new pharmaceuticals.

To avoid the stigma, healthy volunteers often limit how much information they disclose about their participation. As we have seen, healthy volunteers have many tactics for doing so, including keeping the activity a secret from others. Despite some participants' efforts, certain aspects of their involvement are hard to hide, including venipuncture and other marks on the body, long absences while in studies, and the unexplained money with which they return home. Additionally, experienced stigma, whether it is through interactions with others or projections of what others might think, must be deflected away from the self. The compensation can serve this purpose when participants highlight the material improvements to their lives wrought by studies. Many participants further deflect stigma by asserting the moral superiority of earning money from studies as opposed to from crime, as if those were the only two paths available. Participants also mobilize strong narratives that highlight the societal contributions they make by means of their clinical trial involvement and emphasize their self-sacrifice, bravery, and importance to medical research. These claims' legitimacy does not rest on any altruistic motivations to enroll; rather, when "altruism" comes up, it is as an effect of their participation. Self-comparisons serve as a final attempt if not to convince others then to persuade themselves that earning money through clinical trials is normal and acceptable.

Clinical trial stigma can be more or less threatening to one's identity depending on imbrications of other discredited and discreditable stigmas that characterize one's life. Race, ethnicity, gender, class, age, country of origin, legal status, criminal record, education, employment history, and so on create both social advantages and disadvantages depending on the groups to which one belongs. As the next chapter illustrates, there are significant regional differences in clinical trial participation that manifest from differing patterns of inequality and material disadvantage throughout the United States. When disadvantages are greatest, participation in clinical trials—even with the risk of increased stigma—can reap the most material and cultural rewards. Although many healthy volunteers employ narratives about a single event, normally job loss, that led to Phase I participation, this story occludes the profound disadvantages embedded in the racialized social system (Bonilla-Silva 1997). Hence, healthy volunteers do not simply find ways to deflect clinical trial stigma; they ultimately attempt to deflect the adverse events systematically caused by their social positions.

3

A Tale of Three Cultures

Healthy volunteers across the United States have similar economic motivations to enroll in Phase I trials. Yet, the *regions* in which they participate have their own unique clinical-trial cultures. To grasp these cultures, let's begin with three clinic scenes I recorded in my field notes:

Scene 1: At Pharma Phase I, healthy volunteers from one of the ongoing studies collected their lunches and gathered together at two tables in the clinic cafeteria. Adorned in matching chartreuse t-shirts emblazoned with the Pharma Phase I logo, they obviously belonged to the same study. While they ate, they talked animatedly in small groups. As I alternated my focus from one conversation to the next, I noted that the topics consistently coalesced around Phase I trials. Some participants compared the food on their trays to the "nasty" food they had gotten at other clinics. Other participants shared stories about other drug trials, particularly reflecting on negative experiences they personally had or heard about from others. Still others talked about the "spinal tap" study that was keeping a group of participants confined to their bedrooms; they debated vigorously not only the study's risk but also how much money would motivate them to consent to the insertion of a needle in their spine. Although clinic policy required participants to finish their meals in twenty minutes, many lingered in the cafeteria to continue their conversations even after they returned their meal trays. The pleasure they got from talking with each other about clinical trials was as obvious as their t-shirts.

Scene 2: Cottage Phase I had only one study in-house, but the healthy volunteers had been instructed to stay together in the procedure area, stationed in their assigned recliner chairs located in one of several rows facing a 60-inch television. In the afternoon, the TV endlessly broadcast soap operas to the room. A volunteer in the front row of recliners conspicuously held the TV's remote control, making it clear that she controlled the afternoon's entertainment. Although the volume was turned up rather loud, most of the two dozen participants ignored the television as best they could. Many watched movies on their laptop computers or listened to music on mp3 players. Some dozed. Facilitated by the recliners' close proximity, a few pairs of participants conversed about television shows, movies, and books or chatted about their jobs and families. Until one of the nurses began a new round of blood collection, it would have been easy to forget that we were in a research facility.

Scene 3: At least 70 healthy volunteers had just been admitted to Mega Phase I, and they waited in a massive room divided into multiple sections. The largest portion of the space had fifty or more armchairs facing a large-screen television. Above the TV hung a conspicuous sign declaring, "Keep TV set to Spanish Programming," and the TV was indeed tuned to Univision. In a little nook off to a far side of the room, a dozen armchairs faced a much smaller television, with the complementary sign, "Keep TV set to English Programming." The segregated space reflected the composition of healthy volunteers in the clinic, the vast majority of whom conversed with each other in Spanish or watched the Spanish-language TV, whereas a much smaller number spoke in English or sat in that area. Regardless of the language, conversations appeared to center on study participation. Some discussed the study that was about to begin while others recalled studies they had done previously. I also noticed that some of the Spanish-speaking participants greeted each other warmly with hugs and slaps on the back, indicating they had met before. Finally, the clinic staff arrived to begin the proceedings. After quieting the room, an administrator welcomed the volunteers to the facility and forecast the events scheduled for the remainder of the day, speaking in Spanish, then in English. While he delivered information in Spanish, I observed a cluster of people in the English section of the room exchanging anxious or frustrated looks.

In these representations of each Phase I clinic, we see one characterized by the predominance of conversation about clinical trials, one by the absence of such conversation, and the third by spatial division according to language and demographics. Pharma Phase I was located on the East Coast, Cottage Phase I was in the Midwest, and Mega Phase I was on the West Coast. Phase I participation cultures are partly determined by the demographics of volunteers in each region, which in turn are shaped by regional economies and opportunities for work. Differing patterns of imbricated stigma both catalyze individuals' trial enrollment and inflect their orientation to their current and future participation.

By clinical-trial "culture," I mean the shared norms and values that structure how healthy volunteers understand their participation in Phase I trials, which in turn dictate their behavior and shape their identities. Specifically, healthy volunteers on the East Coast tended to be well-networked as part of their long-term, active pursuit of clinical trials, but even so, they often expressed anti-capitalist critiques of the industry. In comparison, Midwesterners tended to be more passive about their trial participation, thinking of it as a short-term financial opportunity to counterbalance a temporary setback. Finally, West Coast participants occupied a hybrid culture between those of the East Coast and Midwest, actively seeking out new studies while wanting to limit their participation due to their distrust of the clinics. These regional cultures act as a prism on healthy volunteers' perceptions of Phase I trials, shaping the extent to which they adopt identities as research participants and become model organisms for the industry.

East Coast Participants

If one is looking for "professional guinea pigs," the East Coast is the best place to find them. While there is little empirical research on healthy volunteers, most has focused on serial participants who treat clinical trials as their sole or primary source of income and may even see studies as their job (e.g., Abadie 2010; Elliott 2008). Scholars have also written about professional healthy volunteers who are so motivated to maximize their clinical trial income that they routinely break trial protocols by ignoring washout periods between studies or enrolling simultaneously in two or more studies (e.g., Devine et al. 2013; Dresser 2013). While certainly not true of all healthy volunteers on the East Coast, this profile nonetheless applies to many individuals. It also forms a critical piece of the culture of Phase I participation that I observed at Pharma Phase I and Academic Phase I.

Because the extant literature emphasizes or assumes that healthy volunteers are young and white, it has fallen short of an accurate description of East Coast participants. In fact, the majority are black men in their thirties who are experienced healthy volunteers. For example, of the participants I interviewed at Pharma Phase I and Academic Phase I, most were black and roughly half had participated in ten or more studies, with a quarter having enrolled in more than 25.[1] Additionally, these experienced East Coast participants traveled throughout what they referred to as the "Northeast circuit," the roughly 300-mile region from New Haven, Connecticut, to Baltimore, Maryland, screening at any clinic recruiting healthy volunteers. Some even journeyed farther, going to Florida, Texas, or Wisconsin for particularly high-paying studies. Interestingly, even individuals in their first study and people with infrequent trial participation traveled a few hours to enroll. This willingness to travel for studies indicates the centrality of Phase I trials to many East Coast participants' lives: they actively kept tabs on the study clinics and went to great lengths to participate.

As the opening scene from Pharma Phase I illustrated, East Coast participants are talkative and sometimes gregarious when it comes to their clinical trial experiences. Several participants even told me that people *should* be interested in who they are and why they enroll in clinical trials. Because Pharma Phase I was the first clinic I visited, the healthy volunteers there made sure to educate me about the right questions to ask, starting with how far they had traveled to participate. Additionally, several wanted an audience for their interviews, and when I suggested relocating to a more confidential space in the clinic, they waved the idea away as if it were crazy. At the same time, it was rare for anyone listening in to interrupt or comment on what an interviewee was recounting. In one such instance, a man I had previously interviewed interjected briefly to propose we complete a follow-up interview because his friend's stories reminded him of some he had not yet told me.

Beyond their social function, conversations about clinical trials also serve a strategic purpose insofar as healthy volunteers share information that could be beneficial for their future participation. Importantly, the value of the information is ongoing, not just for newcomers. As Desmond, an African American in his thirties who was in his third study, explained, "It's like one told the other, you know? You try to help out a friend, help out a friend; that's how it goes around. Say, 'Hey, there's a study here, there's a study there.'" Likewise, Simon, a white man in his forties who had participated in about 18 studies and self-identified as a "professional guinea pig," asserted, "The core group of people I know who do many studies, if they tell me [something about a study], it's as if I had done it myself. . . . I might not have been there, but one of my extremely well-respected colleagues has been there." In this way, the so-cial networks and information flows about Phase I studies are key char-acteristics of the East Coast clinical-trial culture.

The formation of this culture is also influenced by the social and eco-nomic circumstances that make finding studies in which to earn money an imperative. We have already explored the backdrop of economic in-security that propels some individuals to enroll in clinical trials. For East Coast people of color, economic challenges are fundamentally linked to racial inequality, with social disadvantages accruing through a dys-functional education system and limited opportunities for employment. Some evidence suggests that blacks are more discriminated against in the job market on the East Coast than they are in the Midwest or on the West Coast (Bertrand and Mullainathan 2004; Cohn and Fossett 1995). These factors are felt as adverse life events but form patterns of imbricated stigma. The majority of participants at Pharma Phase I and Academic Phase I, particularly the black men, were struggling with ob-durate economic disadvantages. Too many did not finish high school, few had college degrees, and several suffered the consequences of a his-tory of incarceration.[2] Even though my visits to these clinics in 2009 and 2010 took place at a time when many in the United States were hit by the worst effects of the economic recession, East Coast participants rarely mentioned it. This is because for many of them, the recession had not substantially changed their everyday lives, even though some noted an increased competition for low-wage jobs. On the whole, the stories they told about themselves indicated that life was a constant struggle, and they hoped that clinical trials would relieve some financial pressure or possibly allow them to get ahead.

East Coast participants' pernicious economic troubles also structure their expectations about their future involvement in studies. Thus, even when healthy volunteers *hope* to stop participating, they are often care-ful to leave the door open. For example, Janae, an African American in her forties, signed up at Academic Phase I for her first trial after her neighbor, a long-time serial participant, recommended she do a study. She had confided in him about how strained her finances had become after one of her teenage sons was murdered, and he gave her the infor-mation for the clinic. Reflecting on her experiences in the study, she said, "I don't think I wanna just keep on doing this [enrolling in studies], but you never know what's gonna come up. I'm not gonna say I won't, and I'm not gonna say I am. It all depends." Rather than committing to a bleak financial future, participants engage in the rhetoric of "never say never" as a safety mechanism, allowing them to assert that they do not plan or even want to continue in studies but that they remain open to doing so.

Despite claims about the impossibility of predicting the future, participants generally expect that their economic instability will persist. This was certainly the case for Wesley, an African American in his early thirties who had enrolled in an average of three studies each year for the past ten years. Unlike Janae, Wesley did not voice a desire to quit participating. Instead, he declared, "I think I'll keep doing 'em [studies] until I get old, [until] like I can't do no more. I mean, I'm gonna always do studies, you know, 'cause I know I can always count on the cash. . . . 'Cause sometimes you can get a big chunk of money and you can get out of your debt for a little bit of time, you know. But you're gonna always be in debt, you know, unless you hit the lottery . . . because the bills keep coming back. As fast as you pay 'em, they come back." Wesley's view of the economic benefits of clinical trials hinged on his assessment of being unable to subsist—barring a lottery win—without supplementing his income from a string of retail and restaurant jobs he had held over the past decade. Thus, the motif for East Coast participants is that clinical trials are a long-term financial solution because times are either always tough or constantly threaten to be tough again. For those participants who do not want to commit to a future of clinical trials, the option to go back to studies as needed always remains on the table.

A primary reason they remain open, if not fully committed, to future participation is that many East Coast volunteers judge the compensation to be an unparalleled source of income. Not only does Phase I participation help make ends meet, but many believe they can earn more in studies than they can in a regular job. As I previously noted, it is difficult to earn even $20,000 from studies per year, but the worse someone's employment options are, the better that clinical trials look. Indeed, many East Coast participants whom I met consistently made less than $10,000 a year outside of studies, and to earn any wage income often meant working undesirable, insecure jobs. Kevin, an African American in his early forties from New York City, affirmed this when he said, "I'm affiliated with a temporary agency, but I haven't been going there too much. . . . I'm making twice as much money [doing studies] as I used to make when I was doing 9 to 5. These checks are really big—$3,000 to $9,000." For Kevin and others, a history of unstable and low-paying jobs makes clinical trials all the more attractive.

Searching for work can also be demoralizing when good positions seem impossible to obtain. For example, Alexandra, a white transwoman in her forties, held a seasonal job at a department store, but she contrasted her spotty work history with idealized, yet atavistic, notions of employment: "I couldn't survive without the studies really. . . . I hear about people, like, in jobs for 20 years and getting their gold watch, and that's never gonna happen to me. . . . Especially with the economy the way it is, if you don't measure up, there's like 100 people down the line that might take your job. So, I mean, things aren't the way they used to be, you know. It's tough out there in the job market." Add to this the perception that studies are "easy" work, and many East Coast volunteers are absolutely sold on monetarily relying, at least in part, on clinical trials. Describing why studies are an easy source of money, Rashid, a Pakistani immigrant in his forties, explained, "You stay [in the clinic], you relax, and you get paid like $200 a day to get a little bit of blood out of you." Imbricated stigma, of course, adversely structures these participants' employment opportunities. Being black, an immigrant, or perceived as gender transgressive not only creates barriers to obtaining stable, well-paid jobs, but also makes the compensation from clinical trials appear all the more substantial.

Even though most East Coast participants see clinical trials as a great source of income, they are simultaneously highly critical of the pharmaceutical and clinical trials industries. This, too, becomes an integral part of the clinical-trial culture in their region. For instance, having witnessed a recent decline in study compensation, some participants speculated that the 2008 economic downturn provided an excuse to offer healthy volunteers less money. Rather than perceiving the industry as struggling economically, most participants thought the clinics and particularly the pharmaceutical industry were buffered from the recession's effects. Shirley, an African American in her late thirties, became impassioned as she analyzed the change: "The drug companies, the academic institutions, or whatever it is, this huge wheel that turns, you know, to power clinical studies, . . . yeah, it's just so flippin' capitalistic, you know, when you think about it. . . . Everybody lowering their prices, the sponsors are just . . . cheering themselves, you know, because they're actually making more profit off of people [healthy volunteers] who are ignorant and desperate, I would say." Similarly, John, a white man in his early thirties, averred, "I think we could get paid more, and I also think, considering the kind of money the drug companies spend, they pay the smallest amount that they think that they can get away with. It's just good business, I guess. And most of us take it." Study compensation is not open for negotiation, which means that companies can offer less money as long as people continue to sign up for studies. John could not help blaming himself and others for accepting less than they should, which—from Shirley's standpoint—results in further profits for the industry.

East Coast participants did not use the word "exploitation," but it nonetheless encapsulates their understanding of the situation: the money is good but not as good as it could or should be considering how much revenue companies make from drug development. When bemoaning the drop in compensation, Marshall, an African American in his thirties, declared, "They [pharmaceutical companies] make billions, so they would pay other people [the clinics running the studies] millions, [so] why can't I get thousands [more] for it? That's how I look at it. . . . Don't cut *me* off from getting my money, especially when you gonna make money off the pills that we buy, you know?" Marshall's frustration underscores that participants discern that clinical trials are a big business, a savvy perspective formed by observing how the industry operates. Moreover, recognizing how valuable healthy volunteers are to drug development but being unable to set the terms of the exchange can create mixed feelings about their participation. For example, despite his positive perceptions of the compensation relative to temp work, Kevin complained, "And they need people to test 'em on. [Laughs.] That's the whole thing about it. They need people to test 'em on. . . . They're not actually paying volunteers enough money, actually." Hence, participants like Kevin feel taken advantage of while still acknowledging their trial earnings are an unprecedented source of income.[3]

Critiques of the industry have also given rise to calls for a "guinea pig union." While the majority of healthy volunteers do not actually want to create a union, the idea is part of the fabric of East Coast clinical-trial culture because participants strongly believe their criticisms of the industry should be addressed (Abadie 2010). Such views also become a core component of their *identities* as healthy volunteers by adding a different type of solidarity to their social networks. If the industry is exploitative, the information participants exchange can help people earn more money from trials or possibly even protect themselves. This could mean cheating the system by ignoring washout periods or breaking other rules set by the trial protocols. It could also mean sharing intelligence about clinics to avoid or studies that generate too many adverse events. Yet, a vocal minority of East Coast participants cautioned that rather than disrupting the system, healthy volunteers' response to exploitative conditions largely makes them complicit with the industry and ultimately might make companies more money. These were the people who argued for organized collective action. For example, Simon, the self-identified professional guinea pig, proclaimed,

So, myself and a few other people who do a lot of studies are actually trying to get something started where they won't be able to go any lower [with the pay]. . . . There's power in numbers. . . . We're definitely doing something where we just won't do studies. And then, all of a sudden, now, you know, these places [clinics] . . . if they keep continually not being able to fill a study, it doesn't matter if they bid for it or not, [the pharmaceutical companies] they're . . . gonna tell them, "We're not gonna give it [the trial] to you." . . . There's ways we can play the game as well. So, I mean, there are things that we can do. We are in more control than a lot of people give us credit for.

While the idea of a guinea pig strike might be exciting, most healthy volunteers doubted its efficacy, fearing they would instead just lose income. Or as Manuel, a Puerto Rican in his thirties, observed, "There's no union in this thing. So, you know, it's like when you're doing a protest, you've gotta watch out for the scabs." The threat here is that there are always more people—perhaps those new to clinical trials who do not understand how the industry works—who could take their place. When participants want Phase I trials to remain a long-term option, this could be a risky outcome, persuading them to channel their criticisms as information flows within their social networks rather than as a call to action.

East Coast healthy volunteers have created and actively maintain a clinical-trial culture based on social networks. These networks have the intended effect of providing tips about studies, but they also encourage long-term serial participation as well as contribute to people's identities as research participants. In this way, East Coast culture can be seen as cultivating model organisms for the industry by deeply embedding savvy healthy volunteers within the Phase I world. Even for individuals who feel exploited by this industry, the financial benefit prevails, and the industry pays healthy volunteers just enough to motivate a standing reserve of East Coast participants to continuously enroll. Indeed, the largely African American participant pool in the Northeast is no stranger to exploitation; these individuals are already systematically disadvantaged and provide underpaid labor to powerful corporations in many sectors of the economy. In this way, clinical trial participation becomes just another component of a broader pattern of social inequalities.

Midwest Participants

Having started this ethnographic project on the East Coast, I found myself unprepared for the vast cultural difference when I visited CRO Phase I and Cottage Phase I in the Midwest. While CRO Phase I was similar demographically to the East Coast clinics in that African American men were the majority group, healthy volunteers' experience with clinical trials was the polar opposite. On the East Coast, it was rare to meet someone who was in a trial for the first time. In contrast, nearly three-quarters of the participants at CRO Phase I were enrolled in their first study. Although only a third of Cottage Phase I participants were first-timers, this clinic also stood out from the others. It was the only one in my sample where non-Hispanic whites made up the majority of healthy volunteers. Moreover, there was only one immigrant present across both Midwest clinics—Clark, who was a white student from the United Kingdom—and no Hispanic participants at all. Finally, Midwestern participants were largely younger than their East Coast (and West Coast) counterparts, with people in their twenties predominating. The differences between the East Coast and the Midwest clinics, however, went well beyond these surface characteristics.

One of my first impressions of the Midwestern healthy volunteers was that they were incredibly friendly but unexpectedly terse. Everyone I met was so eager to be interviewed that one day at CRO Phase I, I felt as though I had become hostage to the interviewing process as participants literally lined up outside the examination room I was using to conduct interviews. As soon as someone left the room, the next entered. Notwithstanding their enthusiasm, most had little to say about their Phase I trial participation. They smiled as they laconically answered my questions, and many seemed stumped by my interest in their perceptions of clinical trials. For example, Eric, a multiracial man in his twenties, was a first-time participant, and he became truly confused by my request to recount his experiences in the study. After a long pause, he offered, "I mean it ain't really no experience in here. You wake up, you get your blood drawn, eat what they tell you to eat, and then go to sleep. I mean we just find stuff to pass the time. For real, but there's nothing to tell."

Unlike most East Coast participants, Midwestern healthy volunteers typically see clinical trials as a temporary source of income and not a part of their identity. This different orientation means they spend much less time thinking and talking with each other about Phase I studies. Perhaps just as the participants were uncertain about what to tell me during interviews, they might have felt equally at a loss for how—or why—to talk about clinical trials with each other. As described in the scene above, they talked instead about their lives outside of studies—their families, homes, and jobs they had held.

Another important element contributing to the Midwest clinical-trial culture is the more explicit connection between healthy volunteers' participation and the 2008 recession. Many of the first-time participants had recently found themselves in the sudden and unaccustomed position of being unemployed, and they had learned about Phase I trials at job fairs where the clinics had booths. Their new status as unemployed was the shared catalyst to participation that connected them, rendering the clinical trial that had actually brought them together almost incidental. In this context, many viewed the study as a simple stopgap measure to help pay the bills until their employment was restored.

Both Curtis and Adam were recently unemployed and had enrolled at CRO Phase I in their first clinical trial. It was a 25-night confinement study testing the interaction of an investigational drug and a blood thinner. After losing his job in a nursing home, Curtis, an African American in his twenties, had given his information to a clinic representative at a job fair. Several days later, the clinic called and invited him to screen for the study. Curtis explained, "I'm unemployed right now. I recently got laid off. So, it was like, well, for $4,600, as long as I don't grow an extra finger or anything like that, I should be fine. So, . . . I just took the offer." Adam, a white man in his early thirties, similarly narrated his introduction to clinical trials: "Actually, I was looking at the [news]paper for a job and seen that [advertisement] and just, you know, called around. They said they're [paying] forty-six hundred bucks. . . . [Later] they called me back, and they were like, 'You've been approved for the study. Can you come in?' I'm like, 'Yeah,' you know, 'okay, sure.' And then I came in and found more information out about it, and I was like, 'Okay, that's fine.' . . . Forty-six hundred bucks, I mean, you know, for 25 days, it's not too bad of a deal, I wouldn't think." While motivated by the compensation, neither man conveyed much interest in pursuing the lead; both seemed to have merely gone along with it. Likewise, even Midwestern participants who had done more than one study reported that the clinic had contacted them about a new study, not that they had been actively seeking one.

Unlike East Coast participants who often work hard to find available studies, Midwestern participants' approach to seriality is much more passive. In addition, most are unlikely to travel outside of their home city to enroll in studies despite relatively short drives to other Phase I facilities in the region. Tyler, a white man in his twenties, was unusual for the Midwest in terms of his level of experience with Phase I trials, but his passivity about his participation was nonetheless striking. Tyler's primary income came from waiting tables, but he had supplemented it with 14 studies at two clinics over three years. He explained, "When you do your first study, you're kind of on their list. They'll call you; they'll let you know when they have studies. And then I found out about this [other] facility and kind of bounce back [and forth] between the two."

The clinical-trial culture of passivity regarding study participation is rooted in Midwesterners' priorities for earning income. Participants' clear preference for regular employment creates ambivalence, especially among men, about study compensation. On one hand, they perceive the amount of money that studies offer to be substantial. For those in dire circumstances in particular, many feel grateful for the financial opportunity that clinical trials afford. For instance, Nelson, an African American in his thirties who had been at risk of becoming homeless, credited enrollment in his second study for getting him back on his feet. His gratitude was especially pronounced because he had been an alternate in his first study at CRO Phase I and made only $250 for spending the night before being dismissed. A few days later, the clinic called him and offered him a guaranteed spot in another study: "But the second study, Dr. Scott had me in mind, and I really appreciate him for that. He called me and told me about the overweight study [I'm in]. . . . Of course I was up for it, and I did it. I needed the money. I felt like it was a godsend because I was going through some things and that really helped me." With job loss, people's financial situations become precarious very quickly, and the compensation from clinical trials can make a dramatic difference, as it did for Nelson.

On the other hand, Midwestern healthy volunteers do not see clinical trials as a substitute for a full-time job. This was, of course, true for first-time participants who believed their unemployment would be short term. Ted, for one, had never expected to find himself in a clinical trial. A white man in his forties, Ted had recently lost his management position in an information technology firm. He had found out about clinical trials through a friend, and both he and his wife decided to screen to keep up with their mortgage. When we talked, Ted's wife had completed her study, and he was three weeks into a primarily outpatient, eight-week study. Speculating about his future participation, Ted said, "I suppose if I don't find work right away, yeah, I'd be open to it, you know. . . . But I probably won't do many of these 'cause I'll get working again and won't have time." Even participants with a longer history of enrolling in Phase I trials rejected the idea that clinical trials could be anything but short-term income between jobs. For example, Ryan, a white man in his thirties, expressed surprise that he was already doing his third study. He had joined his first study a year before when his job with a security company had been cut back from full time to part time. Reflecting on the studies he had done, he became a bit defensive when justifying his decision to enroll: "I'm not working that much anymore. I'm working just a couple hours a week. . . . Times are tough, and I kind of have to do what I need to do. . . . Which is unfortunate. I'm not proud of being a guinea pig. . . . I'd prefer to get a full-time job, Monday thru Friday. But until then, yeah, I'd probably continue to do the studies." Supporting Midwestern participants' conviction that clinical trials would be short-term was their expectation that their next job was right around the corner. Just as they would not have considered enrolling in trials when they had been working, they anticipated that their employment situation would return to normal and studies would no longer have a place in their lives. Within such a frame, the money from studies might be good, perhaps even great, but no substitute for the stability and wages of a permanent job.

Another important component of the Midwest clinical-trial culture is that participants have a sweeping notion of what count as "studies." Although most people I met were new to Phase I trials, many had a long history of getting paid for their opinion in consumer-product research. Unlike East Coast healthy volunteers, however, many did not distinguish between these marketing studies and Phase I trials. For example, Gabe, an African American in his late forties, counted his study at CRO Phase I as his second, but his first study had been for a breakfast cereal. Similarly, Grace, an African American in her early sixties who worked full time for a health insurance company, proudly identified as a "veteran of studies," having tested potato chips, hot chocolate, skin care products, and antiperspirant in addition to an allergy medication. Dana, an African American in her early twenties, had a similar involvement in marketing studies. Now in her first drug trial, she remarked, "I've probably done at least about eight to ten studies . . . ranging from probably about $10 to about $200. . . . And this is the first one that I've done that's been this big [that is, paid so much]!" Like Dana, many participants differentiated these studies not by the product being tested or the procedures used but by the amount of compensation. By lumping together Phase I trials and marketing research, Midwestern participants unwittingly frame clinical trials as trivial and safe, just something to bring in a few extra dollars.

Yet, even those Midwesterners with a history of pursuing diverse types of studies to earn extra money do not integrate this activity into their identities. Instead, they might see it as a quirky thing they do from time to time. For example, Hattie, an African American in her late sixties, was a retired school teacher who had begun by participating in toothpaste and mouthwash studies and then enrolled as a patient in sleep and blood pressure studies. After discovering Phase I trials, she waited for an opportunity to try that as well, and eventually she became a healthy volunteer in an osteoporosis study. When I asked how long she planned to continue participating in studies, the question visibly bothered Hattie, and she responded as if to set the record straight: "Well, it's been over a year since I did my last study, and I just do 'em when I need some extra money. I mean, I'm not always looking for them, and I turn a lot of 'em down. If I don't need the money, there's no point in doing it. . . . I'm not hooked. I'm not a research junkie—uh uh—because I like doing other things with my time." Comments like Hattie's are not made with any reproach for how *others* might choose to participate in studies. Indeed, a dominant motif among Midwesterners is that enrolling in studies is "a personal choice" and not something to be judged by others. Their comments nonetheless contain a recurring critique: study participation should never become a way of life; it should only be a temporary or occasional way to supplement one's income. Because of their limited trial experience, these participants were unlikely to have crossed paths with the East Coast healthy volunteers who traveled to the Midwest to enroll in trials, but these imagined professional participants served as a touchstone against which Midwesterners could reject the stigma of participation and justify their own involvement in clinical trials.

In sum, the Midwest clinical-trial culture counterintuitively deemphasizes Phase I studies themselves, including their importance to participants' lives. The fact that so many Midwesterners were relatively new participants meant that many had only recently experienced major financial setbacks, and because these had largely been due to job loss, many people expected to secure work soon, which would obviate any need to enroll in future trials. Midwestern participants also differ from their East Coast counterparts in that they made no critique of the pharmaceutical industry or capitalism.[4] Instead, Midwesterners expressed gratitude for the opportunity to earn income that might tide them over until they were again gainfully employed. These characteristics of Midwest clinical-trial culture can be read as stemming from incredibly different social and economic conditions than those that structure the lives of participants on the East Coast. This is not to say that they are not disadvantaged by imbricated forms of stigma, but it does indicate that many Midwestern healthy volunteers do not suffer the same intractable economic adversity as participants on either coast. As a result, Midwestern healthy volunteers are less likely to become the model organisms upon which the Phase I industry relies for its data.

West Coast Participants

If we envision Phase I clinical-trial cultures on a spectrum with East Coast participants on one end and Midwestern participants on the other, we would find West Coast participants very nearly in the middle. There is no single West Coast "type," however; professional healthy volunteers who resemble East Coast participants intermingle with others who, like Midwesterners, eschew that formal identity. Yet, regardless of how many studies they have done, West Coast participants enjoy talking about Phase I trials and form social networks to help find new studies. Even though many of the Spanish speakers can communicate in English, at least to some degree, healthy volunteers' networks coalesce around their primary language. In an important sense, the most salient characteristic of the West Coast clinical-trial culture is that it consists of antagonistic subcultures, even though individual healthy volunteers rarely clash.

Unlike those in other parts of the country, West Coast clinics are more likely to allow participants who speak only Spanish to enroll in studies.[5] Both Mega Phase I and Local Phase I heavily recruited healthy volunteers from Spanish-speaking populations—largely immigrants from Mexico and Central America. During my visit to Mega Phase I, there were more than 70 participants in the clinic, and the vast majority were Spanish-speakers. Local Phase I had a more even match of English- and Spanish-speakers with a slightly larger number among those who spoke English as their first language.

West Coast healthy volunteers have, on average, participated in more Phase I trials than Midwesterners but fewer than people on the East Coast. Almost no one at Mega Phase I was in his or her first clinical trial. At Local Phase I, first-time participants constituted more than a third of those enrolled in various studies, and they were evenly divided between non-Hispanic and Hispanic recruits. However, across both clinics about half of the participants were in their third through fifteenth study. Notwithstanding their greater trial experience, most participants were similar to their Midwestern counterparts in that they had enrolled in studies at only one or two clinics. This limited number of clinics was likely due to the greater distance between West Coast clinics, fewer long-distance public transportation options, and restrictions on where non-English speaking participants could enroll. As on the East Coast, a handful of non-Hispanic participants also identified as "professional guinea pigs" and traveled throughout the country for studies. Notably, two of them, Brian and Louis, flagrantly disregarded the washout period by leaving Local Phase I and immediately joining a study at Mega Phase I.[6]

The earlier scene from Mega Phase I illustrated how the clinic space separated participants based on language, which profoundly affected the clinic culture. Beyond the practical problem of communication, this division along ethnic lines was also symptomatic of the region's broader political economy. The 2008 recession particularly affected the West Coast's housing market, including the rapid end to new home construction throughout Southern California, Nevada, and Arizona (Florida 2009). With the massive job loss that followed, longstanding xenophobic concerns about illegal immigration swelled, leading to even greater animosity in the region toward undocumented workers from Mexico and Central America (Ellis et al. 2014). This culminated in the 2010 passage of Arizona Senate Bill 1070, a broad and discriminatory anti-immigration law intended to make it impossible for undocumented residents to secure work. Although this law applied to the State of Arizona only, and although its constitutionality was immediately challenged and some of its provisions were blocked by court-ordered injunctions, popular support for the measure across the United States accentuates the tense relationship between some native-born and naturalized citizens and Spanish-speaking immigrants (Brown 2013).

My visit to both West Coast clinics in October 2010 occurred after the passage of Arizona SB1070, and immigration politics were on the surface of healthy volunteers' perceptions of each other. Because clinical trials are a competitive source of income, they foment the same anti-immigration narrative about job theft, and for undocumented immigrants, speaking Spanish is all the more stigmatized within Phase I clinics. In interviews, non-Hispanic participants expressed anger toward Spanish-speakers in the clinic, accusing them of taking their place in studies just as they had in the regular employment sector. For instance, Frank, a white man in his forties who had participated in about ten studies, declared, "You're like competing [in studies] against, you know, the minorities, the Hispanics. And then it started becoming a little bit more of an issue trying to get in the place [i.e., clinic] because, you know, nobody's ID'd. . . . It's still not fair . . . if they make $5,000 on a study and they're not paying the taxes on it or they just came from the border from a coyote and they're hiding out here!" Because healthy volunteers are not employees, they are not required to be US citizens; they do need a tax identification number, such as an Individual Taxpayer Identification Number (ITIN), but a Social Security number is not mandatory. Frank and others clearly wished that conventional labor laws applied to Phase I trials. Take Louis, a multiracial man in his fifties—even though he had participated in about forty studies in the past eleven years, Louis insisted he was disadvantaged: "Mega Phase I was a nightmare. When I was doing studies there, they really were . . . they were totally unfair. They were totally [showing] favoritism. . . . And I have nothing against Latinos, trust me. I don't. I love 'em, but it's just flagrant favoritism." Given that Louis was one of the individuals who had participated back to back at Local Phase I and Mega Phase I, it would appear that he was not having difficulty enrolling, but he likely felt the pressure of competition from people he perceived as less entitled to earn money through studies.

At the same time, immigration politics also shape Latinos' perceptions of non-Hispanics. Specifically, many were astounded by non-Hispanics' involvement in Phase I trials. Latinos explained their own participation as due to a lack of work but assumed that non-Hispanics must be lazy. For instance, Hector, a Latino in his thirties enrolled in his third study, asserted, "The anglos, they *can* work, and they don't do it" (translated from Spanish). Similarly, Vera, a Latina in her twenties whose husband also participated in studies, succinctly explained, "Because we are not here legally, we don't have another option left." At the heart of these immigrants' perspective is the belief that native-born healthy volunteers—who can work legally—do not face the same employment challenges, so if they enroll in clinical trials, they must be *choosing* not to work a regular job.

Despite English- and Spanish-speaking participants' perceptions of each other, they have more in common than they grant. In particular, most West Coast healthy volunteers do not want to participate in clinical trials full time or long term. Many even mentioned having known about studies for a long time but deciding to enroll only when their financial need became urgent. This was the case for Frank, the participant who was angry about undocumented immigrants being allowed into studies. He described how Mega Phase I had initially pursued him:

> A few years ago, . . . they were actually calling *us* to come in. . . . I don't know where they got the list, but they were calling us. . . . People had jobs then, and . . . it wasn't like how it is now with the recession and people not having jobs and having problems and stuff like that, and foreclosures and things that we're dealing with. . . . Back then, it was good. . . . And I just was like, "I'm getting this call from these people, and . . . I don't want to be in a research study."

Frank called Mega Phase I and finally joined a study after he had lost his job and his unemployment benefits ran out. Similarly, as a first-time participant, Tiffany, a Native American in her thirties, revealed the desperation that propelled her enrollment, seemingly against her better judgment: "I'm hoping and praying that I'm not gonna be in this situation again, as far as financially, just to where I would pretty much do anything, and this is really like my last resort."

Latino/a participants share the perception that studies should not be done lightly. Many claimed that they could no longer find any work at all and promised that as soon as they did, they would never enroll again. Alma, a Latina in her fifties, had already participated in four studies, but she declared, "I think that no, in fact, we shouldn't do these studies, right? [Laughs.] But it's the necessity. Necessity has made us do this" (translated from Spanish). Mirasol, a Latina in her twenties, refused to say how many Phase I trials she had completed but had frequented two West Coast clinics, and when asked about her decision to enroll, she responded, "What made me decide? Truthfully, hardship. . . . The people that go [to these clinics] very often—, well, there are people who—, how can I explain it? There are people that because of lack of work, we take part in many studies consecutively. And there are people who do not go [to places like this] because they have a stable job. . . . Like years ago when there was steady work like that, we would not even go near [studies]. They would offer [studies] to us, and we would not go near them" (translated from Spanish). It is striking how similar Mirasol's narrative is to Frank's. Both remembered a time when Phase I clinics called them and they had no interest in enrolling.

Most West Coast participants did not have the same optimism as Midwesterners that they would get full-time employment soon, but they believed the economy would eventually rebound, which would mean more work for everyone. For instance, even though he had already enrolled in four studies, Aidan, a white man in his thirties who claimed his participation was temporary, feared the very possibility of it becoming a long-term source of income: "[I] could not imagine doing this, like, for a living, so. But it is kinda scary to come and see people that you've seen [before]. . . . It's like, oh my god, that is becoming me, this cannot be me!" He made a commitment to himself that as soon as the economy improved, "I'm not coming back to do it, no."

Whereas East Coast and Midwestern participants typically perceive that the compensation is phenomenal for the time and effort, West Coast healthy volunteers are more ambivalent about the study stipends. Pointing out that all studies are not equal, many participants noted the wide variation in compensation. Patrick, a white man in his thirties who had done "many" studies, avowed that "the pay is not worth the time" for a lot of available trials. This is particularly interesting to contrast with Patrick's opinion of regular work about which he said, "In this day and age, you take anything you can get." Patrick worked a string of part-time and temp jobs that, unlike studies, held the promise for him of future steady income. This indicates that at least for some West Coast healthy volunteers, study compensation is not seen in absolute terms; the monetary value of the pay—which might be equivalent to low-end wage labor—is moderated by the symbolic value that clinical trials are not actually jobs. At the same time, however, the compensation for some studies is framed as too good to pass up. Representing this position, Alan, a white man in his forties, said, "I knew I wanted to do it [the study] because I needed the money, so once I knew I qualified and the money was good, I'm like,

'I'm doing it.' It would be kinda foolish not to. That's like winning the lottery and not taking the money, [laughs] you know?" By describing the compensation in this way, Alan exaggerated how much money he would earn while also defending his decision to enroll.

West Coast participants' mixed perceptions of the compensation also inflect their view of the clinics and pharmaceutical industry. Because of how grim some participants' financial situations were, many expressed sentiments echoing those of Midwesterners about their gratitude for the opportunity to enroll in studies. For example, Claudia, an unemployed Latina in her thirties in her fourth study, asserted (in English) that "the studies is very good for me, for everyone, for their economics. . . . Everything [I do in] this clinic is [for] my family, is for food, for the money. It's for my children, everything. . . . This clinic, these studies, is my salvation and my family's." Pablo, a Latino in his thirties who was participating in his second study, put it even more simply when he proclaimed, "I thank God that there are studies" (translated from Spanish).

West Coast participants' gratitude, however, is not uncritical. Believing that the clinics take advantage of their financial desperation, many articulated their distrust of them. Thus, for example, Honesto, a Latino in his sixties participating in his second study, professed, "The economic situation of this country forces us to be here in one form or another—Americans or not Americans—to do this thing that goes against our health. This is for animals, these experiments should be done on rats" (translated from Spanish). Like others, Honesto had strong feelings about how the economy was driving healthy people to endanger themselves. However, Honesto also worried that nonlegal residents are even more vulnerable to harm from the clinics. He continued,

> And we have clear examples that have been on the news, I believe it was in El Salvador. . . . This [US] government is recognizing that they did a study that infected more than ten thousand people with HIV. . . . I've heard that in some studies they come from Mexico, they cross the border and then return because they have the opportunity to do a study. . . . They showed a documentary that people were gathered for the studies, and they gathered people and took them to the [clinics] and afterward they received [only] 50 percent of the study [pay]. . . . On Telemundo they showed that there were Mafias [involved]. (Translated from Spanish)[7]

While Honesto's concerns about shady research clinics that exploit undocumented immigrants might smack too much of a conspiracy theory to be given much credence, his underlying worry about the trustworthiness of clinics is one to take seriously. I also heard echoes of these sentiments from other Latino/a participants. For instance, even though Carlos was in his third study, his nervousness about the risks was right on the surface. Carlos was a Latino immigrant in his thirties and had been struggling to find work for years. As soon as I turned on the recorder and before I could ask a single question, he confessed, "[Studies] are the only way we can get money, but I have a question about it. I don't know if this is gonna affect, you know, like affect me in the future if I keep doing this, like two or three [more] times. So I don't know is it gonna be bad for my health. . . . I have that question, but I don't know. They're not gonna tell me if I ask them. They're not gonna tell me the truth. I don't know." Carlos's worry about the staff not providing full and accurate information is another instantiation of Latinos' belief that the clinics are nefarious. Non-Hispanic participants, for their part, generally expressed more trust in the clinics where they had enrolled, but they too conveyed suspicion about places they had never been.

The clinical-trial culture on the West Coast has many more tensions and contradictions than the East Coast and Midwest cultures. Immigration politics are brought into the clinics and, along with language differences, distort people's views of one another, with immigrants being accused of taking study compensation away from American citizens and non-Hispanics being viewed as too lazy to pursue employment options that are superior to Phase I trials. Despite the substantial ethnic tensions in the clinic, the differences among West Coast healthy volunteers seem to be a matter of degree not kind. Regardless of their immigration status or racial or ethnic group, West Coast participants as a whole might be thought of as reluctant model organisms, enrolling serially in new studies despite their profound reservations. They differ from their East Coast counterparts in that their identities are not entwined in study participation, and they articulate a strong desire to quit enrolling. At the same time, West Coast participants espouse a longer-term commitment to enrolling in studies than Midwesterners, but to some degree, this might reflect West Coast participants' greater pessimism about finding other financial opportunities to support themselves and their families.

What distinguishes West Coast clinical-trial culture most from the East Coast and Midwest is healthy volunteers' distrust of the industry. Many feel compelled to enroll in studies to earn income, but they maintain suspicions that the clinics treat them unfairly or worse. Even if there were no basis for these concerns, they are consistent with the region's stigmatizing immigration politics and policies. Ethnic minorities, regardless of their legal status, fear the power of institutions in general to harm or exploit them. At the same time, non-Hispanic, native-born whites believe that institutions are distributing resources, such as jobs and income, unfairly, having assumed—perhaps with little or no evidence—that their personal situations have been adversely affected by undocumented residents. With clinical trials, these forms of distrust are imported into the clinic, permeating how healthy volunteers see each other and the industry. In this regard, being a model organism is both something to struggle to achieve and something to fear.

Comparing Volunteer Cultures

Depicting healthy volunteers across the United States presents challenges when not all individuals are equally representative of the whole. I have sketched out the differences among participants on the East Coast, Midwest, and West Coast in terms of the clinical-trial cultures that coalesce in those regions. East Coast participants who incorporate long-term research participation into their identities are the quintessential model organisms for the industry. In contrast, Midwestern and West Coast healthy volunteers typically expect and want their participation to be temporary, so they tend to see it as something they do and not who they are.

In all three regions, people's adverse life events catalyze their involvement as healthy volunteers in Phase I trials. Social inequalities exist across the United States, but patterns of imbricated stigma vary, creating different ties between the industry and disparate groups of healthy volunteers. On the West Coast, immigration politics infuse what it means to be un- or underemployed as well as valuing or devaluing people as workers based on their membership in different racial and ethnic groups. The 2008 recession exacerbated these relations, as massive job losses led to retaliatory immigration laws in at least one state.

Yet, in spite of this, there remained the sense that clinical trials would no longer be needed to make ends meet once the economy recovered and jobs were again plentiful. Similarly, the Midwest also felt the recession's effects. Joblessness in a place where most individuals participating in trials had previously experienced relatively stable employment gave the region a different character. Among these healthy volunteers, there was a stronger belief that the next good job was right around the corner, and when it came, there would never be a need to give another thought to clinical trials. The sense that participation was temporary was also a product of having healthy volunteers in the clinic who were all relatively new to clinical trials; hence, there were no counternarratives depicting how study participation could morph into a career. Both of these regional cultures are a far cry from popular conceptions of the shrewd "professional guinea pig," a type of participant most clearly associated with the East Coast. Not only is the Phase I industry more established in the Northeast, but it is also a region where racial minorities have been plagued by insecure jobs and wages that are persistently below the cost of living. In this context, it is no wonder that even when clinical trials are not a "career," there is comfort in knowing that when financial times are tough, a study can yield a few thousand dollars relatively quickly.

Clinical-trial cultures are not static, however. At the time of this research, for example, Midwestern healthy volunteers had limited exposure to study participation because of how new the industry was in their local areas. Over the past decade, the Phase I industry has chosen to build new research clinics in the Midwest while closing many older facilities in the Northeast, which in turn has prompted many more East Coast participants to leave the Northeast circuit in search of studies in other regions of the country. These changes, which physically bring together participants from different regions in the same clinics, might result in a gradual blending of clinical-trial cultures. Additionally, national trends in deindustrialization indicate that those lost jobs in the Midwest have largely not been replaced with similar forms of work. While employment has improved more on the West Coast, national politics—especially the blatantly xenophobic discourse of the Trump administration—nevertheless provide endless fuel for abhorrent forms of discrimination against immigrants. The resulting sedimentation of underemployment and economic instability creates the perfect conditions for Midwestern and West Coast healthy volunteers to shift their perception of Phase I participation as a short-term stopgap measure to a viable long-term strategy to maintain their households. These factors combined might even lead Midwestern and West Coast healthy volunteers to become savvier about and more critical of the capitalistic nature of the clinical trials industry. Indeed, as the next chapter illustrates, participants' voices can draw critical attention to the damaging effects of industry changes on the treatment of healthy volunteers across the country.

4

The Commercialization of Phase I Trials

Opportunities for healthy volunteers to participate in Phase I clinical trials have proliferated across the United States in the past three decades. New models of outsourcing clinical research restructured how pharmaceutical companies test their investigational drugs from Phase I through Phase IV trials. Beginning in the 1980s, for-profit companies called "contract research organizations" (CROs) were formed to assist pharmaceutical companies with clinical development, especially by providing statistical and project-management services (Mirowski 2011).[1] These companies also largely supplanted the central role of academic medical centers in conducting clinical trials (Fisher 2009). By outsourcing many of the routine yet complex tasks associated with testing their investigational drugs, pharmaceutical companies were able to expand the recruitment of research participants and putatively speed up drug development (Fisher 2007; Petryna 2009). In addition, by closing their own Phase I clinics, pharmaceutical companies can outlay resources only when they have clinical trials to conduct as opposed to having constant expenses associated with the operational costs of maintaining and staffing a clinic even when its use is low.[2]

Spurred on by these patterns of outsourcing and coupled with exponential growth in pharmaceutical R&D and the generic drug market (Borfitz 2013; PhRMA 2016), the commercial clinical trials industry made large-scale capital and infrastructural investments in its Phase I sector in particular. Departing from previous pharmaceutical industry patterns of concentrating growth in the Northeast corridor, commercial companies instead opened Phase I clinics throughout the United States, including in small cities and areas in the Midwest not previously known for medical research. These clinics included independent research companies specializing in Phase I clinical trials and CRO-based facilities. Unlike independent clinics that do not provide any other services to pharmaceutical companies beyond conducting Phase I studies, CROs' decision to invest millions of dollars building trial facilities or acquiring investigative sites is due principally to the companies' hope that working with pharmaceutical companies from the initial stages of human testing—which is lucrative in itself—will position them to win additional contracts for the entire clinical development process, including ushering investigational drugs to FDA review (Korieth and Zisson 2007).

Not only did the number of new Phase I facilities steadily increase in the 2000s, but also the scale of these facilities changed dramatically. Built to house more participants, newer clinics can accommodate large Phase I trials or conduct multiple studies simultaneously. Most contain no fewer than 50 beds, and several were designed with multiple wards to house hundreds of participants. A far cry from the 12- to 24-bed clinics at most academic medical centers, this is a development that emphasizes the high throughput of clinical trials imagined, if not always realized, by the industry.

While many of these organizational changes are typical contemporary business practices, the Phase I industry has also been plagued by scandal. In the United States, the largest Phase I facility to ever operate was SFBC International in Miami, which was a 675-bed clinic that was housed in a former Holiday Inn and was shut down in 2006 for fire and safety violations and negative press about its enrollment of undocumented immigrants (Evans, Smith, and Willen 2005). In another instance, the massive 544-bed PRACS Institute (Fargo, North Dakota) filed for bankruptcy and abruptly closed, ceasing studies in progress, terminating employees, and failing to compensate hundreds of participants (Redfearn 2013). The FDA has also identified cases of fraudulent data produced by CROs. This has meant that in some instances clinical testing of investigational drugs has had to be recommenced before the FDA would consider pharmaceutical companies' applications to market the drugs (CenterWatch 2007; Redfearn 2012). However, most of the senior management implicated in these scandals were able to survive them by maintaining the same clinics and infrastructure but operating under a different name.

Hence, there are now more types of organizations involved in clinical research than there were thirty years ago, which, in turn, has

encouraged at times questionable—if not unethical—business practices. Indeed, the Phase I industry has often been characterized as
opportunistic, running clinics in ways that can exploit the social and
economic inequalities affecting participants in order to secure significant profits from their contracts with the pharmaceutical industry. Commercial clinics, in particular, are incentivized to reduce the
compensation for healthy volunteers and cut corners on operating
expenses. As I demonstrate below, they often do so by hiring inexpe-
rienced staff, serving low-quality food, and providing few or outdated
amenities.[3]

Notwithstanding these industry trends, not all clinics have prioritized
profits at the expense of participants. In other words, the quality of clinic
accommodations can be read as an indicator of the safety and worth
companies ascribe to healthy volunteers. Indeed, a key feature of healthy
volunteers' experiences at Phase I clinics is the wildly different standards
and organizational schemes they have in place. In some instances, the
industry's disregard for healthy volunteers' comfort also contributes to
the continued stigmatization of trial participation. Organizational priorities not only influence both how participants are treated and how
studies are conducted; they are also critical to understanding the complex industry in which companies, research staff, and healthy volunteers
are enmeshed.

Clinic Configurations

There is no standard template that Phase I clinics follow in terms of their
location, amenities, or staffing. As I have already described, Pharma
Phase I was a state-of-the-art facility. This might not be surprising given
that it was owned and operated by a multinational pharmaceutical company with annual sales totaling tens of billions of dollars. While Pharma
Phase I had its own freestanding building located in close proximity to
a hospital, the other five clinics on my research itinerary deviated from
this model. Examining these spaces provides some insights into the evo-
lution of this industry and healthy volunteers' Phase I trial experiences
(table 4.1).

More than any other, Mega Phase I resembled Pharma Phase I in
that it occupied a new building that was designed and constructed as

TABLE 4.1: Clinic Characteristics by Region of the United States

	Organization Type	Approximate Capacity	Building Type
East Coast			
Academic Phase I	Academic medical center	16	Hospital ward
Pharma Phase I	Pharmaceutical company	50	New, freestanding
Midwest			
Cottage Phase I	Independent, commercial clinic	50	Suite in office park
CRO Phase I	Contract research organization	60	Former factory
West Coast			
Local Phase I	Independent, commercial clinic	80	Former warehouse
Mega Phase I	Contract research organization	300	New, freestanding

a research clinic, but it differed from Pharma Phase I in two key ways. First, it was located several miles from the nearest hospital that could provide medical support should a serious or life-threatening adverse event occur during a study. Second, Mega Phase I was huge. At full capacity, it could house up to 300 participants. Making its space more flexible to accommodate individual studies or varying volumes of participants, multiple self-contained subclinics, including procedure areas, dormitories, and cafeterias, divided the building. While research staff could travel among the subclinics using interconnected corridors, the participants were locked into their designated space for the length of the study. To maximize the number of research participants housed, Mega Phase I furnished the bedrooms with bunk beds, fitting eight to 12 participants per room. Additionally, one of the clinic areas occupied a vast open space, reminiscent in many ways of a school gymnasium, which contained more than 80 hospital beds. These beds were organized head to head in rows two beds wide and six long. During my initial tour of the building, healthy volunteers occupied these beds, lying on their backs with their arms at their sides; many stared blindly at the ceiling above them. Although they were clearly positioned this way for a study procedure, the effect was disconcerting, and I felt relieved to pass through this space and into another. Participants' recreational spaces were more comfortably designed, with warm colors and wall hangings amplifying the homey effect of the oversized chairs facing large-screen televisions. With different spaces for participants to use in each subclinic, Mega Phase I felt ample despite the large number of participants.

In comparison to Pharma Phase I and Mega Phase I, the three other commercial Phase I clinics were less modern and spacious. All three had adopted space originally intended for another purpose. CRO Phase I acquired a defunct manufacturing facility for its clinic, Local Phase I was located in a former warehouse, and Cottage Phase I was situated in an office park, tucked into a larger building containing a wide array of enterprises. All three were miles away from hospitals, and their appropriated buildings profoundly constrained the design of each clinic. Both CRO Phase I and Local Phase I were nearly windowless, so bunk-bed-lined dormitories, recreational spaces, and procedure areas had no natural light. The furniture at all three was mismatched and worn. Cottage Phase I required participants to stay in the procedure area most of the day, where they sat in rows of assigned recliners—many of them defective—which were positioned uncomfortably close together. This might nonetheless have been an improvement over CRO Phase I, where an insufficient number of tables and chairs forced participants to jockey for space, including taking turns at the tables during meal times. Unlike the other clinics, neither CRO Phase I nor Local Phase I had a kitchen on the premises; all participant meals were instead catered from chain restaurants, such as IHOP and Boston Market, and the food was often at room temperature by the time participants were allowed to eat. Cottage Phase I was more connected to the outside world through its large plate-glass windows. I saw participants periodically talking to family members or friends through the glass, a loophole to clinics' policies prohibiting visitors. The sum effect of these three clinics' spaces was rather like that of overcrowded prisons, and those running them seemed quite unselfconscious about the poor accommodations that seemed to have far exceeded their capacities.

In contrast to these clinics, Academic Phase I was located within a large university hospital. The oldest established clinic in my sample, it was also by far the smallest, with just over a dozen beds. The clinic had appropriated a traditional nursing ward of the hospital, so participants had the benefit of staying in two-person rooms with private bathrooms. The facility was, however, more outdated and desperately needed some fresh paint. The recreational space was limited, and participants were generally expected to spend most of the study in their hospital bed. To help them pass the time, the recruiter encouraged participants to bring books, games, and electronic devices. Even though the space was smaller, the clinic did not feel as crowded as some of the others because the participants typically remained in their rooms. This could nevertheless be harder on participants who might feel confined not only within the small clinic but within the even smaller space of their beds.

Clinic Views of the Phase I Industry

While these brief descriptions of the clinics provide some sense of place, the organizations responsible for these clinics tell a different story. The material differences in the clinics operated by Pharma Phase I, Academic Phase I, and the four commercial Phase I companies are products of their divergent organizational values and public reputations. Specifically, Pharma Phase I had an interest in protecting its brand. The parent company of Pharma Phase I spent significant resources building its clinic, making it relaxing and comfortable for volunteers. Pharma Phase I easily had the best facility out of the six that I visited. Although Academic Phase I had the oldest clinic and lacked modern amenities, it emphasized its teaching mission, which enhanced the quality of its clinical and research staff. In contrast, the four commercial clinics—CRO Phase I, Mega Phase I, Cottage Phase I, and Local Phase I—had their profit motive much more at the surface of their operations. This manifested in their second-rate staffing and accommodations. Importantly, these commercial clinics needed to concern themselves with their reputation only *within* the industry (i.e., their standing with pharmaceutical companies), whereas Pharma Phase I and Academic Phase I had reputations to protect beyond Phase I testing. At all six clinics, research staff provided insights into how these facilities operated and how healthy volunteers' worth to the research enterprise was embedded in the clinics' larger organizational values.

Pharma Phase I

In the case of Pharma Phase I, the reputation of one of the most profit-able businesses in the world was on the line for what happened in its clinic. The Pharma Phase I facility was state of the art for a reason. It symbolized the prosperity of the company, and it suggested a deep investment in R&D.[4] While other pharmaceutical companies shuttered their Phase I facilities, the parent company of Pharma Phase I chose instead to invest in and expand its clinical research operations. In addi-tion, by maintaining its own research unit, the company could exert more control over the flow of any information about its investigational drugs, especially safety data emerging from early human testing. Like many other businesses, pharmaceutical companies have highly sophis-ticated public relations teams that engage simultaneously in damage control and "corporate social responsibility" (Banerjee 2008). These teams emphasize the good that companies do while taking the spotlight off the harm their products have created or, more generally, the profits they make from expensive drugs (e.g., Shamir 2005). At Pharma Phase I, these concerns about the parent company's reputation translated into the organizational values of having a facility that represented the com-pany brand, was beholden to a community mandate, and prioritized a participant-centric approach to research.

Explaining her company's investment in their new clinic facility, Gail, Pharma Phase I's operations director, said that "we purposely built a facility like *this*. You know, it's clean. This weekend we just replaced the TVs upstairs. . . . They were six years old and well used, and we want this environment to be comfortable and encouraging." The perspective on the company from the outside was also important, so before Pharma Phase I opened, the company engaged the local community to explain what the research facility was and why they were locating there. As Gail explained, "We weren't expecting to draw a great deal [of healthy vol-unteers] from the neighborhood, although that was gonna be a bonus, but we had to get folks in the neighborhood to understand why we're here. There was a big fear factor. You know, were we experimenting on animals in the area? Were we gonna come in and just take advantage of the situation and then go away? And [Pharma] is a company that doesn't do that. . . . We're encouraged to become part of the community.

It's hugely important to us." Highlighting the anxiety that communities can have about medical research, Gail also conveyed that the decision to build Pharma Phase I in this particular community was not based on its potential pool of healthy volunteers; on the contrary, participants were expected to travel from all across the country to participate, and since this influx of strangers to the community could be another cause for distrust, it was all the more imperative to show that the company had nothing to hide about Pharma Phase I.

The rhetoric around community that Gail and other employees mobilized also inflected their views of healthy volunteers. For Pharma Phase I, the "customer" was the healthy volunteer and not the corporate entity that was feeding the clinic studies. Tanya, an African American woman in her thirties who was one of the recruiters, described Pharma Phase I's focus on participants: "We have a volunteer survey, and every volunteer is asked to complete one. . . . And it asks about our professionalism: were we approachable, do they feel they got enough information, do they feel they were treated fairly while they were here? How was the food, did you like it? . . . I read each and every single comment that is written on the surveys. . . . And that's one of the ways [we] keep a pulse on our external customer and if they're happy with what is going on." Tanya reported a lot of changes in response to these surveys, including fixing problems in the bathrooms, updating the movie library, and revising the menu. This customer-service attitude applied to Gail as well, even though she was at the top of the organizational chart. She emphasized that everyone at Pharma Phase I was responsible for making the experience a good one for healthy volunteers: "We want people to be comfortable. . . . Yeah, if you ask me to get [you] a pillow, I'm [personally] gonna go get a pillow. I'm not gonna say, 'Aaron, go get this.' It's a customer service part of it to keep 'em coming back." The sincerity of these sentiments was quite evident in most of the Pharma Phase I staff. The recruiters in particular took their role as volunteer advocates very seriously. Tanya, for example, spoke at length about the importance of directing people to free clinics to get the care they needed when a screening visit at Pharma Phase I revealed they had diabetes or high blood pressure. She asserted, "It's not just, 'Okay, I'm done with them, they don't qualify [for a clinical trial].' . . . It's an opportunity for us to then educate them about their own health situation and try and . . . point them in the direction of healthcare to be able to do something about it and not to let it linger and go on." Gail and Tanya illustrate how Pharma Phase I's commitment to the community permeated how they wanted to be seen by the larger public as well as how they wanted to treat people who screened for their studies.

Reputation, however, is broader than the work done at Pharma Phase I by its research staff. It seemed that in practice Pharma Phase I was not trying to bolster its parent company's reputation as much as it was struggling against existing negative perceptions of the industry, especially in the healthcare sector if not by the general public. Research staff at Pharma Phase I were keenly aware of these negative views, which became particularly relevant when they needed to make new hires. The medical director of the facility, Paul, a white physician in his fifties, voiced his frustration about this: "I have real objections to the medical schools saying to the kids, 'Look out for some of the marketing practices of drug companies,' and stuff like that. . . . We're losing really bright and dedicated people on our side [i.e., pharma]. . . . It's also difficult to find nurses too, and some of the smearing of pharma, I believe, has produced a certain reluctance of some of our brighter healthcare professionals to have anything to potentially do with pharma research." This image of pharmaceutical companies was salient to a lot of the research staff when they reflected on their transition to Pharma Phase I. For example, Tanya was explicit about her worries about working for Pharma Phase I: "When I first got hired here, I was the only African American person here. . . . And I told [Paul] the medical director, . . . we were talking about recruiting African Americans, [and] I said, 'If you hired me to be the Tuskegee nurse, I am not the person for you.' I said, 'Because if there's something wrong, I am going to whistle-blow like you never heard a whistle before.' [Laughs.]"[5] Once they were in their positions, dispelling their initial anxieties about the industry might even have made the Pharma Phase I staff all the more committed to embracing the company's community-oriented values, thereby illustrating that concerns about the company were baseless.

At the same time, another aspect of the pharmaceutical industry's reputation made some of Pharma Phase I's employees concerned about perceptions of bias in their research. This was particularly true for the physician-investigators and most clearly articulated by Paul. Commenting on their handling of participants' adverse events, he said, "I want the [FDA] auditor to come in and say, yeah, open-and-shut case. . . . No conflict of interest in it because Dr. So-and-So from [prestigious academic medical center] who doesn't work for [Pharma Phase I or its parent company] confirmed it, you know? I'm not gonna make it to the front page of the *New York Times* with that, you know?" Paul's concern about outside scrutiny of Pharma Phase I's conflict of interest in making determinations about the safety of their own drugs is fascinating. On one hand, it underscores the apprehension about maintaining the company's reputation, but on the other, it raises the possibility that it might lead to more careful research. Regardless, these aspects of Pharma Phase I's organizational values and reputation indicate that a pharmaceutical company operating its own Phase I clinic might be confronted with different issues than clinics conducting the trials for them.

Academic Phase I

Academic Phase I was in a unique position. It was technically part of an academic medical center, but because nearly all of its clinical trials came from the pharmaceutical industry, it needed to maintain relationships with companies in order to stay afloat, which could be a struggle when competing with CROs and independent clinics. The academic part of its mission also meant that the clinic was responsible for teaching medical fellows enrolled in the clinical pharmacology program. Neil, the clinic director and a white physician in his forties, explained Academic Phase I's position: "So, for better, for worse, we're a CRO in terms of contracting, in terms of the job that we do and our deliverables. I mean, where we differ is we have other missions. So, we have a training mission. It's a great place for our fellows to train, to learn how to do this. Many of whom go on to [work for] the pharmaceutical industry." Although Academic Phase I was decidedly not a CRO, it is interesting that Neil compared his clinic to the for-profit world and characterized it as a training ground for industry. By this metric, however, he still found his clinic coming up short, adding, "I do feel like lots of times, we're driving blind, so we—, I have almost no competitive advantage." From an industry perspective, Neil might be right. Academic clinics have become outmoded, given how much the scale of healthy volunteer trials has changed. At the clinic level, however, he missed a critical part of what his organization's value for training researchers provides: the strong presence in the clinic of physician-investigators. Academic Phase I differed dramatically from the other five I visited in that I frequently observed a physician circulating within the clinic to examine and interact with participants. This was sometimes Neil himself, but more often it was Andrea, a fellow in the training program. In comparison, the other clinics typically relied on nurses and other staff to conduct procedures or check on participants.

From a healthy volunteer's perspective, the real disadvantage of Academic Phase I's clinic was its lack of amenities. I mentioned above that the space was quite dated and in need of refurbishing. Patty, a white woman in her thirties and the clinic's recruiter, flagged the risk the space created for conducting clinical trials: "It's not a very big place, you know. We don't have a pool table and video games, so I could see why being here for thirty days straight would get a little antsy. . . . You know, like I do try to be as upfront—sometimes bluntly so—with our subjects. . . . 'Well, you know, we had you here [before], you were here for ten days and you dropped out. . . . It ruined all the data we had for you.' . . . It does reflect badly on our group when that happens." Patty drew attention to how the clinic space might hurt retention should participants feel unable to remain confined there during long studies. If Academic Phase I failed to deliver the data they were contracted to generate for the sponsoring pharmaceutical company, their ability to secure future clinical trials could be impeded. Patty's strategy to minimize the chance of volunteers withdrawing from studies centered on being much more lenient about what items participants could bring with them to the clinic. Unlike Pharma Phase I and the other clinics that prohibited camera phones and other items, Academic Phase I encouraged participants to make the space as comfortable as possible for themselves. Additionally, the staff valued their positive interpersonal relationships with participants. Patty explained, "The overall thing that I hear most [from participants] is they don't want to be treated like cattle or a number. We use their names; you know, we don't call out, 'Baseline or Allocation Number Three, come here,' you know? [Instead, we say,] 'Joe Smith, you're up next.'" Although Patty had never visited any other Phase I clinics, she said that from talking with participants, she knew Academic Phase I's approach and relationships with healthy volunteers was different. She confided,

"There's another one . . . I hear a lot of bad things about. . . . [Laughs.] No names mentioned! . . . But they also feel that they're not treated properly [there]. . . . So I think it's that level of trust that they have come to learn with us. You know, Dr. Neil is fantastic; he knows these guys, you know? So he's willing to go above and beyond what needs to be done sometimes for them. . . . It is a level of care that he definitely exhibits towards them."

Because Academic Phase I was a small research unit, it facilitated the kind of relationships that Patty described between the research team and healthy volunteers. With no more than a dozen participants in the clinic at any one time, it was much easier for the doctors and nurses to remember everyone's name and provide individual care. Whereas some of the commercial clinics might have actually treated participants poorly, as Patty suggested, many of these larger Phase I clinics might have simply had a volume problem. With 50 or more participants present at a time, it could become an impossible task for research staff to remember everyone's names. Regardless, the size of Academic Phase I coupled with its training mission created the conditions for the staff to cultivate a hands-on atmosphere prioritizing participants' welfare.

Commercial CRO and Independent Clinics

In comparison to both Pharma Phase I and Academic Phase I, the profit motive was much more front and center in the CRO-based and independent clinics. This does not mean that these companies were purely profit driven, but unlike a pharmaceutical company or academic medical center, they did not have other competing organizational missions. Because their businesses depended on winning contracts for clinical trials from pharmaceutical companies, they had to be attentive to their reputations *within* the industry. As such, they needed to enhance the value of their services to pharmaceutical companies, which, in turn, directly shaped their short-term and long-term business objectives.

At the same time, attention to the bottom line affected their practices because there was more incentive to operate on the smallest budget possible as a way of increasing their profits. Cottage Phase I provided a striking example of this in its staffing decisions. Rather than hiring separate staff to manage the day-to-day operations, senior management instead required personnel to fulfill multiple roles. For example, other

clinics had nurses or phlebotomists to conduct procedures, lab technicians to process blood and other research samples, and kitchen staff to
prepare food. At Cottage Phase I, however, the nurses and phlebotomists
did all three of these jobs. On the first day of my visit to the clinic, I was
truly astonished to see Kristen, a white woman in her thirties and the
lead phlebotomist at the clinic, making dinner for the participants. She
had a break from her responsibilities while the participants were eating, which prompted me to ask her to make time for a formal interview.
About halfway through the interview, I asked how it happened that her
job included cooking. Kristen defensively asserted, "This is actually one
of the things that keeps me happy at this job." As I explained my surprise,
she relaxed and provided a fuller explanation: "Because this company,
I think, only has 25 people full time on the books, everybody has to do
everything or it just wouldn't work. . . . There's only so much income that
the company is gonna bring in—I mean, as a final number. . . . And it
was kind of presented to me like, 'Look, if you learn everything, you'll
make more [money] 'cause then we have to hire less people.' . . . I love
cooking, and I like working in the lab." Although Kristen personally enjoyed performing these duties, she acknowledged the turnover in nurses
at the clinic who had not appreciated such an expanded job description,
remarking, "This job isn't for everybody."

Even though Kristen expressed enthusiasm for her position at Cottage Phase I, she recognized that balancing multiple roles did not necessarily place the clinic or herself in the best possible light for the healthy
volunteers. She wondered, for instance, how they perceived that the person who took their bodily fluids also prepared their meals. Because this
would make her uncomfortable if she were volunteering for a study, she
adapted her behavior to reduce any concerns they might have: "I try
to be very open about my hand-washing procedures, so that they [the
participants] see me. Sometimes perception is everything, 'cause they
know I'm in the lab. They watch me walk away with their pee. And then
they watch me walk in here and make sandwiches. . . . I make sure they
see me put the fresh gloves on when making a sandwich. And some of
my co-workers think that's a little ridiculous, but I make these emphasized movements." Kristen's awareness of how the participants might
perceive the situation indicates that she had not completely normalized
the multiple roles she was asked to fill in her job. Yet, she did not openly

question the management decision to maximize profits by intensifying the labor of the clinical staff. The intentionality of the clinic's strategy was highlighted when the director of operations, an African American man in his fifties named Samuel, boasted, "I'm a Six Sigma black belt, so . . . I knew of some places that we could cut some of the fat off . . . and make things run a lot smoother."[6]

Another aspect of how clinics can run more profitably involves the degree to which they choose to invest in amenities for participants. As noted above, Cottage Phase I had multiple broken recliners that participants were nonetheless expected to use. At CRO Phase I, insufficient and mismatching furniture was packed into a cramped, windowless space, indicating the company's priority was on function not form. Other than televisions, the commercial clinics tended to lack activities for participants. Most had neither the games, movies, and books that Pharma Phase I supplied nor the comforts of a semi-private room that Academic Phase I had. When describing the space at Mega Phase I where he worked, Spencer, a white physician-investigator in his forties, declared, "I think the subject comfort level [at our clinic], just being a newer structure with more modern amenities, is probably greater [than other facilities]. However, interestingly, the average Phase I participant isn't really expecting probably as high level of accommodations as perhaps the general traveling public [is]. So even though, you know, the employees may feel that a newer and nicer facility is better 'cause it's more comfortable and it's fancier for the subjects, they themselves maybe not appreciate it as much as we think that they should [laughs] because they don't really need such fancy conditions." Mega Phase I was spacious and well designed, but with its bunk beds for participants, it would hardly have been considered "fancy" by most people's standards. Still, Spencer's comment about the space not really being for the participants was likely not too far off from the corporate decision to design such a facility. Rather than designing the clinic *for* the participants, the company appears to have invested in its infrastructure to impress clients—pharmaceutical companies whose business Mega Phase I was trying to lure. On the surface, everything was modern, clean, and comfortable, but in actuality there was not much for participants to do during long confinements other than watch television.

There are limits to the extent to which many clinics would be comfortable cutting corners to earn more profits. Many would be concerned about their reputations if they did so. Unlike Pharma Phase I, which was concerned with its reputation with the general public, the commercial Phase I clinics prioritized how potential pharmaceutical company clients might view them. For example, Melanie, a white woman in her thirties who was the operations director at CRO Phase I, reflected on the parent company's relative obscurity: "I don't know that many people would recognize [CRO]. I'm from this area, and I've worked for [CRO] for 15 years. . . . Even people in the industry haven't heard of [CRO], you know, so I don't know if it's any kind of name recognition, other than people very local like within the [city neighborhood] where they've seen our building." CRO Phase I was part of a relatively small but growing contract research organization, which was not only unfamiliar to the general public, but also unknown to many pharmaceutical companies. The parent company had opted to start a Phase I clinic in order to build its reputation in the industry and, as noted earlier, to try to capture contracts for drug development that could span from Phase I studies conducted in the clinic to later-phase studies managed by the larger company. The haphazardness of the clinic space might have reflected the priorities of the parent company, which focused on expanding its broader business portfolio rather than conducting Phase I trials, and it leveraged its resources accordingly. Of course, the clinic had to be adequately equipped to convince pharmaceutical companies that CRO Phase I was prepared to test their investigational drugs, but the comfort of research participants was not part of the calculus.

At the same time, research staff were aware of negative press about other Phase I clinics and CROs more generally. In order to maintain or enhance their reputations, the clinics certainly had to avoid anything in their pursuit of profits that could tarnish their organizations. Kyle, a white man in his fifties who was an executive at Cottage Phase I, took pains to map out the industry for me. When talking about the recent closures of several Phase I clinics, he remarked,

> I have my theories, or hypothesis—whatever the correct word is—as to why those sites closed. I know a couple of 'em are quality issues, significant quality issues. I also know a lot of 'em are financial issues, meaning

the profit margin wasn't what the investment community thought they would be. . . . These things need to be continually examined to prevent fraud and abuse. I just don't have the seeds to cut corners because I know if I ever get caught, that's the end of my business. And I think most research institutions are like that. . . . The risk isn't worth it, 'cause it'll catch up to you. . . . SFBC, . . . that's the greatest example.[7]

Kyle's reference to the Phase I clinic that had been run out of a former Holiday Inn before being shut down is an interesting representation of the risks of cutting corners. Even more fascinating, however, is the fact that he nonetheless seemed to prize taking chances to increase revenue in a way that almost conflated profitability with fraud and abuse. Within this frame, the only reason not to commit fraud was the risk of getting caught and ruining his company's reputation. While this was not literally what he meant, Kyle truly was concerned with making his business profitable. This might be one of the reasons why Cottage Phase I continued to have broken chairs for participants to use.

Although the Phase I industry is relatively small, there are clear differences among clinics based on their organization type. As a general rule, companies that have the most to lose from a scandal are more likely to be cautious about how they manage their Phase I clinics. Pharma Phase I had a global, and very public, reputation to protect as well as an image to *project* with its clinic. Like other university hospitals, Academic Phase I was also concerned about its reputation, especially as research tragedies could have wide-ranging consequences for its entire research portfolio and federal funding (e.g., Kolata 2001b). As for Mega Phase I, CRO Phase I, Cottage Phase I, and Local Phase I, these commercial clinics likely believed they had much less to lose by cutting some corners in the clinic, but these choices affected, to varying degrees, participants enrolled in their studies. These clinic differences raise the question of how these trends are reflected in the experiences and perspectives of healthy volunteers.

Healthy Volunteers' Views of the Phase I Industry

Serial participants were also aware of the shifts in the Phase I industry even if they were not privy to the big picture. They witnessed the closure of clinics and tracked the different names emblazoned on the buildings. Many helped to spread the word about new clinics, the changing availability of studies, and trends in compensation. While they might not have been familiar with the term "contract research organization" or its acronym, they knew that Phase I clinics were run by pharmaceutical companies, private research companies, and universities. Healthy volunteers, regardless of their region of the country and experience in trials, also took note when research staff were professional and cared about participants or when clinics seemingly focused solely on maximizing their profits.

Changes to the Northeast Circuit

As we have seen, not all serial participants are equally plugged into information about Phase I studies. These differences can largely be attributed to the density of clinics and patterns of openings and closures in each region of the country. Historically, healthy volunteers in the Northeast had the readiest access to multiple Phase I clinics. Referred to as "the circuit" by participants, this area included the hub of clinics that were owned and operated by pharmaceutical companies as well as being home to the National Institutes of Health and myriad academic medical centers. Additionally, participants in the Northeast have witnessed more of the closures of pharmaceutical company clinics and experienced a greater decline in study compensation than any other region. For example, Wesley, an African American in his early thirties who had been participating in Phase I trials for ten years, guessed that he had joined about 30 studies based on his pattern of enrolling in three each year. He said, "I've been with GlaxoSmithKline, but they closed down. I've been to Wyeth. They closed down. . . . And Bristol-Myers, I used to go because that's closer to [where I live]. But they closed down." That each place Wesley mentioned was a pharmaceutical company clinic indicated how much the Phase I landscape had changed in the Northeast.

With fewer Northeast clinics available to them, serial participants have not only become more apt to travel within the entire circuit from New Haven to Baltimore, but some have also felt compelled to venture to other parts of the country. In discussing the clinic closures, Eddie, an African American in his early forties with more than 50 studies under his belt, asserted that it had become much harder to earn the same amount of money from studies as he did ten years ago when he began participating. He took this as a sign that he needed to travel even farther to do studies: "They force us to travel. I'll travel from here to Texas, and I'll go from Texas to Chicago, and we'll go to California, and we'll go for where the money is . . . whoever's paying us the most. . . . We'll travel now. So, it's getting kinda crazy." From the perspective of healthy volunteers, traveling for studies could give them a sense of control over their participation because it increased their options for where to screen. Indeed, for participants around the country, Texas, with its cluster of clinics in the Austin area, had become a virtual Phase I mecca, a place everyone should visit at least once because it was believed to offer better studies and worth the travel. Despite this view, traveling for Phase I trials is also risky. Taking trains, planes, and long-distance buses clearly increases people's financial precarity because they spend the little money they might have in the hopes of making significantly more.

Changes in the Caliber of Clinics

Regardless of whether healthy volunteers travel or participate locally, the clinic conditions have also changed, and generally for the worse. Many long-term healthy volunteers spoke nostalgically about the pharmaceutical company clinics that had closed and praised Pharma Phase I.[8] Recognizing that pharmaceutical companies have a different type of investment in the clinical trial process, healthy volunteers viewed these clinics as a benchmark against which to hold other facilities. While decreased study compensation was a key concern, they also stressed that compared with many of the remaining commercial clinics, those pharmaceutical company clinics had been better places to participate in studies. For example, Fred, an African American in his forties who had started participating three years before and had done six studies, fondly recalled his time at one of the pharmaceutical company clinics: "They had like a pool table. They had the TV and the video game [console], but they . . . [also] had a karaoke machine. And they offered like, 'Well, which one of y'all think y'all can sing? Whoever can sing the best, they'll get a hundred dollars.' And they really did it. . . . They had incentives that would pass time by and kept you occupied."

That a clinic structured participants' time through friendly competition for a monetary prize is particularly clever because it helped make studies there more fun and positioned the company as generous with their resources. Likewise, Pharma Phase I was held up as an exemplar for how clinic spaces should be designed. Don, an African American in his late forties, asserted,

> The reason I like about it is that whoever designed it designed it [so] it's perfect for—, it's like a lot of earthy colors, . . . like the paint is like purple and brown. . . . It doesn't look like some units you go to like it's all white walls, [and] you feel like you're in a mental cell. . . . [At Pharma Phase I] they've got some nice pictures of the outdoors, and you can get on the computer. And one thing I really like [is] they have a quiet room that I like, 'cause I like to get away from people sometimes.

Comparing Pharma Phase I to other places, Don even likened his experience there to a vacation. Moreover, Trent, an African American in his late thirties, indicated that differences among clinics could influence where he would enroll in a long-confinement study: "[Pharma Phase I] got a great facility. . . . If you want to do a long study, that's probably where you want to do it 'cause it's very comfortable. A lot of places they don't have as much money as [Pharma], so it's not as comfortable." For Trent, the difference in clinic comfort came down to the wealth of the company and meant that a place like Pharma Phase I should be better than academic or commercial clinics.

Thus, the industry trend was toward closure of the clinics healthy volunteers preferred only to be replaced by ones about which they had many complaints. Because of the vast Phase I trial experience he gained by traveling throughout the United States, Eddie had strong criticisms of the direction the industry had taken:

> Different clinics are different. I understand you have like the major pharmaceutical companies, and you have the middle men actually test [the drugs for them]. . . . It's kinda getting a little crazy now because, like, . . . these different [commercial] places, it's like, you know, it's like a manufacturing plant now [in how they treat healthy volunteers], . . . processing 'em in and processing 'em out. . . . I mean, it's getting a little

out of hand, and there needs to be more regulation in this industry. . . .
All the veterans [healthy volunteers] have said, "That's it, they need to
regulate this; it's getting out of hand now."

Stuart, a white man in his fifties who also traveled the country for studies, was explicit in comparing Pharma Phase I to the other places he had
been: "There are sort of differences, you know. I mean this, because it's
owned by [Pharma] itself is really nice, and then a lot of places are—,
you know, the different drug companies . . . farm it out to 'em or whatever, and they'll just, as far as the physical environment . . . may be a
little more cut-rate. [Laughs.]" Both Eddie and Stuart presented these
industry changes as dire ones, with Eddie even suggesting that the government should step in to manage the declining conditions.

There was a strong sense among healthy volunteers that certain clinics made for a much worse study experience than did others. Several
commercial clinics were mentioned as the worst offenders, with one in
New Jersey repeatedly named as a place to avoid. Participants regularly
described this particular New Jersey clinic as "ghetto," meaning that it
felt rundown and unsafe. Additionally, Alexandra, a white transwoman
in her forties, depicted that clinic as stressful, saying, "It's kind of like the
cattle mart. It's so—, everyone is just bunched up together. . . . And also
they can have like 120 volunteers at one time, and it's a smaller facility
than here [Pharma Phase I], and it seems they just bunch everyone in
[the New Jersey clinic] like sardines." Likewise, Tia, an African American participant in her early thirties, made several negative observations
of different commercial clinics, but her experience of that same New Jersey clinic was particularly memorable: "We had dogs—bedbug sniffing
dogs—come in because there were bedbugs in the facility. In the main
area [for procedures] where they have all the chairs, they had to pull several of them out and dismantle them. The dogs literally were sniffing us
and our baggage and everything. They had to pull beds out. This is the
middle of the summer. Air conditioners were broken. The beds would
stink. . . . It was horrible. Horrible. [Laughs.]" For Tia, these conditions
confirmed in her mind that this clinic was "almost like jail."

Many participants astutely observed that these commercial clinics
were uncomfortable *because* they were more profitable that way. Speaking about the same New Jersey clinic, Terrell, an African American in

his late thirties who had enrolled in an estimated 54 studies, asserted, "When I think of a corporation, like the epitome of the—I'm not gonna say 'evil'—the money-hungry corporation, that's [this New Jersey clinic]. Any way they can cut corners to save a little bit, that's them. And when you're going through this [experience there], . . . you realize that you're going through this so somebody [at the company] can have a bigger boat." Without exception, participants viewed poor clinic conditions not as signs of struggling businesses but instead as intentional cost-cutting measures to increase company profits. Aidan, a white man in his thirties, made a similar complaint about the food at Mega Phase I on the West Coast. Commenting on the clinic's recent change in management, he griped, "The food still sucks, it will always suck, which is terrible. I mean, I can't even imagine the [large amount of] money that flows through one of these studies. . . . I understand it's expensive to do these, but there's no reason the food has to be as bad as it is. Like, I had a turkey sandwich today, maybe ate half of it. How can a turkey sandwich taste bad? But it does. That's pretty sad." Also remarking on Mega Phase I, Frank, a white man in his forties who had participated in about ten studies, thought that the pharmaceutical companies paying for the Phase I trials just had no idea that their funds were not being invested into the clinic:

> The pharmaceutical people that are spending the money . . . doesn't know. . . . Has the client [i.e., the pharmaceutical company] actually ate their food here? . . . The client only sees it printed on a paper. . . . They see the menu, but what you're getting and you're eating is a totally different thing. . . . You got guys that are . . . giving your food with tattoos on their head: "Yo, what's up? Whatcha want to drink, homey?" . . . So the client really doesn't know. The client should actually come in here . . . be like a little secret shopper.

Frank in no way believed that the pharmaceutical companies might be complicit in the poor conditions he experienced in studies; instead, he assumed that they had been duped by a profit-seeking commercial clinic.

Most clinics include detailed information in their consent documents about the specific menu participants are required to consume during a study. This is largely to ensure that participants do not have any dietary restrictions that would preclude them from participating (e.g., pork, gluten, or nuts). Marshall, an African American in his thirties, related an experience at an East Coast clinic that also had terrible food: "So they would tell you—and they actually put that in the informed consent—that the food didn't taste good, 'cause everybody complained about it 'cause it was so nasty." This is particularly condemning because it suggests callousness on the part of clinic management. Instead of actually changing the quality of the food, they simply made people consent to eat bad food—no additional expenditure required.

Not only were the less desirable commercial clinics cutting corners on amenities and food, but some healthy volunteers reported that they also engaged in unscrupulous practices regarding study payment. For example, Brian, a white man in his late fifties who traveled all over the country for studies, accused some clinics of nickel-and-diming participants out of the promised compensation. He fumed, "They're looking to get 10 percent of the money they pay you, they're gonna get it back from you in fines. So they will fine you for every little thing that they can. It's ridiculous." He provided the example of a participant forgetting that he had a blood draw and showing up late to the phlebotomy station. The clinic "fined" that participant $50—meaning that the fine was deducted from the eventual study payment. Participants also argued that clinics took financial advantage of them by making them agree to additional procedures after a study was underway. While not actually reducing their compensation, these participants strongly felt they should be paid *more* for any extra blood draws required by a study. Ross, an African American in his forties who had been participating in Phase I studies for 12 years, became so angry when this occurred at a Northeast clinic that he withdrew from the study entirely: "I checked in in the morning, I wanna say around 7:00 something. That evening they did an orientation, and during orientation, they casually mentioned, 'Oh, well, there are 10 additional blood draws.' And people grumbled but rolled over and took it. And on that 8th day [of the study], . . . they said it involved two more, which wasn't in the informed consent. . . . I complained about it. They said, 'You can leave if you want.' I said, 'I know I can,' and I left. You know, but they were just tacky in their approach." If it was not sufficiently clear that Ross disliked that particular clinic, he added, "I think really the only thing lower than going there is doing that study out of the back of a van."

Healthy volunteers experienced a final type of unfairness surrounding compensation: luring people to screen for a study with the false promise of high stipends. For instance, John, a white serial participant in his early thirties, had received a text message from a commercial clinic advertising a study that offered "up to" $5,700 in compensation, but when he called, the recruiter told him the stipend was only $4,500. In John's view, "They inflated the price to get you to call, and then they just dropped the price. They're playing games with you. . . . That made me not trust them. . . . If they're gonna play games like this, I don't think it's worth it for me to gamble in that way." As a result, John did not enroll in the study, and he told other healthy volunteers about the experience to alert them to the possibility that this clinic might not pay participants as promised.

The biggest complaint voiced by participants about the commercial clinics concerned the lack of qualified phlebotomists on staff. This was in contrast to the academic medical centers and pharmaceutical company clinics, where participants found the staff "professional" and skilled. Tia made the comparison between clinic types explicit: "I love [Pharma Phase I] because it's professional. . . . The staff is very well trained. Most of the people who will draw your blood are actually nurses, and that's not the case with most other facilities. . . . It's kinda, I don't know, I call these the 'hood study spots. [Laughs.] They're like any street corner you can go on, you know? Everything is just so lax." Whereas a lot of participants bemoaned the multiple attempts it took less qualified staff to draw blood successfully, Tia had a terrifying experience at a commercial clinic. In her last study at one, the blood collection was so frequent that the clinic decided to use catheters to facilitate the process. This did not go smoothly for Tia:

> They broke a catheter in my arm! . . . And it took somebody who it was their first day [on the job] to actually get the needle out of my arm. No one else could get this needle out of my arm. I had blood spraying every-where. Thankfully, the point was still sticking out of my skin, so she was able to get some forceps and grab it. And it was excruciating. . . . I said, "Please don't tell me sorry one more time in here. Y'all better get this thing out of my arm. Get it out of my arm!" [Laughs.]

While Tia's catheter experience was anomalous, stories about staff struggling with blood draws abounded. Even though he was in his first study, Eric, a multiracial man in his twenties, observed that half of the staff drawing blood at CRO Phase I were not skilled phlebotomists. Becoming distrustful by the midway point in the study, he stated, "If you're, like, somebody new and you try to draw my blood, get me somebody else. . . . If you don't know what you're doing, you don't need to be sticking nobody in their arm." Interestingly, when describing these situations, many participants claimed to stand up for themselves and request someone with more experience to step in. In Eric's case, it is difficult to know if he was narrating his inner monologue as he encountered new staff or if he really had asked the clinic for someone else to draw his blood. Reportedly, these requests have led to altercations between staff and participants, as Robert, an African American in his twenties, indicated in his criticism of untrained staff: "You're supposed to know where the vein is. . . . I've seen people get mad at the staff. They're ready to fight."

Healthy volunteers' perceptions about the professionalism and expertise of the staff also carried over to their experiences of study adverse events. First, participants assumed that academic clinics and pharmaceutical companies were better equipped in the short term to handle medical problems. Even though he participated at all types of clinics, Marcus, an African American long-time participant in his forties, reflected on enrolling in studies at Academic Phase I: "This is a little bit more safer actually [to do studies] in this environment because you have the hospital here. If something happens, they take care of you right away." Second, participants doubted commercial clinics' commitment to providing medical care should health issues emerge during clinical trials. Indeed, the stories participants told about struggling to get medical attention following a study always involved a commercial clinic. Unfortunately for Javier, a Latino in his forties, he had developed a rash that turned into a "bubble" during an Alzheimer's study at an independent clinic. When the rash went away and what might have been a cyst remained, the clinic recommended he consult an outside physician to have it evaluated. Javier recounted the details of what happened by contrasting his experience with his expectations for how Pharma Phase I would have handled it:

[Pharma Phase I], when there's something wrong with you, they will check you. . . . They will make sure that you're all right. . . . People gettin' reactions and they always take care of you. And not all the places is like that. . . . You know how long it took me to get this [cyst] operated on? But this is a little company called [independent clinic]. They gave me the runaround for about four months because they didn't want to pay for it. . . . And they didn't want to pay for it because they are not like [Pharma Phase I]. [Pharma Phase I] tests their own medicine. They [this other clinic] do testing for other companies. So, they don't wanna dig into their profits. And I try to stay away from those little places like that because . . . do you know what they told me? "If something goes wrong, I'm not there for you." [Laughs.] That's what they told me.

Although the clinic staff did not literally tell Javier that they did not care about his safety, it is nonetheless important that this was his interpretation of their inaction around his adverse event. Moreover, the motif that they were maximizing their profits at Javier's expense echoes all the other critiques of these commercial companies as "cheaper" versions of the best clinics.

In the previous section, Spencer, a physician at Mega Phase I, suggested that the clinic facilities do not need to be high quality because healthy volunteers do not expect or require it. This might be true in the literal sense that healthy volunteers still enroll even when they perceive the accommodations to be uncomfortable and the staff inadequately trained. Russell, an African American in his mid-forties, was irritated by people who complained about the clinics when they knew exactly what they had agreed to. He pointed out, "I know why I'm here, so I signed the consent form and act accordingly. It's that simple. [Laughs.] . . . You wasn't complaining when you wanted to get in there, so just fall back and get paid. I don't care if they have no windows. I don't care, as long as you give me my little three squares [meals]." Russell's focus on the transactional aspect of clinical trials—consent, submit, get paid—supports Spencer's point. Healthy volunteers *do* participate even when clinic conditions are subpar.

Yet, healthy volunteers' willingness to participate at subpar clinics does not account for how they *experience* these conditions. Many, such as Javier and Tia, articulated a strong feeling of being mistreated and devalued. Additionally, Marcus commented on how this was a change in the industry: "Not too many people used to do this [participate in Phase I trials], [so] they needed you. Now it's like, 'Oh well, we got a million people now,' [and] they started to—, they talk trash to you. . . . They treat you like you're actually in jail. . . . That's why . . . over the years I just haven't gone to certain places. You know, my blood is good anywhere, . . . but yeah, it's like you got certain places that they just treat you real, real bad." Narratives like Marcus's about study clinics being like jail also communicate that some participants have felt dehumanized by their experiences at certain clinics. This was particularly salient in Eddie's reflections on the state of the Phase I industry. He lamented,

> We wish it would change for the better, [but] we see it changing for the worse. And we just want it to, you know, "Hey, stabilize it. Don't let it get any worse than what it is, 'cause we're human and, you know, you gotta treat us that way." . . . It's getting to the point where they are, from my point of view, that you are starting to treat me like a guinea pig now. And no, I mean, I'm a human. You know what I'm saying? If you want a guinea pig, just test it on an animal, and that'll be it. They [nonhuman animals] don't talk, they can't say nothing, all you see is their labs: "Okay, his organs failed. Okay." But I can tell you, "Hey, I'm not feeling well. I need some—, I need you to do a blood draw and run that lab, [because] something's wrong."

Eddie's literal comparison between healthy volunteers and guinea pigs is an interesting response to the decline in clinic conditions that he has experienced. It draws attention to the difference that might exist between calling oneself a human "guinea pig" or "lab rat" and being treated like a laboratory animal. In arguing that humans have value beyond that of lab animals because they can verbalize any adverse effects they experience, Eddie was protesting the material changes in the treatment of healthy volunteers. His perspective also serves as a reminder of what the Phase I industry is meant to support.

Reflections on Industry Changes

We have examined the Phase I industry and its relationship to the clinics engaged in healthy volunteer research. Many of the companies that offer clinical research services to the pharmaceutical industry do so opportunistically, seeing the chance to profit from larger trends in corporate outsourcing. There have been numerous documented scandals that have drawn attention to the shady business practices deployed by some Phase I companies, such as SFBC's appropriation of a Holiday Inn with troubling fire and safety violations that forced the company to shut down operations. These same issues were mirrored on a lesser scale in healthy volunteers' experiences of other commercial clinics that seemingly prioritized company profits over participants' welfare.

In examining these industry changes from the perspective of the clinic staff, it becomes clear how reputation and organizational values influence how Phase I facilities are run. Reputation operates in uneven ways in the Phase I industry because the different players have different audiences. Pharmaceutical companies and academic medical centers are generally more concerned about their public reputation than are commercial Phase I clinics because the former are prone to broader and more direct impacts should problems arise during clinical trials. In contrast, commercial clinics are generally more concerned with their reputations vis-à-vis the pharmaceutical industry because this is the source of their business—about which the general public has little knowledge in any case.

The various clinics also had different values that dictated their operations. In the case of Pharma Phase I, the clinic espoused a strong commitment to upholding or enhancing its larger corporate brand, being a good community member, and responding to the needs of research participants. Notably, the customer or client for Pharma Phase I was identified as the healthy volunteer; whereas for all the other clinics, the customer was the pharmaceutical company sponsoring the trial. For Academic Phase I, much of its clinic practices were influenced by its training mission. With its emphasis on teaching physicians to be clinical researchers, Academic Phase I provided better clinical care for and more attention to research participants than any other clinic. In contrast, the commercial clinics were much more obviously business-oriented, looking for ways to increase their contracts with the pharmaceutical industry while lowering their costs in the clinic. Cottage Phase I notably took the approach of combining traditionally disparate job descriptions by requiring research staff to work with participants, in the laboratory, and in food preparation. At CRO Phase I, Mega Phase I, and Local Phase I, there were numerous examples of clinic conditions being less than ideal, either in terms of the space and amenities or the quality of the food. Even though these decisions can negatively affect healthy volunteers, the clinics had a financial incentive to cut corners provided these decisions would not cost them a contract with a pharmaceutical company.

The changes in the industry can be appreciated more directly through the stories and experiences of healthy volunteers. Long-term participants, especially those on the East Coast, have witnessed the shift in the industry with the closure of pharmaceutical company clinics and the proliferation of commercial clinics. Some have responded to this new landscape by traveling for studies, trying to find the best-paying trials in their region or throughout the country. Overall, healthy volunteers have been confronted with less than ideal choices about where to enroll in studies. While their reports of the clinic conditions are concerning, their experiences of unprofessional and untrained staff are much more alarming because they suggest that the commercialization of Phase I trials has led to a decline in the protection of human subjects.

Another effect of these industry changes is to reinforce the stigma of participating in clinical trials. If healthy volunteers believe there is some shame in enrolling in Phase I trials, subpar facilities, in which they are made to feel as though they were in jail or less than human, might just confirm this belief. Additionally, some interpreted their own or others' willingness to participate in studies at clinics with poor accommodations and untrained staff as a sign of financial desperation; to return to those places meant that someone was truly out of better options, which made enrollment all the more shameful. At the same time, the commercial clinics could also be seen as exploiting the extent to which participants are already marked by imbricated stigma. As long as there are healthy people who, because of broader social inequalities, enroll in their trials, what incentive do the clinics have to improve their facilities or to invest more in study stipends?

Moreover, the capitalistic orientation of the Phase I industry precipitates the formation of the healthy volunteer as a type of model organism. In the business model advanced for clinical research, healthy volunteers are constructed in a way that mirrors that of nonhuman animals. Generally speaking, they are present as research material to get the job done and generate profits for the industry; they are not the client whose needs must be met. While the treatment of healthy volunteers might vary from clinic to clinic, their trial enrollment is nonetheless always a part of the broader engine of profit propelling drug development. The next chapter examines what the job of the model organism is in Phase I research.

5

A Laboratory for Human Animals

In Phase I research, the clinic can be thought of as a type of laboratory for human animals. This can be seen in the scientific purposes of the trials and the standardization and control imposed on healthy volunteers. As in nonhuman animal research, the artificiality of clinic confinement creates opportunities for dictating what happens to participants and how often, which generates protocols that differ dramatically in Phase I compared to later-phase clinical trials. The studies' design as well as research staff's practices in selecting and managing participants ultimately define who can enroll in Phase I trials—and who can be transformed in the process into model organisms maximally suited to the research. Here, the configuration of the clinic is itself part of the regimen and bears similarities to nonhuman animal research laboratories.

Despite variations in their spaces, most of the clinics I visited had a centralized procedure area set up for maximum efficiency in executing study protocols.[1] For instance, in Local Phase I's large multipurpose room, where most clinic activities occurred, one area was set up to facilitate blood collection in the most expedient way possible. Thus, two dozen armchairs were arranged in a circle, in the middle of which were two rolling office chairs. On the back of each armchair, a sheet of paper had been safety-pinned displaying a number from 01 through 24 arranged consecutively in clockwise order. The numbers corresponded to healthy volunteers' assigned study numbers, and the office chairs were for staff members. Local Phase I's policy required all study participants to sit in their assigned chairs ten minutes before blood draws commenced for the entire group and to remain there until the group was finished. During the procedure, staff members literally rolled from one participant to the next, a phlebotomy caddy in tow, while the participants simply waited their turns, some reading books or listening to music, others chatting with the person next to them, or more rarely someone watching the blood collection process. In one particular study,

Local Phase I had lost a few participants. The study involved multiple stays, and apparently one person never returned for check-in while two others failed to observe some of the dietary restrictions and were consequently removed from the study.[2] Their assigned chairs remained empty when it was time for the group's blood draws, and the staff gained a short break from their work each time they came upon an empty chair. Depending on the number of healthy volunteers in the study and the frequency of blood collection, the participants and staff could end up spending the entire day in this circle. On days like that, a participant's chair might feel like a cage.

The "events" in a Phase I trial—all the procedures from drug dosing to blood draws to meals—are tightly scheduled and highly choreographed. Accordingly, having everyone assembled in one space is supposed to expedite procedures so that staff can adhere to the precisely defined time-points. The schedule is typically built starting from the first dose of the investigational drug given to the first participant. For example, if Participant 01 received his dose at 8:00 AM and blood draws are supposed to occur at hourly intervals, that participant would receive his blood draws at 9:00, 10:00, 11:00, and so forth. At Local Phase I, they generally timed each participant three minutes apart, which means that Participants 02 and 03 would receive their drug doses at 8:03 and 8:06, followed by blood draws beginning at 9:03 and 9:06 respectively. This could quickly come to approximate a musical round. Because each blood draw sequence could take up to 72 minutes with twenty-four participants present, the next round of blood collection would have to start within this timeframe, necessitating a second staff member to begin those and work in tandem with her colleague. The overlap in events explains why two office chairs were needed for the staff to complete their work within the circle of participants.

Phase I clinics value efficiency because the protocols designed by their pharmaceutical company sponsors demand speed and coordination to execute faithfully. Because the sponsors seek precise data on their drugs' action, the timeframes for each data point are relatively narrow. Any instance in which an event window is missed is called a *protocol deviation*, and research staff must document its occurrence, even if it is only one minute out of range. The threat of additional paperwork and the more significant risk of potentially losing future business from the sponsor incentivizes clinics to develop standard operating procedures (SOPs) to ensure the protocols' proper execution.[3] For example, whereas Local Phase I required participants to be present and waiting in advance of blood collection, other clinics, such as Pharma Phase I, allowed participants more freedom but then issued monetary fines when someone failed to report on time for a scheduled event.

While clinics cannot deviate from the sponsors' overall protocols and frequency of study events, they can choose how much time to schedule between individual participants according to their workflow.[4] At the clinics I visited, there was a range of one- to five-minute intervals allocated between each participant's events. The challenge for clinics is to give staff enough time to minimize the number of protocol deviations while still allowing the schedule to function. If too much time is planned between participants, staff are involved in the same round of blood draws longer, which means they cannot be tasked to do other procedures or engage in other clinic activities; it also means that individual healthy volunteers' schedules can become strange with meals getting pushed into odd hours of the day. Thus, by mandating participants' presence for the procedures of everyone in their group, Local Phase I could ensure that a three-minute interval was sufficient for a single staff member to collect one participant's blood and move on to the next person.

Unpacking the Science of Phase I Trials

Phase I trials' regimentation and control have strong parallels with nonhuman animal research. If the research community tends to have preferred model organisms for their specialized areas, then clinical pharmacology—the science behind Phase I trials—privileges the healthy volunteer as its own. Although healthy volunteers frequently used terms such as "lab rat" and "guinea pig" in jest when they referred to how they or others saw their clinical trial participation, these terms, in fact, convey deeper truths about how humans are used in early-phase pharmaceutical research. Specifically, the high volume of Phase I data generated in a relatively short period of time at precise time-points has more in common with laboratory research than it does with most clinical trials. In addition, confinement to the research facility is a structural feature of both Phase I trials and nonhuman animal research. In Phase I trials, the confinement period imposes standardization where otherwise it would be hard to find among human subjects, and as in a laboratory, it effectively constructs a parallel world of scientific inputs and outputs precisely defined and controlled by the pharmaceutical company sponsor. Study inputs include dosing the participants with the investigational drug or placebo and administering regulated diets. Study outputs of blood, urine, stool, cerebrospinal fluid, sperm, and so on are also systematically collected (no matter the discomfort or embarrassment involved). The confinement similarly serves the important purpose of monitoring participants' actions to prevent them from breaking protocol.

To conduct these trials, clinics must find healthy volunteers who are willing—due of course to the broad array of social inequalities already described—to consent to a host of restrictions and likely adverse study events. As a result, the system values serial participation in particular. The need to identify the *right* healthy volunteers for Phase I trials encourages research staff to select repeat participants based on their proven reliability and adaptability. In so doing, these human animals become model organisms maximally conditioned for Phase I trials.[5]

Every type of pharmaceutical, including those for oncology and HIV/AIDS medications, is likely to be tested on healthy volunteers, and there is no evidence to suggest that the decision to use healthy volunteers instead of affected patients in Phase I trials indicates any difference in expected risks associated with the investigational drug. Not only are healthy volunteers relatively easy to recruit and less expensive subjects compared to affected patients, but they have additional scientific value. Specifically, pharmaceutical companies prefer healthy volunteers in Phase I trials to isolate the investigational drug's "signal" from the "noise" (Lakoff 2007), so that investigators do not have to adjudicate whether symptoms are caused by the drug or the underlying disease. As in nonhuman animal research, the goal is to have a standardized body on which to measure the investigational drug's effects.

Until this point, I have been using the term "Phase I" rather monolithically, as if all clinical trials with this name involved the same type of science. At the outset, I explained that these studies test investigational

Figure 5.1: Myth of Drug Development Process

drugs' safety and tolerability, but the array of Phase I protocol types for measuring these characteristics of a drug is quite broad. A common assumption is that the term "Phase I" is synonymous with "first-in-human" (FIH) clinical trials, or those studies in which a novel compound is given to human subjects for the first time.[6] FIH studies are sometimes called "true" Phase I trials because they are literally the beginning of human testing. In actuality, however, the "Phase I" moniker typically refers to all nontherapeutic clinical trials, particularly those using healthy volunteers and conducted in residential research clinics.

Drug development is almost always portrayed as a linear process (figure 5.1). The phases imply a step-wise progression as if nonhuman animal testing concludes in order for Phase I to begin, which then must be completed for Phase II to commence, after which Phase III testing is conducted, so that finally a pharmaceutical company can petition the FDA or other regulatory body to make the drug available on the market. This ideal of drug development bears little resemblance to how pharmaceutical companies' research programs actually proceed (figure 5.2). Clinical trials begin long before animal testing is concluded because the FDA no longer mandates long-term toxicity data before green-lighting human testing. The agency requires only preliminary nonhuman animal data that indicate that a new compound is reasonably safe and will likely be effective in treating its target illness. As for the clinical phases, they too proceed more in overlapping than linear fashion. Specifically, Phase I trials are conducted during the *entire* drug development process, even continuing after FDA approval, in order to provide additional data about marketed drugs' safety profile (Derendorf et al. 2000). Phase I studies include those that test a drug in single

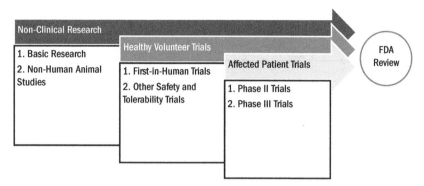

Figure 5.2: Actual Drug Development Process

or multiple doses; compare different formulations, such as a tablet versus capsule; investigate its cardiac, hepatic, or renal effects; measure its interaction with other (usually marketed) drugs; and assess food's effects on a drug's action. Additionally, some Phase I trials are designed to prove that generic drugs are bioequivalent—processed by the body in the same way as brand name drugs—or that racially or ethnically diverse bodies similarly process the same drugs.[7] Many healthy volunteer trials are conducted just prior to a drug's market approval because the data, including those pertaining to drug interactions, become valuable only after that drug's efficacy has been established. Despite occurring at different moments in the drug development process, all these studies count as "Phase I" trials.

Diverse Phase I studies are linked scientifically by their investigations of a drug's pharmacokinetics (PK) and pharmacodynamics (PD). In lay terms, *pharmacokinetics* measures what the body does to a drug after it has been consumed, including how it is absorbed, distributed, metabolized, and excreted. *Pharmacodynamics* refers to how a drug acts on the body—how it changes chemical or physiological processes—and measures how the drug's concentration affects the response (i.e., the dose–response relationship). A drug's PK and PD are measured primarily through blood, which is why Phase I studies have extensive blood collection; particularly on days when the drug has been administered, participants might undergo hourly blood draws for several hours. Other bodily outputs, such as urine, feces, or cerebrospinal fluid, might also be acquired, but systematic collection of these substances is much less common than that of blood.

Even though Phase I trials are designed to answer a range of research questions about pharmaceuticals' safety and tolerability, research staff often focus on the quotidian tasks of executing the protocols, particularly because of the fairly standardized procedures across trials. A single industry term best encapsulates Phase I trials' workflow: "feed 'em-and-bleed 'em." The phrase emphasizes the one input and one output that structure most days in the clinics,[8] but it also situates the clinics' activities in a laboratory paradigm. Because the protocols come from the sponsors, the research staff—from physician-investigators to phlebotomists—are charged with executing the studies, not designing the science. In an important sense, the staff are largely like skilled laboratory technicians playing their part with the study inputs and outputs, rendering healthy volunteers structurally equivalent to nonhuman animal subjects.

Phase I trials can be read as protocols designed to produce harm in healthy volunteers in order to document investigational drugs' safety profile. Put another way, these trials' purpose is to use healthy volunteers to generate adverse events in vivo, in a human model organism. In a classic dose-escalation study design, for example, each cohort of eight to twelve healthy volunteers is given a higher dose of the investigational drug until a preestablished stopping point is reached or the severity or frequency of the adverse events compels the investigators to halt the study prematurely (Chapman 2011). The information gleaned can help pharmaceutical companies select a therapeutic drug dose without unduly burdensome side effects. In addition to PK and PD data, participants' corporeal experiences and subsequent self-reports also form the backbone of investigational drugs' tolerability assessment. There is strong clinical evidence that patients are less adherent to prescriptions when medications produce too many side effects (Osterberg and Blaschke 2005), so Phase I trials help examine the experiential side to a potential therapy. Healthy volunteers become the basis for determining how much of the drug might be too much. This goal of generating adverse events under laboratory-like conditions in at least some participants in each study mirrors that of the nonhuman animal research world.

Producing Harm in Phase I Trials

As with nonhuman animal research (Birke, Arluke, and Michael 2007), the possibility of intentionally harming a healthy organism is not without some angst for many research staff, especially when they take the time to reflect upon it. Patty, the recruiter at Academic Phase I, conceded, "You know that is a chance you take when you come in to do Phase I studies [as a healthy volunteer]. We cross our fingers, knock on wood, light a candle, pray on it. [Laughs.] You know, we don't want to see anyone injured by anything we do here."

Fortunately for research staff, serious adverse events are rare in Phase I trials, and these trials are generally considered quite safe (Emanuel et al. 2015; Johnson et al. 2016). While there have also been instances in which healthy volunteers have died or been gravely injured from their participation (Hawkes 2016; Wood and Darbyshire 2006), most research staff have never experienced or witnessed this type of tragedy firsthand. At the same time, temporary adverse events are very common, with one report estimating that 65 percent of healthy volunteers experience at least one per trial (Sibille et al. 1998). These trends indicate that staff typically expect that healthy volunteers might not feel well during a clinical trial, possibly suffering from headaches, diarrhea, or other common symptoms, but that dramatic problems are unlikely.

Research staff often justify the production of these fairly mundane—even if uncomfortable—symptoms in Phase I trials by highlighting the data's value. Unlike nonhuman animal studies, human trials provide some space for subjects' voices. Research staff routinely query participants about how they feel, collecting data about the subjective experience of having consumed an investigational drug. Although blood provides critical data, symptoms such as nausea and headaches do not have any biological markers in blood, so these data can be assessed only through self-report. Whereas some adverse events, such as gastrointestinal problems, can be observed in both animals and humans, data about others can be captured only from humans. As Paul, the physician-investigator at Pharma Phase I, explained, Phase I trials are needed because "human beings . . . have the remarkable capability of communicating what we feel. I mean, you know, maybe the rats did okay, but is the rat going to tell me they had a headache?"[9] Coupled with the temporary nature of most adverse events, such symptoms are rarely seen as harmful to participants.

When serious adverse events *do* occur, it is all the more alarming because research staff expect their healthy-volunteer model organisms to be impervious to any real harm. These experiences have both professional and emotional components as staff face the role they played in harming someone. For physicians, their identities as Phase I investigators are often developed through their responses to these unusual occurrences. This was certainly the case for Paul at Pharma Phase I. In telling me about the first serious adverse events to affect his participants, Paul narrated it as a rite of passage in clinical pharmacology:

> [It was] in the early 1980s . . . that I would conduct a what would be called today "proof of concept" trial. . . . It had an unexpected and sudden toxicity. . . . So after the first patient [*sic*: healthy volunteer] that that happened to, and the patient recovered without any sequelae, I was permitted by the IRB [institutional review board] and everybody to continue. And they just said, "Well, Paul, you've had your one idiosyncratic reaction, don't see it again." . . . A week later another volunteer came in with the same issue. And the whole class of medications died before my eyes.

Paul described the dramatic fallout from this clinical trial involving the study's sponsor, the IRB, and an attorney when one of the participants threatened to sue. In the midst of this, Paul's mentor from his previous academic training program had suddenly called him:

> He said like, "What are you doing? You know, I've heard these rumors about—," and [he] and I actually talked about the whole story. And the bottom line of the whole thing, which was uncharacteristically for his sort of mode, he sort of asked me about my emotions during the whole thing. He said to me, "So how did you feel," he said, "making someone ill with an experimental agent?" . . . I said I didn't feel very good about it at all. And it was interesting his response to me was, he said, "Well, that's why we need, you know, responsible and good doctors to do this sort of thing." He said, "It's not the stuff of babies." . . . So at that point, I sort of declared myself like an early clinical investigator with drugs and stuff. . . . I decided to commit my life to doing this [work].

While Paul's mentor had affirmed his emotional response to this episode, the real lesson Paul learned was to approach Phase I trials with redoubled resolve to unflinchingly perform work that would make lesser physicians uneasy.[10]

Scott, a white physician-investigator at CRO Phase I, had a similar negative experience that shaped his view of the harm that can come to healthy volunteers from clinical trials. He prefaced the story by reflecting on the ethics associated with the investigator role:

> And, you know, thank God, the government in the last 25 years has made all these regulations as best they can. So, yeah, as far as my participating as an investigator, in terms of the ethics of it, for me, one of the toughest ethical questions comes from way, *way* out front before we've accepted the study, when we're sent the study [from the sponsor], and I read the investigator's brochure, you know, and I read, you know, the rationale and the background [of the study] to decide do I think this is safe? Because I have to look a subject in the eye and say, "I really think this is safe for you to do."

Without pausing, Scott shared that his worries about Phase I studies stemmed from the possibility of unexpected serious adverse events. He explained, "And we actually had one study last year where someone—thank goodness they were fine—but they ended up in the ICU overnight because of a reaction, and it was a study in which in the animal studies, two monkeys actually died three days after getting a high dose of the drug. . . . And we got to that, this high dose, and this guy had a reaction, so we stopped the study. And again, he had complete recovery in 24 hours, but you don't like that to happen at all."

Further details about the clinical trial revealed Scott's prior conflict with the pharmaceutical company sponsor regarding the adverse events that had occurred in an earlier cohort. Specifically, Scott had wanted to halt the dose escalation, but the sponsor refused, disputing Scott's assessment that the adverse events were drug-related (i.e., were adverse *effects*). Scott ultimately capitulated even though he "was gettin' a little bit gun-shy with going up on the dose," and that was when the healthy volunteer ended up in the ICU. Scott expressed ambivalence about pharmaceutical companies when he distinguished himself from the sponsor by saying,

I think most of 'em [sponsors] have a tremendous respect for investigators because we're the guys, you know, with feet to the fire. I mean obviously they feel—, the better sponsors [anyway], clearly you can tell that they feel very, *very* responsible for anything that happens. I mean not only financially, medically, legally, but [also], you know, personally. And it's nice to know that you have backup like that. But at the end of the day, I'm the one here. [Laughs.] So it's easy if you're [2,000 miles away] to say, "Well, give me a call if anything goes wrong," you know?

Scott's lived experience of a clinical trial progressing differently than expected heightened his strong sense of responsibility toward healthy volunteers' well-being. His story also underscores the extent to which Phase I trials' purpose, at least from the pharmaceutical company sponsor's perspective, truly is to produce adverse events. In this case, the sponsor not only denied that the adverse events Scott had documented were drug-related, but also remained untroubled by the prevalence of symptoms that the participants had nonetheless displayed. This story also illustrates an important contradiction between Scott's professed ethical stance of conducting only safe studies and the on-the-ground reality of being guided by institutional arrangements, primarily the lucrative contract his company had signed with a pharmaceutical company.

Stories like Paul's and Scott's are largely exceptions. While the possibility of harm to healthy volunteers is always present during Phase I trials, most research staff do not describe serious problems occurring in their work. Additionally, they discursively minimize the potential harm to participants in how they talk about trial protocols. Staff almost always referred to adverse events simply as "AEs." Language is important for structuring perception, and the abbreviated term further masks the harm caused to participants through the trial because "adverse" is no longer even articulated. In the process, adverse events become normalized. Like the procedures that healthy volunteers must undergo in studies, AEs are simply a normal part of what happens to model organisms. The assumption is that such research subjects will not truly be harmed because they are healthy enough to withstand any long-lasting effects of the drugs. Documenting and managing adverse events become just another routine part of the job.

Cultivating Model Participants

Adapting to the Phase I laboratory, thus, demands a great deal from healthy volunteers. They must be willing to be confined to a clinic, undergo frequent procedures, and experience adverse events. Those ready to consent to these conditions must also qualify for the trials by fitting the parameters for "healthy" that the pharmaceutical company sponsors define. These prerequisites make it difficult for research staff to identify people who can be the right participants for their studies, and they shape research staff's process of cultivating healthy volunteers as model organisms.

Although clinic confinement might be justified by Phase I trials' scientific goals, the experience can be difficult for healthy volunteers. Research staff often articulated the sentiment that this trial design is not a "natural" state, sympathetically noting how adults are not accustomed to these conditions. For example, Gail, the director of operations at Pharma Phase I, told me, "I've done this for 18 years on this side [as staff]. You give me a badge [as a volunteer] and close the door behind me and tell me I have to wear a green t-shirt and I can't go out that door on my own, I'm not gonna do well in this environment." Extrapolating to first-time participants, she added, "When it's our studies that are 19, 20, 21 days [long] and we have five or six [participants] who are brand new, . . . that always makes me a bit nervous, because you don't know how you're gonna react when you're put in a colored t-shirt and given a set of rules to go by. That's a tough thing for an adult to do." For those first-time participants, Tanya, one of the recruiters at Pharma Phase I, emphasized the importance of communicating exactly what they should expect after checking in for a study: "I sit them down and tell them, it's like, 'Look, you're going to have people all day long telling you what to do. So, if you're not the kind of person that can deal with people telling you when to wake up, when to take a shower, when to do this, [you're going to have a problem.]' I said, 'You know, it's not prison, but it's a very controlled environment. This is science we're doing here.' And I think some people don't understand that." While Tanya's articulation fell short of describing clinic conditions as similar to nonhuman animal research, it is telling that she rejected a comparison between the controlled environment and prison by appealing to science instead and hinting at a closer alignment with a laboratory setting.

Identifying the right scientific specimen is also a rigorous process. When it comes to their eligibility for these clinical trials, healthy volunteers are not simply non-ill humans; they qualify because they meet specific, strict inclusion-exclusion criteria. Healthy volunteers have historically been called "normal" in contrast to their sick or diseased counterparts (Stark 2012).[11] This language, however, misses the mark given that healthy volunteers can hardly be said to be representative of the overall "normal" population. Instead, they generally have better than average test results on their blood pressure, red and white blood cells, liver function, cholesterol, and so on. Moreover, they also must adhere to a host of restrictions that require them to deviate from their usual diets and behaviors. Part of this adherence is consenting to the confinement period and subjecting themselves to the surveillance that ensures they are good subjects for the experimental conditions. Even though healthy volunteers are not "purpose-bred" for Phase I trials as nonhuman animals are for laboratory research (Leonelli 2012), being subjected to the narrow parameters typical of these clinical trials distinguishes these participants from healthy populations at large.

There are many reasons why someone might not qualify for a Phase I trial. Provided that a prospective participant does not take illicit drugs and is neither underweight nor obese, that person is then subjected to a plethora of routine tests to determine whether he or she meets the ever-shifting parameters that the study sponsors set for a specific trial. Andrea, a white physician-investigator at Academic Phase I, described some typical screening criteria:

[Those who qualify are] people who their lab values are normal, make sure their liver functions are okay and their kidneys are working properly, that's always a good thing. And we assess for family history, we assess for personal history, we assess for allergies. So, based upon those things and physical exam as well as we check for, we screen for, obviously Hepatitis, HIV, and all those other good things. So, if all those things come back within normal limits or negative, then we consider the patient a healthy volunteer. Also, we do an EKG tracing to make sure that they have baseline normal sinus rhythm, and that's considered to be a normal, healthy volunteer.

I asked Andrea about typical reasons that prospective participants are disqualified from trials. Without hesitation, she responded, "So, what we've been getting is sometimes when the EKG parameters are too narrow, sometimes we get disqualifications based on that. And so sometimes we'll do two or three EKGs, and the numbers still come out just a couple of numbers higher than what they [the sponsors] want in their range and that disqualifies them."

What is important to note here is that often these study parameters are not designed to disqualify people who are not healthy; rather, they reject normal, healthy people based on clinically nonsignificant findings that simply do not match what the sponsor wants. One explanation for this is that pharmaceutical companies adjust the inclusion-exclusion criteria to compensate for the investigational drug's expected action on the body. For example, if a drug is known to lower blood pressure, the inclusion-exclusion criteria might dictate that healthy volunteers must have blood pressure readings above a certain threshold so that the drug will not lower it to a dangerous level. The inverse is also true: a clinical trial might exclude healthy volunteers with blood pressure on the high end of the clinically normal range when the sponsor expects the drug to raise it. In these ways, pharmaceutical companies construct the ideal model organism—one that can produce data to make their drug appear as safe as possible.

Moreover, healthy volunteers must meet the trial criteria *twice*: once when they screen, then when all the same tests are repeated after they check in for the study. Participants can also exercise their right to withdraw their consent or simply fail to show up for the study. For these reasons, Phase I trials—unlike all other clinical trials—have an established system of bringing in extra healthy volunteers, who are referred to as "alternates," "backups," or "reserves," depending on each clinic's lingo. Much as with nonhuman animals used in research, having alternates ensures that the experiment can be conducted on schedule with the correct number of subjects. The clinics can estimate from prior experience the appropriate number of extra healthy volunteers to bring in, anticipating to use some but not all of them. They then send anyone home (with compensation for a single night in the clinic) who does not meet the criteria at check-in or who is not "used," meaning anyone who is not dosed with the investigational drug or a placebo.

Clinics are focused on finding the right bodies for the efficient functioning of the study protocols, and nowhere is this more apparent than in their search for participants with prime veins for blood collection. Given the centrality of blood for generating data about investigational drugs, the clinics want participants with veins that are easy to access quickly. Typically, they want to collect each healthy volunteer's blood within 60 to 90 seconds, from tying the tourniquet to applying the bandage.[12] Tanya, the recruiter at Pharma Phase I, defended selecting participants based on their veins: "But, you know, we're also here to make sure we get the blood drawn, and it's going to be on time, and if we have to use a butterfly [needle] with you to get you [that is, successfully get your blood drawn], that means it takes more time. It means we're going to be late for the next person. And so we really try to avoid that as much as possible." Thus, more difficult veins interfere with the workflow and pose the risk of research staff falling behind on their time-points.[13] As a result, staff rate prospective participants' veins during the screening visit, and this attention to venous access illustrates the extent to which healthy volunteers' bodies must conform to a certain standard to be eligible for study inclusion.[14]

Because of Phase I trials' stringent inclusion-exclusion criteria, research clinics want to have a reliable pool of healthy volunteers who are likely to qualify for any clinical trials they conduct. In a sense, they cultivate a standing reserve that mirrors on a much larger scale the system in place for each study. Indeed, clinics rarely have problems finding appropriate participants who qualify, regardless of the study parameters. This is primarily because clinics have their regular healthy volunteers who, as a group, can be counted on to screen and qualify for Phase I trials. As long as study volume does not outpace the number of people in their participant pool, returning healthy volunteers ensure the clinic's recruitment success. Samuel, the director of operations at Cottage Phase I, voiced concern that their pool of eligible healthy volunteers was inadequate and disclosed that they still needed to appraise how successful their recruitment of participants could be each time they negotiated a study with a sponsor: "Once someone [from a pharmaceutical company] calls us for a study, you know, Kyle and Brent [the business development officers], they look at it to see if it's gonna be feasible, 'cause our healthy database is around 10,000 people. So they'll look and we have a pretty good idea right up front if we're gonna be able to recruit when we're looking at [who is still on] washout from other studies." Although 10,000 healthy volunteers may seem like a veritable army, the clinics must account not only for participants being available and interested but also qualifying for the new study, including having adequate time between studies to complete their washout. By way of comparison, two other clinics in my sample had nearly 17,000 and 14,000 healthy volunteers in their respective databases. Using a lab animal metaphor, Alyssa, a white woman who worked dually in business development and recruitment, joked about her role in bolstering Local Phase I's participant pool: "When I was in college, do you think that I ever said, 'I'm gonna grow up and I'm gonna buy, you know, [human] guinea pigs for a living'? I didn't understand that this world was out there."

Occasionally, a study is designed so narrowly that clinics screen hundreds of people but cannot fill a panel of 24 participants. When this occurs, staff become frustrated and lament that the inclusion-exclusion criteria are based on pharmaceutical companies' unrealistic expectations. During my visits, Cottage Phase I and Local Phase I were struggling with the same "impossible" clinical trial. The study was for a diabetes drug that lowered men's sperm count. Rather than risk long-term reproductive problems for participants, the pharmaceutical company sponsor had designed the study to include only men who had unusually high sperm counts. The inclusion-exclusion criteria for this trial were so stringent that the sponsor had had to resort to hiring multiple clinics across the country to broaden the search for eligible healthy volunteers. George, a white recruiter at Cottage Phase I, had already screened 14 men of different ages and races with and without children, and none had been eligible. Alyssa from Local Phase I told me that it becomes the clinic's duty in these situations to inform the sponsors that they must alter the study protocol: "Frequently you'll say to the sponsor at that stage, 'You know, I don't think this is gonna work, and here's the three inclusions that are the problem or whatever.' . . . They don't realize frequently how much that can impact the success of their study, which means that they're not gonna get *any* data, which means that it's gonna fail miserably." While Alyssa emphasized the role that the clinic must play in evaluating the sponsor's criteria, this did not necessarily produce the desired effect. George did actually contact the sponsor to see whether they would make exceptions to the diabetes study's inclusion-exclusion criteria: "I went in, and I just lobbied for forty [percentile], 'cause I have enough people that are, you know, even had a forty-two percent that can't even do the study." Unfortunately for George and Cottage Phase I, the sponsor refused to grant the request. What this example highlights, though, is that when pharmaceutical companies deviate too far from the ready pool of repeat participants, or the model organisms cultivated by the clinics, they might not obtain the data they want as expediently as they expect.

Meeting the protocol requirements and having excellent veins are necessary but insufficient criteria for being invited to enroll in clinical trials. Even when prospective healthy volunteers pass all the screening tests, research staff might not believe they will make good Phase I participants. "Good" study participants are those who are capable of following direction, punctual for all their procedures, well behaved in the clinic, adaptable to the confinement, and dependable for follow-up visits. In other words, research staff want to avoid situations in which volunteers have problems with authority, cannot get along with others, must be searched for in the clinic every time a procedure is scheduled, and are unlikely to complete a study because they cannot last the confinement period or they fail to show up for final outpatient procedures.[15] While technically any prospective healthy volunteer might qualify as "good," the staff give preference to repeat participants because they are known quantities: they can be trusted to fit the general criteria required by Phase I trials, to adapt to the clinic environment, and to finish any studies they start. By weeding out others, this selection process effectively creates model organisms, people who are maximally suited for Phase I science.

At Pharma Phase I, the recruiters saw their role in the selection of participants as a line of defense for the clinic's safety and as a means of achieving its business goals. Tanya stressed how her conversations with prospective volunteers served as social and psychological tests of individuals' suitability for Phase I trials: "We've had other folks that've come in and have presented with some, you know, abnormal affects, and so we alert each other to that fact and say, 'What do you think?' and 'Watch the person during the screening time.' If we're convinced that this person is inappropriate [to do studies here], then we make that judgment." The judgment in this case would be to disallow a person's trial enrollment if the staff believed the person to be potentially dangerous or disruptive. Yolanda, another African American recruiter at Pharma Phase I, affirmed this holistic rather than biological screening process: "It may sound like we're kinda picking the cream of the crop kind of thing, but in the kind of work that we do, it's very important that, again, we look at the whole individual, not just their labs, that we look at who they are." The Pharma Phase I recruiters were particularly adamant that this process was crucial for the study's safety, given that everyone selected would be confined together in the clinic. Specifically, Erica, one of the white recruiters, asserted, "We are in the business to make studies successful [by filling them with volunteers], so not to rule out people unnecessarily, but by the same token . . . [we must] make it a safe environment for everybody."[16] Although the social and psychological metrics that Pharma Phase I employed were less concrete than the trial inclusion-exclusion criteria, prospective participants who were argumentative, seemed paranoid or delusional, had hygiene problems, or could not follow instructions during the screening process were all likely to be excluded from Phase I trials there.[17]

Research staff's social and psychological assessments of prospective participants also explain their preference for repeat healthy volunteers. As known quantities, the participants have already been vetted and proven trustworthy, which gives them a distinct advantage over first-time participants and even other serial participants who have no prior enrollment at a specific clinic. Given staff perceptions that clinic confinement is difficult, they regard those who handle it well as particularly valuable. Marion, a white woman in her early sixties who was the recruitment director at CRO Phase I, explained, "We use repeats quite a bit, we do. But we do feel more comfortable with 'em. I mean they're in-house for a long time. The girls [staff], by the end of a week or so many days, they have a sense of who's being honest. . . . There's been some we'll say, no, they can't come back; you know, we've used 'em once or twice, and we don't have a good feel for 'em." In this way, the staff intentionally select the same healthy volunteers over and over again. These participants are seen as well suited to Phase I trials, so they are allowed to or invited to enroll again, which with the additional experience, can further affirm that they are the ones with whom the staff want to work. Not only do staff seek model organisms, they actively cultivate them through the study experience.

To truly achieve model status, healthy volunteers must be compliant, flexible, and able to "do what it takes" for the trial protocol. Knowing what is expected during a study does not come naturally in the artificial environment of the Phase I clinic, so the staff have to train participants how to behave. Experienced healthy volunteers are valuable in this regard because they understand how the protocols work and know the clinics' SOPs. Research staff prefer repeat participants for this reason, but some clinics also actively shape more compliant research subjects through strict clinic rules. Pharma Phase I imposed a highly structured environment on participants, and it notably ran much more smoothly than other places. Remarkably, even though healthy volunteers were given more freedom than they were at a place like Local Phase I (with its requirement that all participants be present in their assigned chairs during the group's blood collection), they were nonetheless on time and ready for their procedures. This was because each participant was given a personal events schedule to follow during their clinic stay and was responsibilized through a fining system in which study compensation was docked when participants were late to procedures.

Earlier we heard healthy volunteers' complaints about fines, but Pharma Phase I's system of events schedules and fines had a valuable role in enforcing the protocol. When arriving even one minute late for a procedure could cost them part of their paycheck, this threat quickly trained participants to watch the clock. One manifestation of how healthy volunteers tried to be on top of their schedules was that they almost always had the printout of their individual schedules with them for reference. Typically, when participants observed someone from their study walking toward the procedure area (made more visible by the color of their t-shirt), they instinctively looked at one of the ubiquitous, synchronized digital clocks, grabbed their schedule, and consulted it.[18] From time to time, this led them to jump up and run to the procedure area as well, but typically, they ended up realizing that they still had time before their next event.

Given that participants hated to have their pay reduced,[19] Pharma Phase I's system trained them to adhere to the protocol's expectations through a punishment system. Tanya, the recruiter, expressed this goal explicitly: "It's kind of a teaching thing too for them, as far as being on time, 'cause we try and, you know, build this culture of how essential [being] on time is because once they get here in the unit, everything is based off of time. . . . And they're even told that 'on time' is five minutes *before the time* that they're, you know, actually scheduled." The threat of fines was effective at eliciting the behavior Pharma Phase I expected from its healthy volunteers. Not only did few people have their pay docked per study, repeat participants were well adapted to the system and rarely had trouble adhering to their schedules.

Another important aspect of Pharma Phase I's operations structure was that its SOPs were designed to align with the strictest study protocols a clinic must execute. The idea behind this is that making them routine practice prepared participants (and staff for that matter) for the most exacting clinical-trial demands. Thus, for example, training around meals was, and is, particularly important because typically people do not view eating as a procedure, but that is precisely how it is defined in Phase I protocols, which dictate how many calories or how much fat participants must consume. Because some protocols are more stringent about meals than others, in terms of how much of the food needs to be consumed or how much time participants have to do so, Pharma Phase I generally applied the strictest conditions to all meals. Specifically, participants had to eat every item placed on their meal tray within twenty minutes. This SOP generated one of the worst punishments a clinic could enforce: if participants did not finish their meal in its entirety, the staff made them eat any remaining items before they left the cafeteria. When someone has to eat a pat of butter without any bread or drink a salad dressing packet, everyone present quickly learns what "finishing" their food tray means. Gail, Pharma Phase I's director of operations, underscored the logic behind her decision to make all meals at the facility eaten in twenty minutes regardless of the individual protocol: "I'm a firm believer in the rules, and that's how we train people for the next study. That's how we get data collected on time. That's how you get good data quality standards." In other words, one of Gail's core assumptions behind this decision was that Pharma Phase I would have ongoing relationships with repeat healthy volunteers.

Even at the clinics that did not have as many rules and punishments as Pharma Phase I, the research staff were well aware of the importance of training healthy volunteers to be what I characterize as model organisms. Patty, the recruiter at Academic Phase I, argued that socializing participants to research encourages compliance. She observed, "I don't think they understand how specific the [pharmaceutical] companies are with their time-points you know? We have a small window; you know, they tell us we have to get a blood sample at 8:10, we have 8:10 to 8:15 to get that blood sample, you know? And if not, we have to document why we didn't get it. So, I don't think they're aware of the short timeframes that we have to deal with, you know, to get everything done." Furthermore, not only must participants be trained to understand the workings of clinical trials and to respect the time-points, but staff's interactions with healthy volunteers must also minimize the possibility of error. Elliott, a white project manager, described how this dynamic worked at Local Phase I:

> I think just making ourselves clear is what's required, yeah. You know, for instance, if we have to record the actual stop time of a meal, a pretty common way of doing that would be to ask the patient [sic] to hold onto like the last bite of food and to kinda not consume it. And I mean, if you explain to someone, . . . [it] helps your compliance, because people don't just like automatically finish kinda thing. . . . [Another thing is] never give a participant a dosing cup until one second before the time of dose. Because once it's out of your hands, it's in theirs, and the potential for boo-boo is extremely strong at that point. So, if you're gonna get an early dose, then that'll be the way it happens.

Both Patty and Elliott emphasized the importance of participants grasping the logic behind the rules to ensure their compliance, along with the clinic structuring the procedures for success. Thus, the staff must condition the participants to the exact requirements of how Phase I trials work.

Research staff's cultivation of healthy volunteers to be model organisms illustrates some challenges inherent in the structure of Phase I protocols. Their practices to increase participant compliance are indicative of their investment not only in the clinic SOPs and environment but also in the healthy volunteers themselves. The effort of training healthy volunteers to be good Phase I participants is a valuable investment. As

Alyssa at Local Phase I put it, "When you have those that aren't naive subjects, they're kinda a dream for everyone, you know? I mean they know the routine, they know how to behave, they know everything is time sensitive."

Constructing the Efficient Laboratory

Research staff's practices of selecting and cultivating the right kind of participants for Phase I trials can be read as clinic-level strategies to ensure that studies run as efficiently as possible. Pharmaceutical companies' protocols create demanding study event schedules, and research staff are incentivized to work with repeat participants whom they know they can trust to expedite the workflow. As a result, healthy volunteers become model organisms that are prepared—for the monetary compensation—to be confined to the clinic, poked and prodded for procedures, and subjected to adverse events. Yet, in this construction of the model organism, the staff's attention to the potential harm to participants is redirected so that adverse events are not harms per se but merely a routine part of data collection. Indeed, staff are more likely to perceive participants as *sources* of risk to the protocol rather than as subjects who are *exposed* to risk. This is because as staff manage intense data collection schedules, they must count on healthy volunteers' cooperation to succeed in meeting all their time-points.

Healthy volunteers who understand and anticipate the study protocols support the clinic workflow, minimizing the chaos that could otherwise occur should participants be uncertain about how to handle the artifice and constraints of the Phase I laboratory. Thus, staff's selection of repeat participants is part of making healthy volunteers "good enough" model organisms (Lewis et al. 2012). By training compliance in repeat participants, Phase I science goes beyond what would be possible with nonhuman animal model organisms, fine-tuning their contribution in physiological *and* behavioral ways. Healthy volunteers are collaborators in the process, motivated by their own adverse life events to adapt and adhere to the Phase I laboratory and become the known quantities trusted to generate the data pharmaceutical companies require. But, how good are those data?

6

The Dark Side of the Model

What does the construction of a Phase I model organism mean for the validity of clinical trial results? Or put another way, how much can we trust the data from serial healthy volunteers about the general safety and tolerability of pharmaceuticals? As we have seen, the Phase I clinic aspires to be a highly controlled and efficient laboratory that enrolls healthy volunteers who are suited to confinement. Yet, the picture of Phase I trials running like a well-oiled machine masks validity issues caused by the very structure of the protocols and how they are conducted. In particular, the use of model organisms in science aims to achieve standardization and predictability across laboratory contexts, but it has its own set of intrinsic and extrinsic drawbacks that often remains hidden from view. On one hand, as with nonhuman animal research, questions arise about how data from model organisms can be extrapolated to the "real world" of patients who will ultimately consume these drugs. This is not only because participants are not representative of the general population, but also because the laboratory demands do not mirror patients' environments and behaviors when taking pharmaceuticals. On the other hand, the practices of both research staff and healthy volunteers further undermine study validity as they bend trial rules to make the model fit the protocols. For example, the required washout periods between trials become an inconvenient obstacle to recruitment, so staff routinely ignore signs of rule-breaking. Rather than a symptom of "bad apples" involved in research, these validity threats are deeply embedded in Phase I trials' design and execution.[1]

One way to examine these validity problems is by analyzing how the use of healthy volunteers as model organisms supports various actors' interests in Phase I trials. These interests are both individual and structural, and they typically hinge on economic incentives for a desired outcome. In the case of the pharmaceutical industry, clinical trial designs—especially inclusion-exclusion criteria privileging young, healthy men—produce results that depict companies' products in the safest light and limit their liability for harm to participants. The clinics are also not free from commercial interests; they require pharmaceutical companies' return business, placing pressure on staff to fill studies quickly and deliver the right kinds of data. Finally, healthy volunteers have their own interests in maximizing the money they earn, and they find ways to exploit the system that exploits them. As model organisms, healthy volunteers are distinct from their nonhuman animal counterparts in that they can exert more agency over their participation, from when and where they enroll in studies to how much they adhere to trial demands. Thus, the Phase I trials' model-organism approach is deeply flawed, but in ways that actually serve the interests of clinics, healthy volunteers, and especially the pharmaceutical industry. Because these interests often conflict with those of future patients seeking safe drugs, the hidden validity problems they generate are what I consider to be the "dark side" of the model organism.

Intrinsic Validity Threats

Even when a study proceeds precisely as dictated by the protocol, there are serious questions that must be asked about how well it succeeds in measuring investigational drugs' safety and tolerability. Specifically, one might wonder what Phase I data mean and for whom. All clinical trials are designed to answer specific research questions, and the choices investigators or sponsors make about the protocols service those questions while simultaneously foreclosing other lines of inquiry.[2] Given that Phase I trials are conducted in a controlled environment with healthy volunteers, there are clear limitations on what can be known about the action of these drugs in sick patients. Rather than answering the general question "How safe are these pharmaceuticals?," Phase I trials instead tackle the narrower question "How much of an investigational drug can be given to healthy volunteers without inflicting too much harm?" Yet, even posing the question this way is not specific enough to represent what actually occurs in Phase I research. The question has to further account for how the protocols define "healthy" through the inclusion-exclusion criteria, how the dietary and lifestyle restrictions and the confinement radically depart from real-world conditions, and how serial participants restrict the overall number of healthy volunteers involved. For research staff and healthy volunteers, these validity issues become puzzles on which to ruminate.

It is important to probe how well healthy volunteers represent the general population. Individuals who are best suited to Phase I trials must have sufficient available time, and often limited economic opportunities, to have the motivation to consent to study confinement. Additionally, the fact that participants are typically young, minority men could raise alarm about these trials' generalizability.

Sex

The existing scholarly literature focuses much of its concern on women's underrepresentation in clinical trials.[3] Specifically, increasing attention has been given to sex-based differences in both the safety and efficacy of medical treatments (Clayton and Collins 2014; Mazure and Jones 2015). With regard to Phase I trials in particular, inadequate numbers of female participants in these pivotal safety studies create the risk that future prescription drugs could have a higher probability and magnitude of harming female patients (Miller 2001; Rademaker 2001). Indeed, drugs removed from the market for safety reasons between 1997 and 2000 were shown to have disproportionately harmed female patients, generally by adversely affecting their hearts or livers, regardless of the type of drug (US General Accounting Office [GAO] 2001). Sex-based differences might result from females' (usually) smaller size and weight, their higher percentage of body fat, or their smaller organ size (Meibohm, Beierle, and Derendorf 2002), and such findings underscore the importance of including both sexes in biomedical research. Owing to mandates for women's inclusion in all clinical trials they fund (Epstein 2007), the US National Institutes of Health (NIH) recently reported that more than half of all Phase III (therapeutic) trial participants are female (NIH Office of Research on Women's Health 2017). Yet, such inclusion requirements do not apply to non-NIH studies, and female participants continue to be underrepresented in industry-funded Phase I trials (Chen et al. 2018).

Research staff and healthy volunteers also voiced apprehension about women's underrepresentation in Phase I trials. Namely, they pointed to the restrictive inclusion-exclusion criteria as the crux of the validity problem. For example, Charlotte, a white physician-investigator at Pharma Phase I, discussed her struggle with her parent company to open up protocols to female participants:

> There is a major [sex] bias in the way the protocols are written that we're trying to fight for more opportunities [for women]. . . . [Our parent company defaults to] you cannot put women who are of childbearing potential in studies. . . . We sometimes get protocols that *could* enroll women of childbearing potential, and we have won the battle many times . . . [when] we said, "Listen, you *have* to open it to women of childbearing potential. There is *no* reason not to in this case." So, we try . . . to see if there's a real reason for which there are no women of childbearing potential [in each protocol] . . . because eventually the drug will be given to everybody down the road.

Charlotte went on to explain that when Phase I trials commence, the long-term toxicity and reproductive teratology studies often remain pending in nonhuman animals. This allows the company to argue that women of childbearing potential must be excluded from trials due to the absence of data indicating fetal harm is unlikely. Thus, the nonlinear process of drug development provides a structural justification to uphold the paternalistic position that women are always potentially pregnant and their hypothetical fetuses must be protected (Corrigan 2002).[4]

For their part, female healthy volunteers emphasized both how unfair it is to exclude women of childbearing potential from many Phase I trials and how safety data suffer as a result. Shirley, an African American woman in her late thirties, had a doctoral degree in the natural sciences and frequently identified with the research staff, but she found it frustrating that pharmaceutical companies were not nearly as concerned about men impregnating women as they were about women getting pregnant during clinical trials. The iniquity generated by sex-based inclusion-exclusion criteria is worsened, from Shirley's perspective, because of the validity problems that arise when younger women, in particular, are underrepresented in these trials: "A lot of that age group [of nonchildbearing women] is now going to be like fifty and above. So, I mean, now you've got, you know, data coming in for women who are older, not for younger, so I mean that's also going to be skewing the results." In other words, by restricting the participation of women of childbearing potential, Phase I protocols do not simply reduce the *number* of women who can qualify but they also ensure that female participants are, on the whole, older as a group than are males. This in turn compounds the sex-based validity problems inherent in most study protocols.

Race/Ethnicity

In comparison to questions about Phase I trials' representativeness in terms of sex, the inclusion of minorities is an altogether different issue. Race and ethnicity are thorny social categories because of unsubstantiated assumptions that different groups are demarcated by discrete, shared genetic characteristics.[5] Although biological differences among racial and ethnic groups are largely overblown or misrepresented, these groups might nevertheless be subject to a host of material inequalities, such as differential access to medical care, that exert real effects on patterns of health and illness (Marks 2013). In medicine, a persistent racial/ethnic disparity is that clinical trials have historically enrolled mostly white research participants (Epstein 2007). This dilemma, however, is turned on its head in Phase I research because of its enrollment of primarily non-white healthy volunteers.

While the scholarly literature constructs the problem of race in research as the *under*representation of minority participants (e.g., George, Duran, and Norris 2014; Hussain-Gambles 2003), it is virtually silent on the implications of an *over*representation of these groups. Scholars even disagree in their assessments of why racially and ethnically diverse clinical trials are desirable, pointing to biological and social factors and oftentimes conflating the two. On one hand, some authors advocate for including minorities in clinical trials in order to have data on biological differences about how racial and ethnic groups respond to drugs (e.g., Evelyn et al. 2001; Johnson 2000). This argument places race/ethnicity on par with sex by assuming that there are important biological differences undergirding the most efficacious and safe treatments for patients once drugs receive market approval. On the other hand, some commentators refute any underlying biological differences between racial and ethnic groups and contend that these groups' inclusion in research is a social justice imperative (e.g., Corbie-Smith 2004; Mwaria 2005). Averring that biomedical research is a positive enterprise with which to be involved, these scholars criticize the exclusion of minority groups as denying people the opportunity to reap the potential benefits that can come from trial participation. This standpoint is more problematic with Phase I research, however, when the primary advantage of enrolling is financial compensation, which can be regarded either as a positive opportunity for an individual participant or as part of a system that exploits the economically vulnerable (Elliott 2017; Elliott and Abadie 2008). Following this latter logic, the overrepresentation of minority groups would be cause for alarm rather than celebration.

Both biological and social understandings of race and ethnicity were present in research staff's narratives. Espousing a biological view on race was Tanya, one of the African American recruiters at Pharma Phase I. She asserted,

> I really am a firm believer that early science is good science and that . . . there needs to make sure that there's minority inclusion. One of my goals has been to make sure that we have enough people represented in order to make sense of that. We do a lot of genotyping in Phase I, so, you know, having African Americans and Latinos and Caucasians in equal numbers take part in those tests, to me, is very important because that science is what's going to propel what happens in Phase II in the [patient-]subject population. And if you don't have a really good picture, . . . I firmly believe you're setting yourself up to have a drug that goes to market that's going to exclude a lot of people, and it's not going to work well with a lot of other types of ethnicities. . . . There's plenty of cardiovascular drugs on the market that do not work for African Americans. And the primary reason is because they're [not] involved in the clinical trial process.

Criticizing the status quo of drug development, Tanya took both a biological and political stance on the inclusion of diverse groups in clinical trials.[6]

Paul, the white physician-investigator at Pharma Phase I, had a different view: "You often can't make systematic conclusions [about race or ethnicity]." He continued, "It actually turns out that in a lot of basic, sort of bread-and-butter pharmacokinetic and pharmacodynamics [studies] that demographic or racial distinctions, especially in the United States where we're such a hodgepodge of backgrounds, we don't find—as often as one might think—a whole lot of differences there." Paul all but described race and ethnicity as social, rather than biological, in his position on why Phase I science has little to offer on racial differences. This is fascinating, in part, because despite what could be seen as a recruitment "success," racial and ethnic data are nearly invisible in Phase I research. Perhaps this is simply due to the low numbers of participants, which disallow subgroup analysis, relative to larger-scale efficacy trials, but it suggests there is little evidence that the current racial and ethnic composition of Phase I trials threatens validity. Hence, even if there are race-based biological differences in the action of pharmaceuticals, Phase I research is underpowered to find them. This means that African Americans' inclusion in early-phase trials cannot achieve Tanya's desired results. Moreover, it might even tip concerns about minorities' inclusion in Phase I trials away from a focus on validity to exploitation because these studies cannot add appreciably to the knowledge base about racial health disparities.

Study Design

I have already outlined how pharmaceutical companies can make a drug appear safer than it really is through a study's inclusion-exclusion criteria. This is one of the reasons that recruitment can prove challenging, especially when the sponsor seeks participants who are far outside the range of what would be considered normal for healthy individuals. This protocol design effectively counterbalances any potentially harmful effects of the investigational drug, such as lowering or raising blood pressure, with participants' baseline health. While inclusion-exclusion criteria that are difficult to meet cause consternation among staff and among healthy volunteers, whom are fixated on their respective goals of executing and enrolling in studies, these improbable parameters also raised doubt about the trials' validity. Joseph, an African American healthy volunteer in his thirties, commented, "Some things, they'll make you wonder, you know, about the intentions of the pharmaceutical companies, but whatever." When I prompted him for an example, he explained,

Some studies, they wanted—because the drug dropped your heart rate down so much—they wanted people with an abnormally strong heart rate so they could make it seem like whatever it drops 'em to, the normal levels, it didn't hurt them any. And when they're disclosing it to [future] patients, they didn't say, "We tested it on people with an abnormally strong heart, or—." You know what I mean? So, by the time it gets out in the public, people with normal hearts are gonna be taking it, and then they're gonna be screwed, you know what I mean? . . . Let's be for real. Somebody's gonna get it, and it's gonna screw 'em up, a couple of people, I mean. And [the pharmaceutical company] you're gonna weigh out how much you're making off the drug versus how much you're paying out in lawsuits, and if it's greater, you're just gonna be a calculation, and you're gonna keep the drug on the market.

The connection Joseph made between the study protocol and its implications for future patients is quite perceptive given that clinical trials' limitations are often invisible once drugs are on the market (Henwood et al. 2003; McGoey 2012a). Further, Joseph underscored how economic priorities influence knowledge production. Like other industries, the pharmaceutical industry indeed utilizes a harm-liability calculus that permits consumer injury and death when the product's overall profits outstrip what might be paid in lawsuits.[7] Although Joseph did not provide an actual example, this type of corporate decision-making was a key part of the scandal in which Merck wanted to keep Vioxx, its blockbuster drug, on the market as long as possible despite evidence of the drug's damaging, and at times fatal, cardiovascular effects (Biddle 2007). In this way, Joseph's criticism of clinical trial inclusion-exclusion criteria astutely homed in on how companies prioritize their profits over public health when they make their drugs look safer than they should.

Phase I study confinement and restrictions from normal activities also generated concern. Staff and healthy volunteers were quick to criticize the artificiality of the clinic environment by comparing it to how people, particularly future patients, behave in their everyday lives.[8] Even though the controlled nature of Phase I trials is part of what transforms a healthy volunteer into a model organism, clinic conditions were perceived as unnatural and therefore capable of throwing the data into doubt. This theme occurred regularly when staff and participants appraised the food required by study protocols. Thinking about healthy volunteers' experience of nausea, vomiting, and diarrhea during trials, Roxanne, an African American study nurse at Academic Phase I, suggested these gastrointestinal issues "could be food also, I guess. It's hard to tell sometimes. Like maybe it just doesn't agree with them, since it's hospital food."

Healthy volunteers were often even more explicit in their assessments of how Phase I trials' confinement structure biases results. Take Annie, a white woman in her forties who was enrolled in her second study. Annie's curiosity about the validity of the trial design was piqued when she felt so drowsy that she had trouble reading the books she had brought with her to Cottage Phase I. She wondered whether it was simply the lack of caffeine that she would have normally consumed or a consequence of remaining in one chair all day. Summarizing her daily clinic activity, she said, "I just look a little bit at the TV, read a little bit, and drool a little bit." In her view, it was the environment that made her feel so out of sorts, not the investigational drugs. She opined, "See, and that's why part of me is frustrated with [this set-up]. . . . What guidelines do you need to still do these studies but in a more natural environment? Like if you gave me a shot [of the medication] and let me go home and do my natural day, you know, would I have different side effects? . . . It's unnatural situations, circumstances, and then [do they] pull that data and then figure it's about half right?" Annie's position on eliminating confinement to increase the trial's validity assumes participants could be trusted to follow the rules. Based on the numerous "confessions" I heard of how they inadvertently neglected study restrictions when out of the clinic (not to mention blatant rule-breaking, which is discussed below), Annie likely gave healthy volunteers too much credit. Without reducing the number of restrictions for healthy volunteers to follow as part of the protocols, the bias problem would only be compounded.

As a physician-investigator, Paul was well aware that research staff and healthy volunteers think about the confinement and restrictions in these terms. He did not disagree with people's assessments that Phase I trials' artificiality could profoundly affect the results. He even took the criticism further than participants did by declaring that it is a problem endemic to research: "Humans will report adverse events . . . just as a result of the fact that they're living and they're under observation; all of us have bodily sensations all the time that our brain conveniently suppresses for us." Through this articulation of the power of a Hawthorne (observer) effect, wherein observation alone produces change and might therefore introduce bias into any experiment, Paul claimed that the protocols control for this through the use of placebos: "So that's why we do double-blinds, . . . so that nobody knows [who is taking the investigational drug or the placebo]. . . . Every sensation that a person feels is recorded, and then breaking the blind [to reveal who got the drug] only knows ultimately for sure whether it's of any sort of significance."

A story I heard at CRO Phase I underscored the putative value of the placebo-controlled design. The physician-investigator, Scott, delineated how a class of drugs they tested had known gastrointestinal effects, including loss of appetite, nausea, and diarrhea, so when two trial participants developed these symptoms, Scott assumed they were drug-related. After notifying the sponsor, the company unblinded the trial, and it turned out both participants had been on placebo. Summing up his experience, Scott remarked,

> It's a very humbling experience . . . [and] a good lesson of human nature, you know? Someone starts complaining a little bit, and then maybe a staff member says, or I might even say, "Well, tell me more about that." . . . You sort of feed into each other, you know, and before you know it, you've got a full-blown AE [adverse event]. Shut the study down, but they got placebo. . . . And to this day, I don't have a good explanation for that. I mean you have to say, okay, well, maybe, *maybe* it was the diet they were getting, but everybody was getting the same diet. And again, these are young, healthy guys; I mean, they could eat nails and probably have nothing happen to 'em, you know? [Laughs.]

The power of the nocebo effect—negative bodily symptoms produced by people's expectations that they could occur—surprised Scott and his CRO Phase I colleagues, especially because he perceived healthy volunteers to be rather invincible model organisms. More broadly, the incident underscores the usefulness of the placebo design in adjudicating causes of adverse events.

At the same time, however, the placebo-controlled design paints the development of adverse events in very black-and-white terms.

Specifically, if only the participants who have taken the active drug experience headaches, those adverse events are more likely caused by the study drug. If, however, participants in both groups experience headaches, then is that "proof" that the confinement or restrictions are the likely culprit, or can some headaches still be caused by the drug? This approach seems scientifically robust because the clinical trials' design accounts for this type of bias. However, the small number of healthy volunteers in Phase I studies reduces the likelihood of meaningful statistical differences between the two groups, with advantages to the investigational drug in the analysis.

Model Organism

Clinic recruitment practices also contribute to intrinsic validity threats to Phase I trial results. As previously discussed, all model organisms are selected for attributes that investigators expect to facilitate the research. Healthy volunteers are selected for the efficiency they bring to Phase I trials, but as with all model organisms, they also come with validity risks. To put it another way: as individuals are selected for their adaptability to confinement and further trained to meet the clinic's needs, their representativeness of the general population is called into question. As Scott asserted, they are usually "young, healthy guys . . . [who] could eat nails," not more typical humans. Further, when the same serial healthy volunteers join study after study, the possibility exists that the science is predicated on large-scale selection bias. The bias can work in multiple ways. First, it could be that serial participants are only those individuals who usually do not experience any adverse events, which prompts them to continue to enroll (see also Sibille et al. 1998). Second, it could be that serial participants have varying tolerance to investigational drugs—as opposed to high tolerance across the board—but individuals have fairly consistent adverse events when they have them. For example, a participant might be especially prone to gastrointestinal changes, so these are more likely to occur to that person irrespective of the investigational drug. A third possibility is that serial participants might have increased tolerance over time, particularly for specific classes of drugs, so they are less likely to experience adverse events as their exposure increases.

That much of new drugs' safety data is drawn from a relatively small pool of healthy volunteers can be a disquieting thought, but there are no data to determine what the real implications are for the science. Paul from Pharma Phase I parsed this issue for me as he evaluated the effect of serial participation:

> There's two issues mixed up in this. One is whether I take the same drug multiple times in multiple studies. . . . If I participate in ten studies of the same drug, then I've introduced bias across ten studies as opposed to one. But that's with the same drug, right? Most companies don't usually—although it's not a universal thing—most companies don't allow participation with the same drug across multiple studies. . . . Now multiple different drugs, like taking different drugs and things like that, I don't know that if Paul doesn't get side effects to Experimental Drug 1, that that's necessarily going to be predictive of the fact that I'm gonna be immune to side effects from Experimental Drugs 2 through N. That, I think, is a bit of a leap of faith. . . . [Does] frequent participation bias the adverse event database? . . . I'd need to see some proof to be convinced of that.

Paul was optimistic that serial participation does not introduce any or only negligible bias, but not everyone involved in Phase I trials follows the protocols. For instance, if Paul assumes the same person's data cannot bias a drug's safety profile because the sponsor restricts repeat participation for that drug, then a system must be in place to ensure that this restriction is upheld. In practice, however, serial participants frequent multiple clinics, and they cannot be expected to give full reports of which investigational drugs they might have taken elsewhere. This is acutely challenging as fads in drug development translate into multiple companies working on products in the same chemical class, making it all the more difficult for participants to know which drug they took, at which clinic, and who was the sponsor. Without a centralized database tracking enrollment, it is easy to imagine there could be little enforcement of prior studies as exclusion criteria for new clinical trials. Thus, even when people try to follow the rules, there are multiple gaps in research oversight that could cause bias. Moreover, this appraisal does not account for *intentional* subversion of the clinical trial protocols.

Extrinsic Validity Threats

Validity concerns stem not only from Phase I trials' design but also from the practices of research staff and healthy volunteers. Many random occurrences during a clinical trial could threaten its validity. More alarming, however, are the routines or conventions that undermine trial protocols and introduce systemic bias. Many of these practices can be traced to the use of healthy volunteers as model organisms. Even though model organisms are selected in order to expedite science, reliance on *humans* creates problems. Unlike nonhuman animals, healthy volunteers cannot be ordered for a laboratory; they must be identified as qualified to enroll. For their part, the staff often adapt the model organisms they have (i.e., repeat participants) to fit the study protocols. At the same time, being valued as a model organism can embolden serial participants to break protocol rules, including washout periods and other restrictions. In both cases, as this section illustrates, the actions of staff and healthy volunteers could distort trial results.

Forcing the Model Organism to the Protocol

As outlined earlier, qualification for Phase I trials can be a moving target. First, each study's inclusion-exclusion criteria vary according to the type of data the pharmaceutical company wants about its product. Second, normal fluctuations in humans' vital signs and blood can make someone eligible one day and ineligible the next. Yet, research staff must match the pharmaceutical companies' inflexible trial protocols with the healthy volunteers they count on to enroll. Thus, to find the "right" model organisms for each trial, staff might tinker with the inclusion criteria to force their preferred volunteers to fit or make them "good enough" (Lewis et al. 2012). In practice, this manifests in staff helping serial participants qualify for studies through both subtle and extreme manipulations of the inclusion-exclusion criteria. Intervening in this way might be within the protocols' parameters or could be blatant examples of breaking the rules to facilitate their workflow.

Clinics are normally given a surprising degree of latitude in how they screen prospective healthy volunteers. The sponsor stipulates clear-cut specifications dictating acceptable results for all the tests and measurements, but oftentimes the clinic can determine how criteria are met. For example, the sponsor might require that each participant has a certain level of iron in his or her blood, while allowing clinics to run "repeat" labs to give them additional chances of qualifying. Likewise, if a prospective participant's blood pressure is too high, the staff can wait several minutes and take another reading. Before repeating the procedure, the staff might coach healthy volunteers to breathe deeply in order to lower their blood pressure. Staff are motivated to help participants qualify because it facilitates their workflow, possibly reducing the amount of screening they must do for a trial, or because they are invested in enrolling specific people into a study.

For most staff, providing prospective volunteers with multiple attempts to qualify for studies went unremarked, even if it was quite easy to observe on any screening day. Within the logic of the clinic, the practice was hardly improper, except perhaps to the uninitiated. Sandra, a seasoned African American nurse who was new to Phase I trials, having started her job at Cottage Phase I only a few weeks before my visit, was troubled by what she perceived of as the clinic "pushing" ineligible participants into studies. When I met her, she was full of questions about the ethics of her work, and the screening process was one of the things that nagged at her. She confessed hesitatingly, "You know what my impression [of Phase I] is? It's gray. I thought research was—. Well, before I got into it myself, . . . I thought it was just a little bit more cut and dry, or you know, a little bit more black and white. . . . [But] the whole process seems gray." Sandra stopped and wondered out loud, "Should I even tell you this?" I encouraged her to continue, and she sighed as she picked up where she had left off:

> No, I just, you know, that's one thing that I think about sometimes is it just seems like there's several attempts at getting somebody in[to the study], and I'm sure the SI/PIs [subinvestigators/principal investigators] know what they're doing, but I don't know. . . . You go by numbers [lab values and vitals], but . . . you also push them into "healthy." You repeat until you get the number you want for them to be healthy [for the protocol]. . . . [With] blood pressure, blood [work]: "Oh, we'll have them come back and repeat it." "Oh, we'll have them come back and repeat it." "Oh, we'll take it a few more times."

Sandra reflected on our interview, joking that, "Oh boy, it's like having a conversation with my lawyer!" Sandra might have felt she was transgressing in telling me her ethical qualms about the screening practices she witnessed at Cottage Phase I, but her description of these events would no doubt appear quite normal to most Phase I clinics. As long as the prospective participants eventually pass the tests, these practices would likely be sanctioned by the pharmaceutical companies, even if they feel like cheating to someone new to this research context. Either way, Sandra's narrative elucidates the extent to which the staff might work at getting healthy volunteers to fit the protocols.

Although there have been documented cases of clinics falsifying data (see CenterWatch 2007; Redfearn 2012), neither Sandra nor other staff at the clinics I visited related any stories of themselves or colleagues engaging in research misconduct by "fudging" the numbers, so to speak. Nor was this something I observed during my field work. Yet, serial participants related personal stories about how far staff had gone to get them into studies. Typically, these instances occurred at clinics without electronic data capture systems designed to automatically record results of procedures. Clinics using conventional paper-based systems created opportunities for screening information to be captured aspirationally rather than with actual results. For example, a staff member takes a participant's blood pressure, which is 145/90, but to allow the person into the study, she records it as 135/80. This also occurs with participants' heart rates and weights. Ross, an African American who traveled the country enrolling in clinical trials, had benefited from these occurrences. Thinking about a Northeast clinic (which was not part of my study), he related,

Well, they weren't above board the way they do their vitals and things. . . . Give you an example, they did the blood work and they brought you in to do vitals. As soon as you sat down, they slapped a cuff on, and in most cases—not in most cases, a lot of cases—your blood pressure would be out of range because they normally have you sit minimally two minutes before they'll run that, and they did it immediately. If it was out of range, they would record it as a good range. They put me on the scales, and I had weighed . . . 100, 101 kilos [220–222 pounds], and they weighed me at, I wanna say, like 176 pounds; they had wrote down a weight and height that is acceptable for the study.

When I asked Ross why he thought they had done this, he grinned, "'Cause I'm a regular." His experience clearly shows a disturbing side to clinics' preference for healthy volunteers with whom they have relationships.

Whether staff operate within the protocols' parameters or commit research fraud, the common theme here is that they find ways to get healthy volunteers into clinical trials. Not only do they have to fill the studies with eligible participants, but staff are primarily interested in enrolling healthy volunteers with whom they have personal experience and know to be good research participants. From their perspective, then, the means might justify the ends. They must moderately force the model to have the organisms with whom they feel most comfortable working. This, however, exacerbates Phase I validity problems as staff become complicit in the myriad ways that serial participants willfully break protocols.

Fostering a "Rule-Breaking" Model

The preferential treatment that repeat participants receive at clinics fosters a culture of rule-breaking. Scholars have previously identified this as healthy volunteers' subversive and deceptive behavior designed to increase their Phase I participation (e.g., Devine et al. 2013; Dresser 2013). Importantly, a key part of what the existing literature ignores is how the current *structure* of Phase I trials enables validity-compromising behaviors. Interactions between serial participants and staff indicate that when healthy volunteers become model organisms, the research context shifts to accommodate that organism's needs and preferences. In other words, serial participants are emboldened by how much clinics depend on them to enroll, and they subsequently push the boundaries set by trial protocols.

The clearest example of this dynamic is seen in some serial participants' disregard for mandatory washout periods. Most Phase I protocols dictate that healthy volunteers wait at least 30 days before joining a new clinical trial. These washout periods, intended for participant safety and data integrity, limit the number of studies in which healthy volunteers can enroll over time and thus the amount of money they can make. As a result, many serial participants break the washout period, if not routinely then at times throughout their study careers. Washout periods can also be an inconvenience for the clinics. When clinics and staff rely on serial healthy volunteers, washout periods create a barrier to recruitment. This might be one of the reasons why the industry has no centralized clinical trial database or registry, making washout enforcement nearly impossible.

Healthy volunteers' nonobservance of the washout period is an open secret in the industry. To meet their obligation to sponsors, clinics' practice is to ask prospective volunteers for the dates of their last study. Staff are not naïve—that is, they cannot be unaware that their preferred repeat participants are likely enrolling at multiple clinics—but they can enforce washout periods only for their own studies and otherwise must rely on the information healthy volunteers provide. Without objective, third-party information about participants' trial history, staff claimed they should presume that participants are honest. This sounds like a perfectly reasonable assertion because how could staff be expected to do anything else? For example, Neil, the physician-investigator at Academic Phase I, emphasized his trust in healthy volunteers to give him truthful information about their last study: "At the end of day, they're putting their trust in me to look out for their wellbeing; I put my trust in them to do the same and to provide them with knowledge that it's not good to do two studies at once."[9]

Taking participants at their word, however, is challenging when there are physical signs that suggest the prospective volunteer has recently completed a study. Staff at all the clinics I visited had stories about the evidence of clinical trials being clearly written on prospective participants' bodies when they came for a screening visit. Denise, the nurse manager at Pharma Phase I, reported, "We've had subjects come and screen, and they've got, you know, needle marks on their arms. And I've been doing an ECG on someone and they've got the telemetry [adhesive on their skin]. I'm like, 'When was the last time you were in a study?' you know, and I don't always believe them because how can that still be on there? You know? So, I don't know. And then you can't call people liars, so." Denise became uncomfortable when I inquired about why the clinics could not do more to police the washout periods, and she answered defensively, "You don't really have any control over that, so. But the way I look at that is it's their life. They know the risks because we tell them." From this perspective, as long as staff ask participants about their last study and inform them of the risks, they have fulfilled their duty, and those individuals are eligible to enroll no matter how obvious it is they are gaming the system and potentially undermining the validity of study data.

The lack of centralized enforcement of the washout period emboldens serial participants to be dishonest. Jeffrey, an African American man in his twenties who estimated he had screened for 100 studies, had regularly broken the washout period rule. Never fearing that he could get caught, he observed, "There's really no way they can really detect if you've had any other [investigational] drug or not. So, you know, they have to go by our word. So, they don't really know." When talking about her experience with the washout period, Tia, an African American woman in her early thirties who had participated in more than 35 studies, cited the lack of studies for women as an obstacle to her following the rules: "I would want to flush everything out of my system, and for the most part, I really, really try. But like I said, for women, it's really hard to find studies so you have to be calling and you're hoping that the date winds up giving you sufficient time to really, really flush out your system. . . . But if something [a new study] comes up, I'm gonna take it. I'm gonna take it. And that means I'm not gonna tell the truth [to the clinic]."

Additionally, healthy volunteers acknowledged the staff's complicity in participants' failure to observe the washout period. Although he personally observed the washout period, perhaps as a function of enrolling only at Academic Phase I, Sidney, an African American man in his forties, griped, "I think that these facilities know that they [participants] are going from here to there to there to there. . . . And when you kind of look the other way, you know, you're endorsing it. And, you know, you're basically not gettin' the results of what you're doin' this [clinical trial] for. . . . But if I see it and I know, [then] I'm sure the staff knows it." What is remarkable is that it was Sidney and not the research staff who expressed concern about the implications for clinical trials' validity when participants can seemingly lie with impunity.

Beyond the washout period, healthy volunteers often test trial protocols' boundaries and find ways to break the rules even while in confinement. Given that the confinement's purpose is to control all study elements, one might suppose that the staff would be diligent about enforcing all the rules, especially any prohibitions against the consumption of outside food, but staff, at least at some clinics, are prone to ignore these activities when they are not done flagrantly. Rule-breaking can include participants clandestinely exercising, such as doing sit-ups in bed or pull-ups in the shower stalls; swapping or finding ways to dispose of unwanted food during meals; and sneaking food or personal care items into the clinic. I can attest that during my clinic visits I detected a fair number of minor infractions, such as participants clearly wearing cologne, chewing bubble gum, using lip balm, and eating mints. None of these seems particularly serious, but they are also explicitly against the rules and easily observable.

Much of the rule-breaking revolves around clinic food. Healthy volunteers understand that meals are dictated by the study protocols, but they cannot help but want to throw away items they find unpalatable. These instances are not necessarily premeditated but are responses to what is served at each meal. However, Marshall, an African American in his thirties, related an unusual story about how far participants might go to make a clinic's food more appetizing:

> [A clinic that closed] had the worst food ever. . . . It was like the food didn't taste like anything; it was like no salt, no pepper, no butter, no sugar. . . . It was crazy! . . . You would see people come in there, like in the cafeteria, you [were] eating and you see someone pulling sugar out of their arm [that is, sleeve], you know? You have scrubs on and the pocket right here [on the chest]? Hot sauce, soy sauce [in there]. . . . I was in there for 27 days, that's when I was askin' for it; some guy got some hot sauce: "I sell it to you, $5.00," . . . "$2.00 for a little pack of soy sauce." People would pay it 'cause the food was so nasty, like you had to make do.

The idea of an underground economy of condiments is both comical and intriguing. It highlights some serial participants' entrepreneurialism that they would come prepared to sell these items, all the while knowing they might get caught and risk losing the much larger compensation from the study. In a case like this, it is implausible that the clinic staff could remain unaware when money exchanged hands and the plastic packets had to be disposed of somewhere.

Blatant rule-breaking is most likely to happen among serial participants because they are the ones who are more comfortable in clinical trials and know how far they can push these activities without getting caught.[10] These behaviors become characteristics of the healthy volunteer as a model organism, so common as to be expected. Even when such wrongdoings are visible to participants' peers, most of those peers would never inform the staff, as Sidney indicated regarding washout periods,[11] but that these protocol violations might bias trial results is an important concern. In that context, the inaction on the part of staff, who would have to exercise willful ignorance of the situation, is alarming. Whether it is fresh venipuncture marks and traces of ECG adhesive on the skin or evidence of contraband in the clinic, staff are simply not incentivized to confront cases of noncompliance. Enrolling repeat participants is advantageous to recruitment, and when staff ignore any rule-breaking that occurs once a clinical trial is underway, they minimize the number of protocol deviations they must report to the study sponsor. Plus, staff might perceive some incidents as innocuous. Does it really affect the study data when someone applies cologne or throws away a tomato they are required to eat? There might not be a clear answer to this question, but not observing the washout period or exercising could alter the trial results because of their effects on participants' liver and kidney functions, blood pressure, and so on. The fact that these things happen routinely suggests that the control component of Phase I trials is much more illusory than planned and thereby calls into question both the intrinsic and extrinsic validity of the trials.

Adverse Event Reporting as a Validity Calamity

Perhaps more than any other source of extrinsic validity concerns, the biggest threat to Phase I trials revolves around reporting adverse events (AEs).[12] One could argue that healthy volunteers are model organisms who are constructed to simultaneously produce *and mask* adverse events. The point of these trials is for healthy volunteers to describe any bodily changes they experience after taking an investigational drug (or placebo), but the process is not without its complications. As with the deviations from screening procedures, washout periods, and the myriad study restrictions that suggest collusion between research staff and healthy volunteers, there are structural disincentives for adverse events to be reported and recorded thoroughly and accurately. In this domain, the pharmaceutical industry's role is also central to the problem.

As described above, the placebo-controlled trial design aims to determine which symptoms are drug-related by comparing participants who receive the investigational drug to those who do not. Of course, this method can work only if participants are thorough in reporting how they feel during the trial, no matter how minor the physical complaint. Yet, healthy volunteers are disinclined to communicate their symptoms for at least two reasons. First, many interpret their symptoms as being caused by something other than the investigational drug (such as caffeine withdrawal or boredom), so by that logic, they do not believe that the staff must be apprised of their symptoms. Earlier, Annie exemplified this position by claiming that her drowsiness was likely caused by the confinement, positing that she would feel fine if she were allowed to have a "natural day." Second, many healthy volunteers fear that should they report a symptom, the staff would kick them out of the study and they would not receive their full compensation.

Participants were aware that by choosing not to disclose adverse events, they could be compromising the study. However, some noted that the financial disincentive to report overpowered most people's commitment to science. As Javier, a Latino in his mid-forties remarked, "Sometimes people [participants] don't report things like they supposed to because . . . sometimes they'll stop dosing you and some guys just are in it for the money. . . . I've seen people not say anything, and they could be sick as a dog and still take that medicine. And in all reality, [by doing that] right now you're not helping the study, you're just deceiving the purpose of what you're supposed to be doing."

It is not literally true that healthy volunteers are removed from studies when they report adverse events. Rather, what is more likely to happen is that a participant may be discharged early if the investigator or sponsor determines that the person's health could be compromised by continuing. For example, a headache is highly unlikely to cause enough alarm to remove someone from a study, but a cardiac event would precipitate this course of action. That said, it is the case that participants might not receive the full compensation if they are withdrawn. Therefore, healthy volunteers might conclude that it is not worth the risk of reporting even minor adverse events.

Staff were fully aware of the prevalence of AE underreporting in Phase I trials, but most saw it as fully the participants' responsibility. The staff envisioned their role was to inform healthy volunteers that their bodily experiences were important data and to ask participants how they feel throughout the study. They did not believe they should have to draw information about adverse events out of people. Elliott, a white project manager at Local Phase I, illustrated this well: "One of the things I always like to try and get over to people is that one of the principle responsibilities *they* have on a study is to be upfront with us about anything that's occurring with them medically, that we're gonna put the onus specifically on them to let us know if there's any changes in their health. . . . But the point is, it's not down to me to do." Similar to their position on washout periods, many did not feel obligated to investigate whether participants provided complete and truthful information about their adverse events.

With AE underreporting an expected part of Phase I trials, there was general consensus among staff that pharmacokinetic (PK) data are more objective and reliable than participant-derived data. This makes sense in so far as PK data are available for each blood collection time-point whereas with self-report, there is no way to assess what data might be missing or inaccurate. However, as staff discussed PK data, new suspicions about participants' trustworthiness crept into their narratives. Neil, the physician-investigator at Academic Phase I, declared,

At the end of the day [for the study results], mostly it's going to be the PK, which is hard to fake, right? . . . Let me put it a different way: You get a PK value that you do not trust. Did the patient cheat the med? Was it a bad blood draw? Was it stored in improper conditions? Was the assay batch bad? Did the statistician make an error? So, you want to chase down all of those [variables]. [In contrast, if] you get a whole bunch of AEs in the study, was it somebody who wanted to get out of the study? Was it three people who were in cahoots together? So, you want to approach findings that are abnormal with the same sort of rigor to get to what you think the truth is regardless of what the type of data [that] the data is . . . but I see it really as ultimately, and fortunately for the PK, it's much more objective because you have a number.

The interesting twist in how Neil described why PK data are more reliable is that he identified the problem with AE data not as underreporting but as fabrication. But for him, both PK and AE data are open to a certain amount of skepticism, especially when a study generates unexpected results.

Rather than focusing on healthy volunteers' trepidation that an adverse event could get them kicked out of a study, Neil and other staff constructed participants' self-reports as tainted for the opposite reason: they have motives to leave the clinic early. Paul from Pharma Phase I also held this view, believing that healthy volunteers would feign symptoms to get the entire study canceled, which hypothetically could result in all participants receiving their full compensation despite the shortened confinement:

> Now what sponsors worry about, to be frank, is that volunteers catch on to—and I've only had that happen to me once in my career—where they all caught on to the fact that if they *all* complained of a certain sort of thing, they could get out [early from the study] with the whole fee; that's what people worry about, okay? And sometimes, granted it's only happened to me once, and I just had to take them [at their word], 'cause how am I gonna challenge a head-banging headache? I have no clinical basis on which to say so.

Although Paul expressed angst when recalling this incident, staff rarely expected events like these to occur. Dishonesty about symptoms occurs primarily in the other direction, but it nonetheless indicates how pervasive the distrust of participants can be. Indeed, returning to Neil's scenario of "bad" PK data, his suspicion even carried over to the PK data so that his first thought about why the number might not be accurate was that somehow the healthy volunteer "cheated the med," meaning that they had managed to avoid taking, in part or in full, the investigational drug. Additionally, while Neil flags how bias can affect both PK and AE data, PK data are generally trusted until they reveal something unexpected, whereas AE data are always suspect because they come from healthy volunteers.

Phase I trials' use of healthy volunteers as model organisms has another important effect on the production of AE data. Depending on any adverse events healthy volunteers develop in one clinical trial, staff can restrict those individuals' access to future trials. Patty, the recruiter at Academic Phase I, discussed this knowledge of people's past adverse events as part of her recruitment for new studies: "We do have some people who tend to get rashes easy from certain drugs. I don't call them for certain studies 'cause I know, oh, so-and-so reacts to [a specific antibiotic], you know. There's no point in even attempting to contact them because it will just end badly for both of us." From the healthy volunteer's perspective, it would be hard to blame Patty for this recruitment strategy. Saving those who are sensitive to the drug from the rashes they could experience is a caring act. However, this selection process has the potential to skew the data about the drug, potentially making its effects look different than they might actually be in the broader population. Model organisms, with their known, reliable characteristics, enable this.

Beyond trying to make the study more positive for healthy volunteers, selecting participants based on past adverse events can also be geared toward the pharmaceutical companies hiring the clinics. Neil from Academic Phase I perceived this approach to enrolling subjects as providing the sponsor with the right kind of data: "So, it's a balance to make sure that we get the appropriate amount of AEs without getting too many AEs. And I would say some of that goes into judgment if you know people. And so, the advantage of repeat individuals will be you sort of know who's going to have a crazy AE each time and some people who are stoic, laconic, and you may need to draw it [that is, information about their symptoms] out a little bit more." Here again the repeat participant offers an advantage to the clinic because the staff can anticipate the number and kind of adverse events they might report. Taking Neil literally, this could allow the clinic to give the sponsor more positive data about the investigational drug because participants could either have a higher tolerance for medications or reliably underreport their symptoms.

Clinics' relationships with the sponsoring pharmaceutical companies are even more fraught than Neil's perspective on AE data indicates.

Concerned about securing future clinical trials, staff are sensitive to both the contracted and tacit expectations pharmaceutical companies have about their performance. Conflict with the sponsor is prone to manifest in how physician-investigators interpret participants' adverse events. Investigators differ in their willingness to attribute symptoms as drug-related, with some taking a conservative approach to safety by assuming the investigational drug is the culprit. This is not how the sponsor wants investigators to interpret the data, and they exert pressure on those physicians to reevaluate the data. This happened to Scott at CRO Phase I. He recalled a startling encounter he had with a representative of a pharmaceutical company: "One of the safety people over there, she made some comment the other day, . . . 'Usually it seems like you err on the side of saying it's drug-related.' Which was sort of news to me, but I mean if I, basically, if I can't figure out an alternate plausible explanation for it, . . . that's [got to be] drug-related." This interaction with the sponsor had given Scott pause because even though he was not in charge of the clinic's business development, the comment had struck him as a corrective, a warning about how he interpreted the data. Scott found this upsetting because he was highly invested in what he saw as a scientific and objective process.

In contrast, Lucy, an Asian American physician-investigator at Local Phase I, did not have the same level of confidence in her AE assessments. In responding to my question about how adverse events were coded, she immediately noted her deferral to the sponsor: "So far I have not been able to say 100 percent certain that it is caused by [the drug], but I often choose 'suspected' because you're never gonna, I mean no one's gonna know 100 percent. And as far as I'm concerned, I cannot say something's definitely related unless I know 100 percent, and I'm never gonna know 100 percent, and that's what it boils down to." In both examples, there is a question of what is the burden of proof for a drug to be deemed safe. The sponsors prefer an approach mirroring that of the criminal justice system, innocent until proven guilty, and Lucy aligned herself with this orientation. Scott, however, felt it misrepresented the drug to ignore strong evidence to the contrary.

Andrea, an Academic Phase I physician-investigator, had similar experiences with the sponsors. Compared to Scott, however, she did not have a stake in being "right" or having her interpretation of AEs prevail.

Yet, unlike Lucy, she felt frustrated by the games the sponsors played in minutely scrutinizing adverse events. This process was fresh in her mind when we spoke because Academic Phase I had recently battled with a sponsor over its interpretation of whether its investigational drug was the cause of several adverse events. She described the scene for me:

> We have conferences [with the drug company] like every week just to make sure we can list every single AE, . . . and then it's a humungous hour-long back and forth about whether or not that AE was drug-related and what it should be called. . . . Then based upon the conversation that you had at the meeting, you can determine, "That one, this is an AE. We're gonna call this that. We're gonna say this is this. That one sounds like this." And it's a panel of like ten people on a conference call . . . [and] people just nitpick. [Laughs.] . . . It's like, "No, this is, you know, this is blue." "No, no, no, this is sky blue with a touch of periwinkle and a hint of lime." And you're like, "No, it's just blue." [Laughs.]

Given that some potential risks of the investigational drug are already listed in the consent form, I wondered why the sponsor opposed attributing those AEs to its drug. Andrea chuckled and explained, "Yeah, *especially* with the expected ones because they want to be very clear what, you know, this drug causes as a side effect profile. It determines the scheduling of the drug. It's nuts. It's much more than I thought. . . . It's serious stuff. It's not like something that you just, you know, say, 'Oh, this is that.' . . . [It] has to go through like a whole panel [laughs] of people—hot potato, hot potato—until it gets accepted [as caused by the drug]." Andrea's story underscores the extent to which pharmaceutical companies actively resist the production of AE data about their investigational drugs. Panels like these suggest that the stakes are high for a clinic that wants to continue to conduct Phase I trials for a particular sponsor. It is not hard to imagine that investigators—at least those with an interest in their facility's financial success—would feel pressured to adopt the sponsor's interpretation of the data.[13]

AE reporting is clearly a complex process that threatens the validity of Phase I trial results beginning with healthy volunteers' underreporting of symptoms, staff's selection of participants to minimize illness, and the pharmaceutical industry's resistance to interpreting bodily changes as drug-related. This essentially means that even though the production of AEs is the very purpose of Phase I trials, none of the actors involved *wants* documentable adverse events to emerge from clinical trials. Importantly, economics structure everyone's interests. For the healthy volunteers, there is a fear that AE reporting could result in their discharge from a study with less money than what they counted on when they enrolled or that they might not be selected for future studies.[14] The research staff are beholden to the sponsors because of the nature of contract research and therefore must negotiate their clinical judgment through the lens of how the pharmaceutical industry wants Phase I data to be produced. Finally, pharmaceutical companies have financial incentive for their drugs to look as safe as possible in order to facilitate market approval and the eventual uptake of prescriptions. Hence, the reporting problems generated in Phase I trials truly could be calamitous for what we know about new drugs' adverse effects.

The Science We Get Is the Science Pharma Pays For

Despite how highly controlled Phase I trials appear, their structure undermines how valid the data can be. First, young, healthy male participants are not representative of the general population, particularly sick individuals who will be the ultimate consumers of the drugs being tested. Second, Phase I trial conditions are not comparable to real-world contexts, making safety data even less translatable to the treatment of illness. These intrinsic validity concerns stemming from how Phase I trials are designed and conducted mirror the problems that emerge when extrapolating from nonhuman animal research to human medicine.

Adding to these validity issues, however, are the extrinsic features that are part of healthy volunteers', clinics', and the pharmaceutical industry's practices in how these trials are conducted and the data interpreted. With the use of serial healthy volunteers as model organisms, Phase I trials promote instrumental behavior among staff and participants to facilitate the science getting done and mask adverse events. The trials are certainly efficient this way, but it is unclear how robust the data are not only for translation to future clinical uses but also on their own terms when everyone manipulates the protocols. This happens during the screening process when healthy volunteers can blatantly defy the washout-period requirements between studies and staff find ways to ensure that repeat participants qualify. It also can be seen with healthy volunteers finding myriad ways to disregard restrictions while the staff manage to ignore these protocol transgressions. Finally, when it comes to documenting adverse events, the system guarantees that these data are suspect through incentives for participants and staff to underreport investigational drugs' effects. Although there has been scholarly attention to healthy volunteers breaking the rules, it is equally if not more troubling that the research staff and pharmaceutical companies are engaged in their own subversive practices. These practices can be seen as adverse events for science because they profoundly undermine the knowledge produced about new drugs.

Ultimately, pharmaceutical companies get the data they pay for, the data they want. The system of Phase I research downplays validity problems and shows investigational drugs in a more positive light. All scientific knowledge is partial (Haraway 2001; Harding 1991; Longino 1994), but the use of healthy volunteers as model organisms capitalizes on structural incentives in ways that threaten validity. Thus, prescription drugs can never be as safe as what the Phase I data suggest. The next question I consider is how safe these trials are for healthy volunteers.

7

Consenting to Adverse Events

When I arrived for my first day of field work at Academic Phase I, a receptionist ushered me to a small waiting area in the facility's spartan administration suite. She told me the clinic director had been delayed because some medical issues had occurred in their current study. I was not there long when a woman who was seated in a nearby cubical offered to get me some tea or coffee. After I declined, she picked up her cell phone and made a call. Without any small talk, she launched into a frantic description of the hallucinations healthy volunteers had nearly unanimously experienced after being dosed with the investigational drug that morning. As I involuntarily eavesdropped, it dawned on me that the woman did not actually work at the clinic; she was a representative from the pharmaceutical company sponsoring the study.

Later when I met with Neil, the clinic director and a physician-investigator, he confirmed that the woman had come to observe the trial. His team had previously reported to the sponsor these same adverse events with earlier cohorts, and the company wanted one of its own employees to witness the next dosing. Neil disclosed that the majority of healthy volunteers had experienced sleep paralysis—an often-frightening conscious state in which one experiences vivid hallucinations and cannot move or speak—as a result of the study drug, and many had wanted reassurance that this drug effect would be short term.

When I finally entered the clinic and met the participants, many complained about how drowsy and "off" they felt. Lying languidly in bed, most still wanted to be interviewed and talk about their side effects. This study was Kim's first. An African American woman in her early twenties and a mother to two young children, she had enrolled at the encouragement of her father, Marcus, a veteran healthy volunteer in his forties, who was in the next room, participating in the same study. I asked Kim whether she had experienced any side effects. Yawning noisily, she replied, "Yeah, but the only thing really was sort of a hallucination. . . . I had a really crazy dream, but that was it. . . . And that was a side effect [of the drug]—vivid dreams. They was sticking IVs in my cheeks, and my dad was actually coming to do it. I was like, 'Dad, you're not sticking no IV in my cheek. You better send me home.'" Surprisingly, Kim claimed to be unperturbed by the adverse event, crediting her father's long-term study participation: "I have a lot of faith in my dad. He's been doing this for however many years he's been doing it, and he took a study before and it has to be okay."

Given the low probability of dramatic symptoms occurring in Phase I studies, it was serendipitous for me to be present at a clinic when healthy volunteers experienced something as unusual as sleep paralysis. This also provided the opportunity to observe how trial participants made sense of and minimized their experience of adverse events. Notably, as the investigational drug's soporific effects subsided, the participants engaged in a process of normalizing the study risks so that even sleep paralysis became banal and insignificant. For example, during my interview with Kim, her study roommate, Janae, an African American in her forties and also a first-time participant, chimed in about her nightmares from the study drug as well as her initial and ongoing fears about clinical trials. By the end of the day, however, Janae's perceptions had changed. She reflected nonchalantly, "I went to sleep and had kinda dozed off once. I had a little dream, and then dozed off again [and] had another [dream]." That even first-time participants could become so blasé reveals how powerful the experience of recovering from such adverse events can be. For many, it confirms that any long-term harm from trial enrollment is unlikely.

Healthy volunteers' risk perceptions are interwoven with their status as model organisms. As participants gain experience in clinical trials, they become more accepting of and less concerned about Phase I risks. Yet, having detailed information about each study remains a critical part of participants' assessment of risk and ultimate belief that they will not be harmed. This is ironic because the formal consent process often presents a worst-case scenario of what might occur. Specifically, each trial's informed consent form details a wide variety of potential symptoms participants might experience, ranging from headaches or nausea to organ failure or death. However, as we have seen in participants' experience of sleep paralysis, most adverse study events are temporary, with participants returning to their baseline health by the trial's conclusion. Thus, the risks spelled out in consent forms of what *could* happen can be unnerving, but all the experiential evidence of what is *likely* to happen points to the relative safety of such studies. This view of risk positions healthy volunteers as model organisms who are prepared to consent voluntarily and serially to Phase I trial risks.

It is critical to explore how research staff and healthy volunteers engage and understand information about the risk of adverse events in Phase I trials. By examining formal and experiential sources of risk information, we can see how the consent process both normalizes risks to participants and stigmatizes healthy volunteers as apathetic model organisms. Although both staff and healthy volunteers typically agree that Phase I trials are safe, both groups perceive most serial participants to be desperate people too focused on the financial compensation to assess appropriately the risks of their participation. From this vantage point, study participation is contradictorily regarded as safe unless someone does not take the consent process seriously. In their simultaneous acknowledgment and denial of the possibility of study harms, staff and healthy volunteers demonstrate ambivalence about study risks.

Characterizing Phase I Trial Risks

To contextualize staff members' and healthy volunteers' risk perceptions, it is important to ask what the *actual* risks of Phase I trials are. Calculating these risks is no easy task because, as we saw previously, these studies are diverse and include a wide variety of investigational drug types with differing study designs. Depending on the study drug, the dose and frequency of its administration, and the medical procedures involved, these clinical trials can range from very low to fairly high risk. Of course, a purpose of Phase I trials is to produce adverse events, so it should be no surprise that even accounting for the underreporting problem described earlier, physiological and bodily changes are very common, but they are generally mild and of short duration.

To better characterize the risk of adverse events, some authors have attempted to quantify their occurrence through meta-analyses of varied Phase I trials. In one of the earliest such studies, Sibille and colleagues (1998) used 10 years of adverse event data from 54 clinical trials (testing

23 different investigational drugs) conducted on healthy volunteers at a single clinic in France. The data included 1,558 adverse events generated both through participant self-reporting and medical testing. There were no deaths or life-threatening events in that 10-year period, but 65 percent of all the healthy volunteers had at least one adverse event; of these the authors deemed only 4 percent to have been severe. The most common issues were headaches, diarrhea, and indigestion, and even participants receiving a placebo experienced these same symptoms. The authors also labeled nine adverse events as "worrying": six healthy volunteers had "malaises with loss of consciousness," one had an atrial fibrillation (an irregular and rapid heart rate), one had hyperthyroidism, and one developed bicytopenia (a reduction in bone marrow production). Even these unusual adverse events resolved fairly quickly. All but the bicytopenia, which lasted 12 days, cleared up in 24 hours or less. Longer-term adverse events in their dataset included the participant who experienced a "permanent" increase to his/her PR interval (a measure of the heart's functioning) and others who experienced increased liver enzymes (suggesting possible liver damage) lasting almost two weeks. In sum, the data from this meta-analysis indicate that healthy volunteers are very likely to experience temporary adverse events, and a small percentage of participants could develop problems that take longer to resolve or need more monitoring and/or intervention. These findings have been corroborated by more recent analyses of the published literature and from other Phase I clinics' adverse event data (Emanuel et al. 2015; Johnson et al. 2016).

While meta-analyses emphasize the statistical safety of Phase I trials, they fail to account for the notable cases of death and serious harm to healthy volunteers that have occurred. Two such deaths received considerable media attention. Ellen Roche, a 24-year-old, died in a 2001 asthma-related study at Johns Hopkins University (Kolata 2001a), and Traci Johnson, a 19-year-old, committed suicide during an antidepressant study at an Eli Lilly facility in Indianapolis in 2004 (Harris 2004). In 2006, six healthy volunteers who were enrolled in a study in London nearly died when the investigational drug caused rapid multiple organ failure (Wood and Darbyshire 2006). More recently, a 2016 clinical trial in France resulted in the death of one healthy volunteer and long-term neurological impairment in three others (Hawkes 2016). While journalists and other observers have speculated about mistakes and problems that might have endangered the trial participants, these tragedies happened in the normal course of how studies are managed and overseen (Hedgecoe 2014). To a large degree, this is what makes Phase I trials appear so risky: the investigators and research ethics boards neither expected nor could prevent such catastrophic results.

The field of bioethics disagrees about how much ethical concern is warranted for clinical trials involving healthy volunteers. Some argue for a higher ethical burden to reduce risks to healthy volunteers because they cannot benefit therapeutically from the research (e.g., Chapman 2011; Miller 2003; Stein 2003), whereas others argue that the rarity of serious adverse events discredits any ethical qualms (e.g., Emanuel et al. 2015; Johnson et al. 2016). In the latter case, it is striking that the prevalence of adverse events in Phase I trials does not give these authors pause. The fact that two-thirds of healthy volunteers *routinely* experience headaches, gastrointestinal problems, changes in liver and kidney function, and so on should not be ignored, minimized, or dismissed. Moreover, the estimated 1–4 percent rate of severe adverse events should generate some apprehension because these are bodily changes that pose a greater threat to the short- and long-term health of a not-inconsequential number of participants.

Despite—or perhaps because of—the sensational cases of healthy volunteer trials gone awry, Phase I investigators are keen to demonstrate evidence that participants are rarely harmed (Emanuel et al. 2015; Kumagai et al. 2006; Sibille et al. 2006). Some even frame participation in relative terms, as being safer than many blue-collar professions, for example (Kupetsky-Rincon and Kraft 2012). However, the tragedies that have occurred in Phase I trials are well known to research staff working with healthy volunteers, and they foster staff's ambivalence about trial risks.

Informing Healthy Volunteers about the Risk of Adverse Events

Bioethicists and others often ask: Do healthy volunteers *truly* understand what they are doing? That question is often followed by another: How well do they read and comprehend the informed consent forms for studies? These questions highlight the stigmatized nature of research participation as well as healthy volunteers' socioeconomic positions. With the taint of financial desperation surrounding healthy volunteers' decisions to enroll in Phase I trials, there is an ethical worry that either they cannot fully appreciate the risks or they are not sufficiently free to refuse participation. Examining the formal consent process provides a window into how healthy volunteers understand study risks and also how their model organism status shapes research staff's perceptions of them.

Informed consent is the federally mandated process that requires researchers to give prospective participants detailed information about their studies, and it provides the basis for voluntary decisions to enroll in research (Faden and Beauchamp 1986). To meet this ethical and regulatory requirement, Phase I clinics use screening visits to communicate study information, and they document that the consent process occurred by requiring staff and participants to sign consent forms. Unlike later-phase trials that enroll eligible study participants as they are identified, Phase I trials enroll healthy volunteers concurrently in groups or cohorts. As a result, many clinics assemble prospective participants on designated screening days to convey the details about a specific clinical trial to the whole group. Those individuals who give their consent then undergo the relevant screening procedures together. This industry practice for group consent is an efficient way to screen participants because it requires only one staff person to read through the form (often literally reading the consent form out loud) and answer questions from the whole group, potentially responding to multiple people's concerns about the same issue.[1]

Throughout my field work, I had the opportunity to observe many consent sessions, many of which are referenced in this book. The most memorable, however, was at Pharma Phase I, likely because it was my first time witnessing group consent. The session was run by Carol, a white nurse in her forties whom I spent time shadowing during my visit. Like many clinics, Pharma Phase I had a designated area for the consent process. At first glance, it looked like a doctor's office waiting room, but unlike those clinical spaces, the rows of chairs all faced the same direction, allowing a staff person to command everyone's attention.

When Carol and I entered the room a little after 9:00 AM, 17 men sat and chitchatted with each other while they waited for the consent process to kick off their screening visit. Carol introduced me, and as I made my way to the back of the room and took a seat, she added that I was "giving away" gift cards to anyone who participated in an interview. The men eyed me with curiosity, but Carol quickly redirected their attention to the consent form they had been given when they arrived. Going through the form page by page, she explained that the study was part of a larger clinical trial for an investigational tuberculosis drug. Curiously, they were screening to participate in a control group ("Cohort E") that would not test the investigational drug and would take instead an FDA-approved antibiotic that was already in use for treating other infections. I followed along in my copy of the consent form, and I noticed that Carol accidentally kept referring to the antibiotic by the wrong name. At least one of the men also heard the mistake, and he asked her to clarify what drug they would be testing. Carol was good humored about her error, and this only improved her rapport with the participants. She encouraged them to interrupt her at any time to correct her or ask questions. In response, one man asked how the drug would be "dosed," wondering whether it was a pill or liquid suspension. Another asked whether they would be dosed before or after breakfast. Someone else asked about the drug's half-life. Carol answered each question and cited the page in the consent form where the information could be found. As the questions continued, the men started answering each other's questions, and Carol suddenly looked more like a discussion moderator than a trial spokesperson. It was a livelier session than I had expected, and I was particularly struck by the savviness of the questions. I knew that these men could not be screening for their first studies.

Once questions about the clinical trial were answered, participants focused on the study payment. Although they had already known that this five-day study paid $1,525, some wondered how quickly they would receive that payment and how they would get their checks. One man pointed out that Cohort E paid much less than the others. Because the consent form detailed the entire clinical trial, it also included information about how much each study cohort would be paid. Specifically, Cohorts C and D, which were slated to take the investigational drug and stay at Pharma Phase I for 30 consecutive days, paid $6,275. Carol told them compensation was based on confinement length, but she also divulged that the cohorts were being recruited out of order and that Cohorts C and D had not yet begun recruiting. Eager to find out how they could join those cohorts, several men wanted to know the recruitment schedule. Carol explained that the dates had not yet been set, but warned that participants would be eligible to enroll in only one group of the entire trial.

In response to this news, an African American man in his late thirties—whom I later found out was Ken, who had traveled nearly 2,000 miles to screen at Pharma Phase I—argued that there were no scientific grounds to exclude the control group from the other cohorts. To his mind, because they would not take the investigational drug at all, being in Cohort E was basically like enrolling in a completely different clinical trial. Carol seemed genuinely persuaded and promised to speak to the pharmaceutical company's project manager. Notwithstanding the stunning logic Ken deployed, most of the men were not particularly concerned. Of course, they were intrigued by the possibility of a study paying more than $6,000, but that study required a very long confinement and still did not have set dates. Besides, they knew in advance that the study they had come to screen for that day paid $1,525. The men's willingness to enroll in Cohort E, even with its lower pay and consequences to their eligibility for Cohorts C and D, was fortunate because after her call to the project manager, Carol later confirmed that participants could enroll only in one cohort of the trial.

Carol wrapped up the official consent process by instructing the men to read through the consent form individually and to keep asking questions as they had them, even throughout the medical screening. She emphasized that they must not sign the form without a staff person present to witness their signature and that she would remain at the front of the room for that purpose whenever they were ready. Most of the men jumped up immediately, clearly not interested in taking the time right then to read the consent form more thoroughly.[2] The ones who remained behind had remembered me and asked how to participate in my study.

Debriefing afterwards, Carol rated this consent process as pretty typical for Pharma Phase I. She noted that people's personalities influence the process, which often demands improvisation on her part to fully cover all the information. The pattern she observed was that while participants usually asked questions about the study drug or procedures, they focused primarily on the compensation and not the risk. In this instance, the men had not asked a single question about expected or possible adverse events, but Carol did read them aloud. Their lack of questions could have been because the list included many common side effects, such as diarrhea, headache, nausea, rash, vomiting, and fever. There were, however, several others that should have signaled some additional concern, including anemia, colitis, and seizure. Carol postulated that despite the staff's efforts, the consent process fails to ensure participants really understand the risk they take each time they enroll.

Staff Perspectives on the Informed Consent Process

Phase I research staff almost universally articulated that there are deep, troubling problems with the informed consent process. As evidence, they pointed either to healthy volunteers' alleged lack of engagement with the process or the very fact that, after hearing the risks, they nonetheless enroll in studies. At the same time, staff widely acknowledged that these trials are generally very safe and that healthy volunteers should not fear being harmed by their participation. By holding these opposing views, staff manifested their ambivalence about Phase I risk. The consent process clearly contributes to this ambivalence because the staff must communicate to prospective participants the formal details about what could occur, regardless of these adverse events' likelihood of developing. Understandably, staff want healthy volunteers to take this information seriously. Yet, what it means for healthy volunteers to take it seriously is surprisingly unclear in staff members' narratives.

At the heart of why many research staff doubt healthy volunteers' understanding of Phase I risks is that they personally would never enroll. As Denise, the nurse manager at Pharma Phase I, put it, "We have people who do it [participate in studies] all the time. But I mean it always still kind of blows my mind when I have to say [during the consent process] 'and death' [is one of the risks]. I mean, that would—, I'd walk away right there!" Perhaps feeling the irony of that position, Denise equivocated, "I'm not sure if I would do it, *but* we rarely have anything serious happen. So that's something else you have to consider, you know." Denise illustrates the staff's ambivalence: somehow studies pose too much risk for staff to enroll but are generally very safe. By highlighting how seriously they personally take the risks outlined in consent forms, staff construct an implied universal against which they believe everyone should be measured, thereby stigmatizing anyone who falls short. In practice, this means that staff interpret healthy volunteers' decision to enroll as proof of their ignorance of the risks.

Although staff might agree that the consent process is flawed, they hold differing views of the root of the problem. For some, consent forms are too detailed and technical for most people to understand. This was the conclusion arrived at by Scott, the physician-investigator at CRO Phase I: "I say to myself often [that] it would be interesting to know how much they got [from the consent form]. . . . I mean if I weren't in medicine—let's say I was teaching English, okay?—and someone handed me an 18-page consent form to sit down and read, there's a lot there, as you know. And it's so repetitive and so tedious that you could lose your way." Whereas Scott blamed the consent forms, others, like Denise at Pharma Phase I, presumed healthy volunteers' limited education placed much of the information "over their head."

Another staff interpretation of the problem with informed consent is that psychological processes impede individuals—no matter their education or class background—from feeling at risk. Having this perspective, Charlotte, a white physician-investigator at Pharma Phase I, argued that consent forms should exclude unnecessary risk information, particularly warnings about how death might result. Although she acknowledged the possibility of "all the horrible, possible things that can happen" in certain studies, "including death," she challenged how meaningful this information could be: "I don't even know what's the point of writing it, 'death is a possibility,' when actually nobody really thinks about [how] it could happen. You know what I mean? The fact that they [participants] sign, [that means] they are accepting that they can die? I don't think so. Right? So, so what is the meaning of that?" When I probed about improving the consent process, she reiterated that the possibility of death should simply be removed from consent forms because it was psychologically impossible to have the intended effect. Charlotte also did not seem to think that death was included in consent forms as part of pharmaceutical companies' strategy to protect themselves from liability should catastrophe strike.

Beyond healthy volunteers' comprehension of study details, staff also flagged the difficulty participants have remembering that information. For instance, Roxanne, an African American study nurse at Academic Phase I, complained that participants need constant reminders about all aspects of the studies in which they have enrolled. She lamented, "And some of them, . . . it's like they don't have *any* recall. So they may read the consent, and they may understand it at that moment, but they can't—, they don't have any recall. Like, 'We *just* talked about this.'" These issues challenged many staff members' patience, but some were sympathetic about how difficult it would be to retain the myriad details contained in consent forms. Overall, they believed that the consent process must be fundamentally flawed when participants routinely have no idea what adverse events might befall them in a clinical trial.

For other staff, the problem is not with the consent process itself; it is with the healthy volunteers. These staff perceived healthy volunteers, especially serial participants, as indifferent to risk and interested only in the financial compensation. Examples of this sentiment abounded in my conversations with staff members. Patty, the recruiter at Academic Phase I, accused serial participants of being willfully unaware of study risks: "Those who have been repeat subjects, they don't even read the consents any more, and I know this because I will question them, 'Well, do you realize what dose you're gonna be taking? Did you see what that side effect was?'"

Serial participants' perceived apathy frustrates research staff because they feel as though they must work all the harder to force the information on them. Staff often quiz participants, forbidding them from signing their consent forms until they can describe basic study details. By taking these measures, staff feel more confident they have fulfilled their ethical responsibility. To this point, Neil at Academic Phase I asserted, "At the end of the day, my feeling is and the ethos of this country is— compared to other countries' interactions with medical systems—is that individual autonomy is a key determinant. . . . [If] you choose not to read that thing [the consent form], and we go back and forth and discuss just briefly what's going on, ultimately I think that's on you as the individual." Thus, in Neil's opinion, participants have the right to remain uninformed yet still enroll in trials provided staff make a concerted effort to deliver all the information participants need.

Despite their concerns about uninformed participants, staff also criticized prospective healthy volunteers who take risk information *too* seriously. While staff assume serial participants largely ignore consent forms, they fault some first-time screeners for overreacting to information about the possibility of adverse events. George, a white recruiter at Cottage Phase I, illustrated how these rare participants are treated almost as a joke by staff: "The other people that crack me up, and I'll be honest with you, they read the informed consent—, and then we call 'em 'the runners.'. . . . They read the informed consent. . . . However, they don't like what they're reading, and all of a sudden just leave their stuff and– [whistles]. I mean, literally run. . . . They just get up and leave, gone! We all look out the window at 'em as they're walking, running to the car. It's like, 'We got a runner!'" Staff perceive it as irrational that participants could have such a strong reaction to the consent form that they would leave the clinic without a word. Yet, this reveals staff members' conflicting assumptions about how healthy volunteers *should* engage risk information, again highlighting their ambivalence about the risks. Declining a study in this way, after all, is not necessarily so different from the staff's own assertions they would never enroll.

Whether healthy volunteers are framed as unable to comprehend risk information or as willfully resistant to receiving it because of their fixation on the financial compensation, research staff rely on stigmatized, and stigmatizing, representations of participants as the basis for their views. In the process, staff construct the healthy volunteer as a type of model organism that is universally uninformed, or at least unconcerned, about Phase I trial risks. That serial participants, in particular, are accused of being the most apathetic about the consent process means that staff believe healthy volunteers become less aware of and knowledgeable about the risks of specific trials as they join new ones. Pivoting on the informed consent process, this two-dimensional conception of healthy volunteers places participants in a double-bind. Without their refusal to enroll, what evidence would suffice to persuade staff that healthy volunteers are engaged with the consent process, understand the information given to them, and weigh the study risks against the compensation they receive? By thinking about the consent process as a finite moment, research staff regard prospective participants as people who either would consent to *any* study or as "runners" who would likely never enroll.

While their frustrations with healthy volunteers are clearly based on their workplace tasks, professional experiences, and personal ambivalence about study risks, research staff fail to account for how participants' experiences in clinical trials change what information is valuable to them and when.

Healthy Volunteers' Views of the Informed Consent Process

In contrast to research staff's perceptions of them, healthy volunteers' discussion of informed consent indicates that they do not underestimate its value. They specifically appreciate the extent to which study details are spelled out, giving them the chance to know what adverse events to expect so that they can decide whether to enroll. Granted, participants often do have poor recall about studies, and they are quick to accuse others of focusing more on the financial compensation than on the risk information. As with staff, a strong current of ambivalence shapes healthy volunteers' risk perceptions: they must attempt to reconcile the fact that the consent forms paint a picture of greater risk than what many have previously experienced in studies. Ultimately, healthy volunteers conclude that the consent process is an important but insufficient information source about Phase I risks.

There is plenty of evidence that healthy volunteers are generally informed about the trials in which they have enrolled. As part of my interviews, I always asked about the study they were in the process of screening for or participating in. Responses ran the gamut from encyclopedic descriptions of the studies to uncertainty about the details. Interestingly, even when some healthy volunteers lacked confidence about the right answer, they still "guessed" correctly. For example, Bob, the white participant who traveled throughout the country enrolling in Phase I trials, got the drug right on the first try but doubted himself as soon as he uttered it: "Diabetes medication, I think. No, wait. I should know this. Stop the tape! [Laughs.] No, I'm just kidding. . . . I forgot." It is easy to imagine how Bob's response might be the kind of comment that would frustrate the staff after they have invested so much energy in the consent process.

Yet, in large part due to staff members' efforts, it would be difficult for healthy volunteers to escape knowing pertinent study details. Just as the staff emphasized, healthy volunteers described being quizzed about the study details to be allowed to enroll. Marshall, an African American in his thirties, joked about how intense this could be: "But when they go over the informed consent, they always ask you questions, just to make sure, like they usually read it—well, they always read it out loud to you—but they always ask you a question to see just if you're paying attention: 'Well, who knows this? Who knows that?' It's kinda like being in school: you don't raise your hand, they gonna call on you anyway. 'What are you taking? What's the drug?' You know? Stuff like that." Learning answers by rote, however, does not translate to how well participants might retain or comprehend that information.

In line with staff assumptions, some participants do struggle to make sense of the details included in consent forms. Carl, an African American in his forties, was in his fourth study, and he said he always asked questions during the consent process because "[there's] a lot of stuff written in the paperwork that you don't understand, you know, when you've got doctors writing sentences and different things. . . . That [study information] stuff is important to me." For others, the problem is a general lack of familiarity with medical procedures. Until they undergo them, participants cannot fully understand what it means to wear a heart monitor for 24 or 48 hours or to have a dozen blood draws in a single day. In one interesting example, Marshall, who referenced the staff quizzing participants, described an 11-night, $4,400 study for which he screened. He declined to enroll after reading in the consent form that participants had to drink feces-tainted water, possibly for a so-called challenge study in which healthy volunteers were intentionally infected with a disease in order to test an investigational treatment. He noted, however, the consent form had used the word "excrement," which made it difficult for people to understand what the trial required: "Well, [another person screening] he was like, 'What does that [word] mean?' . . . I was like, 'Feces!' He was like, 'What?' I had to be like, 'Look, dude, like they want you to drink dookie in a cup of water!' . . . He was like, 'Well, they don't say that.' I'm like, 'That's what the word means.'" Marshall chuckled recollecting this interaction, but then he turned quite serious and added, "I think sometimes the vocabulary [in the consent forms] might trick people."

For most healthy volunteers, the consent form is valuable because it is the primary mechanism for protecting one's life or health when enrolling in Phase I trials. First-time participants were particularly eager to read the consent form carefully. Janae, who was one of the participants who experienced sleep paralysis in the study at Academic Phase I, affirmed, "I was adamant on reading and reading. . . . I was really nervous. It's the first time I'm taking an experimental thing, so I was over that paper, that booklet like this [pretending to hold it tightly and close to her face]. I mean, I must've read that thing 100 time[s]!" While Janae did not explicitly mention the study risks, her description conveys her concern about adverse events that could result. More experienced participants also noted how much importance they had placed on their first consent form. Rodney, an African American in his forties, was still fairly new to Phase I trials having just started 18 months prior, but he participated whenever he could at the clinic closest to where he lived. He recalled, "The first one I did, I read that thing [the consent form] maybe ten times, but I knew what I was signin'. Had a better understandin' of what was goin' on, you know. It made me feel safe and feel comfortable. I did the study, and [then] I felt even better about it."

In the absence of experiential knowledge of studies, consent forms carry more weight as a critical information source. This does not, however, mean that consent forms lose all value as individuals complete more studies. Even the most veteran participants routinely emphasized consent forms' importance. Or, in the words of Russell, an African American in his mid-forties who had participated in over two dozen trials: "I can't speak for the next person, but I make [it] my business to read what I'm getting into. Because this is your life, I mean you're taking a chance . . . so I make sure I read everything." One difference between first-time and more experienced participants is that for the latter, new study information might only make it into their short-term memories; once the trial is complete and especially once another is underway, study details fade away quickly.

These examples demonstrate that the consent process achieves its purpose: it helps people decide whether or not to enroll in specific clinical trials. That people *do* enroll is seen by some staff as a failure of the consent process's efficacy, but healthy volunteers described using the process to decide both to enroll in and to decline studies. Dennis, an African American in his twenties, serves as an excellent example because he had participated in only three clinical trials but had screened for at least double if not triple that number. Reflecting on his decision-making, he related, "I guess it just depends on the product, what I read on the paperwork. . . . [It's] the side effects; again, it always comes to the side effects, symptoms or side effects. Heart attack—I don't know why stroke doesn't always seem to be that much of an issue [in studies]—but heart attack, death should be number one [as a reason to decline a study]." Dennis illustrates how healthy volunteers might use the consent process to identify possible adverse events they believe are too dangerous to risk.

Regardless of the importance most participants claim to place on the consent process, there is a curious convergence in research staff's and healthy volunteers' perceptions of serial participants. Healthy volunteers asserted that no one else (or few others) paid as much attention to the consent information as they did. For example, Sidney, an African American in his late forties and a long-time participant, opined, "I don't think they read the consent. I think they read the payment amount and how long they're going to be in [the clinic] and that's basically it. . . . I would think 75 to 80 percent of the people read the compensation and the length of stay, and the rest [they ignore], you know. . . . I actually read it because I want to know what it's for." Similar to staff, participants often reached this conclusion about other healthy volunteers based on the questions they asked during group consent. Shirley, an African American in her late thirties, stated, "I've been screening side by side with some people, and the first question out of their mouths when they're getting consented is—'cause sometimes they do you in groups—is, 'How much are we gonna be making?' You know, and the thing is, is that it's a weakness in that it shows that they're not really thinking about [the risks of] what they're actually getting into, because it could be very serious."

Of course, empirically it does not add up that the majority of healthy volunteers do not read the consent form or engage the broader process. First, simply too many participants consider themselves exceptions for it to be true. Second, it also directly conflicts with participants' commentary about research staff's diligence in ensuring people are, in fact, getting the study information they need. Instead, Sidney's and Shirley's indictments of other participants suggest that healthy volunteers partake in stigmatizing discourses about each other. This type of self-comparison allows them to demonstrate that they, unlike others, actively protect themselves from Phase I risks.

Taken together, participants' comments about the informed consent process illustrate a fascinating aspect of how healthy volunteers make sense of study risks. Critically, participants do not necessarily make the case that Phase I trials are de facto dangerous, but they argue that ignoring the information in consent forms is a dangerous way to participate. This position exemplifies the ambivalence healthy volunteers clearly feel about study risks. Without consent forms, healthy volunteers would be uncertain when they should decline a trial, but they often need or want more information than the formal consent process provides.

Seeking Experientially Informed Consent

Although consent forms describe what happened when an investigational drug was tested on prior groups of humans or—in the absence of such information—on nonhuman animals, healthy volunteers have trouble determining how that risk information translates into which adverse events they should expect to experience. As a result, they often seek anecdotal evidence either from research staff or other healthy volunteers about what has actually happened in prior trials of the same drug. Placing a higher value on what is likely to happen than on what could possibly occur, healthy volunteers often seek reassurance that others have been through a clinical trial safely. In contrast to the official consent form, this can be thought of as *experientially informed consent,* or unofficial risk information based on one's own or others' clinical trial experiences.

With such experiential information, healthy volunteers hope to adjudicate where clinical trial risks might fall on a scale between death and no bodily changes at all. This informal intelligence might then help them choose clinical trials with acceptable adverse events or at least minimize their ambivalence about a particular trial's risks. This type of negotiation came across in Kim's earlier comments, when, even after having experienced sleep paralysis, she appealed to her father's long-term history of study participation to convince herself that she would not be harmed in her first Phase I trial. More often, however, participants desire information about specific studies in order to limit their risk exposure. This can become an imperative when some of the possible adverse events listed in the consent form cause alarm. For instance, James, an African American in his late twenties who estimated he had participated in 25 studies, vividly remembered an example of one consent form in particular that prompted him to ask the research staff some follow-up questions:

> I saw once where it said one of the side effects was jaundice and like yellowing of the eyes, and that really bothered me. . . . And I was like, what are the chances [of that happening]? 'Cause we were, I think we were the third group to do it. And I wanted to know like what the statistics were, like had it ever happened to anybody prior, like in other studies? And they said, no, [it hadn't]. . . . I ended up doing it. It was fine. But yeah, that gave me—, I don't know why, it just stuck out to me. I was like, whoa.

Rather than basing his decision to participate on the consent form alone, James relied on others' experiences to feel comfortable with the risk, even if this information was simply filtered through the staff. In another example, John, a white man in his early thirties who had participated in three studies, declined a study in which a friend had been in a prior group and reported to him that "it also turns your body fluids orange, so your teardrops would be orange. . . . If you wear contacts, those will turn orange." Whereas James was reassured by the information he received, John used his friend's experience to determine he was not prepared for the risk of that particular adverse event.

Research staff are also well aware that healthy volunteers want this information. On one hand, they believe this provides more relevant information to participants, especially when adverse events are expected. Patty, the recruiter at Academic Phase I, explained the clinic's strategy of providing direct, experiential information to participants during the consent process. She asserted, "I think people appreciate it more if you're honest and they know what they're heading into, you know? . . . I did try to tell them [when they screened] that you're gonna have hallucinations, you know, people have had vivid dreams, they have had sleep paralysis, you know, these things that I think are important before you sign a consent form to know what you're signing." On the other hand, staff worry that participants place too much stock in what happened to earlier groups. The problem is that adverse events might not have occurred in a prior group but could manifest in subsequent studies. Neil, the physician-investigator at Academic Phase I, explained,

"Occasionally you'll have a drug in which people do, in fact, get these [adverse events] in a dose-dependent fashion. And when people have not been warned . . . in an explicit fashion verbally, then sometimes they get upset." Experiential information, therefore, is prone to backfire when staff are limited in their ability to predict which adverse events might occur.

Perceptions of "Normal" Phase I Risks

Although the informed consent process stresses the gravity of Phase I risks, most healthy volunteers do not *feel* particularly at risk once they enroll in a trial. Essentially, healthy volunteers acknowledge adverse events can occur, but they develop counternarratives that construct trials as safe, *even when* they experience bodily changes during a study. This view is possible because they trust their assessment of the information about the trial they receive as part of the consent process, asserting that they can identify and would decline risky studies. Moreover, as long as any adverse events are short term and resolve on their own, participants usually take this as confirmation that the study is harmless. Their experiences, by and large, "prove" that Phase I trials are safe.[3]

Serial participation contributes to healthy volunteers' minimizing of Phase I risks. In becoming a type of model organism, well adapted to the needs of the clinics, participants undergo a twofold process of, one, becoming desensitized to risk and, two, building their trust in the research enterprise. As with consent, this process is experientially informed and based on their personal and collective experiences in trials. These themes of desensitization and trust have already been hinted at through the examples and discussion above, but they are essential to understanding serial participants' relationship to risk, especially how they justify or rationalize their decisions to enroll—and continue to enroll—in Phase I trials.

Take, for example, Pete, a white man in his late fifties who had participated in more than ten Phase I trials in several parts of the country. As might now be expected, he acknowledged the risk studies pose and faulted others for how "the money overshadows" the consent process. Yet, Pete's personal experience of miserable short-term adverse events paradoxically persuaded him of studies' general safety. Specifically, in an Alzheimer's disease trial, he and other participants had suffered so much vertigo and vomiting that the clinic stopped administering the investigational drug to confer with the sponsor. When they reinitiated the study, the sponsor included a dose of a second (marketed) drug to minimize vomiting. Pete recalled,

> It was the first study I've been in where there was a lot of sickness. . . . I mean it was a pretty strong, strong dose. . . . It was rough. We dosed 26 [people] and 18 got sick. And then [the staff] they went, "Oh my god!" So then they called us all in the cafeteria and go, "Oh boy, obviously we need to rethink this study," so they postponed it for a week. . . . That's really the only time I've actually seen physical illness. . . . Yeah, it was [laughs], "You guys better go back to the lab and rethink that one."

Pete could laugh about this experience in large part because his symptoms had been short term. Additionally, the fact that the staff had not simply allowed the participants to suffer, choosing instead to postpone the study and change the dosing protocol, increased his trust in the clinic and sponsor. Furthermore, seeing that the study had not affected his long-term health, Pete developed a different idea about the risks, contrasting his initial shock at seeing his first consent form to understanding that some side effects are just "common." His experiences, as with many other healthy volunteers, desensitized him to the "normal" risks of Phase I trials, including the occurrence of adverse events, and increased his trust in the research enterprise.

Desensitization to Risk

As with the repetition of many other risky activities in life, serial Phase I participation desensitizes healthy volunteers to risk to the point where some even sound cavalier about the possibility of experiencing adverse events. For example, when I asked Wajid, a Pakistani immigrant in his forties, about his perception of Phase I trial risks, he replied, "The reason why I don't too much think about the risk [is] because I've done it so many times. If something was supposed to happen to me, it would have done happened already." Similarly, Maria, a Latina participant in her thirties, told me, "I start . . . in 2001 with one pill, and nothing happened, . . . and

I see nothing happened and I continue to [participate] and I have [done] like five studies." These experiences often become more salient sources of information about participants' personal risk of harm than consent forms are. In other words, healthy volunteers acknowledge there are risks but believe they are personally safe from harm (see also Fisher et al. 2018a).

Participants often narrated a trajectory from feeling fear or panic at the thought of enrolling in their first clinical trial to confidence that studies are generally very safe. Julius, an African American in his late thirties participating in his eighth study, mocked his initial concerns about the risks: "I was like, oh my God! You know, I was freaking out, but my friend assured me, 'No, it's nothing.' . . . I was like, 'Yeah, but . . . this is serious; anything can happen.' . . . But I did it, and everything worked out. . . . [laughs] I'm still here." Living through their first study—and however many after—reassures participants they will not be harmed, especially not in the long term.

The absence of adverse events, or the presence of only very minor ones, further contributes to healthy volunteers' desensitization to risk. Getting safely through a study provides a striking contrast to the dooms-day scenarios many had feared when they read the consent form for their first clinical trial. When thinking about his first time screening compared to the second, Lars, a white man in his twenties, observed, "I realized all the studies were gonna say 'possible death' [on the consent forms], 'cause everything can kill you. Yeah, so that didn't bother me [the second time]." Likewise, Kevin, an African American in his early forties, was dismissive when I asked him directly about study risks. He proclaimed, "I never had experienced too many adverse events in four years. I've experienced like two. . . . I don't feel nothing. I feel just the way when I came in. I'm going home tomorrow [from this study]; I have no headache, I'm not dizzy, I'm walking straight, and my teeth didn't fall out yet." Moreover, short-term adverse events can be normalized by contrasting them to sickness outside of studies, such as the flu, food poisoning, or hangovers. In this vein, Graham, an African American in his early forties in his first study, made light of his adverse events: "And the dosage was so minimal! I'm like, I already know I can get more side effects from a shot of Patrón [tequila] than I can get from what I just took on this study. [Laughs.] I think I've had more party days in college dorms worse than I've had from this pill they just gave me." Despite

Kevin's and Graham's bravado about adverse events, they also both acknowledged the potential risks of study participation and the importance of reading consent forms. Yet, their awareness of the risks did not translate into *feelings of being at risk* when they participated because their experiences reassured them that doing so was safe.

Also contributing to serial participants' desensitization to the risks is the perception that the potential adverse events for each study are always the same. Even though the investigational drugs differ, consent forms appear to have a standard list of possible risks, such as nausea, vomiting, diarrhea, and headache. This can lead participants to believe that if they did not experience any of those symptoms in one clinical trial, then they are equally unlikely to experience them in another. For instance, Jeremy, a white man in his thirties who had participated in six studies, said, "I've seen the same side effects on every one of the studies I've done, but I personally haven't had a lot of side effects from it. Like the first couple I did, I got like the rashes they showed [in the consent form], but I don't remember anything going wrong in the last couple that I've done. So it's been all good." Jeremy's experience is especially remarkable because he *had* experienced an adverse event commonly listed in the consent form, but this did not make him feel any more vulnerable to trial risks. Indeed, cases like these might promote the importance of gathering experientially informed data from staff or other participants about which adverse events of the "usual suspects" listed they should expect.

It might be counterintuitive that the consent process could contribute to serial participants' risk desensitization, but it appears to have this effect on some. However, the long list of possible adverse events coupled with the rare experience of any serious ones also contribute to participants' ambivalence about Phase I risks. They are informed that study risks can be severe, but their personal experiences of adverse events *up to that point* have shown clinical trials to be safe. This means that desensitization to risk is a fragile state because it can be replaced by a greater sense of risk should participants experience or witness more serious adverse events during a study.

Trust in the Research Enterprise

Beyond desensitization, healthy volunteers' trust in clinics—and in research more broadly—attenuates their perceptions of risk. Oftentimes this trust manifests through assertions that the research staff's job is to ensure participants are not harmed in studies. Sidney, one of the participants who previously emphasized the consent process's importance, made this point particularly forcefully: "[Since] the very first one [study] here, . . . I basically had trust that the staff here [at Academic Phase I], they wouldn't want to see anything happen to me because it's not in their best interest. . . . [And] being in a controlled environment where if something did go wrong, that they could correct it or I would be safe, like I wasn't going to die in here or anything." Salvador, a Latino serial participant in his forties, held the same view about Mega Phase I: "I mean, they are always monitoring us. I mean, it's not like they are going to give us something that we can't handle and we are going to die" (translated from Spanish). These articulations of trust also communicate Sidney's and Salvador's struggle with their ambivalence about the risks: anything *could* happen during the study, but the staff ultimately protect participants from harm.

Trust in the research enterprise extends even beyond the clinics' walls. Gleaning information from consent forms, many healthy volunteers trust that the drug development process creates important safeguards that minimize participants' exposure to risk. Participants' faith is rooted both in the science leading up to Phase I trials and in the institutions that oversee the clinics. Many participants find it comforting that clinical trials on humans occur only after (some) nonhuman animal testing has been conducted. In her appraisal of risk, Alexandra, a white transwoman in her forties who had participated in about a dozen studies, argued, "Normally, they sort of talk about how like we test these [drugs] on rats, but they've had at least 10 or 12 times the dose that we're having. So if like a one-pound rat can get through it alright, I'm sure I should be okay, you know? . . . So I just figure I'm safe enough." Comparing relative body size to dose was a common refrain healthy volunteers deployed in their interpretation that Phase I trials are minimal or low risk. Additionally, some participants pointed out that not all study drugs are investigational; some are already on the market in some form, which implies that unexpected and dramatic adverse events are even less likely.

Not everything participants believe about the drug development process is completely accurate, but some of their misperceptions also diminish their sense of risk. In one such example, Lisa, a white first-time participant in her twenties, described the impression she had gotten from the consent process: "I was told that [the drugs] they're tested on animals first, and that they test 'em on other humans in Europe before they test 'em on Americans, and that they just aren't on the market [in the United States] 'cause they have to test it on Americans, and it was [already] tested on animals and humans in Europe." What Lisa likely read in the consent form was that the study was designed to test a drug that had not yet received FDA approval but was already on the market in Europe. The FDA does not require human studies to be conducted on American participants. It has, however, been true historically that new drugs are approved for the European market before they are in the United States, which can mean there is more safety information about a drug still in clinical trials than would otherwise be the case (Abraham and Davis 2005). While Lisa might have had some details wrong, she generalized out from this information about drug development to vocalize her trust in a research process she believed makes US clinical trials safe.

Additionally, healthy volunteers flag how the FDA and/or institutional review boards (IRBs) provide oversight of clinical trials. The information participants have about this aspect of drug development might be even shakier than the science, but they know that other organizations are charged with looking out for participants' safety. For example, some participants discussed how IRBs ensure healthy volunteers are informed about study risks, including when new information about risk arises after a clinical trial has begun. Arnel, an Asian immigrant in his fifties, was in only his second study, but he explicitly tied his trust in the research process to the IRB: "I'm kind of trusting in that they have to adhere to the IRB, whatever it is, you know. So I kind of have faith in the process they're doing, and whatever they catch, whenever they catch something, I know that it's part of protocol to let it be known to everybody, like immediately, you know what I mean? So if something happens to a prior group, . . . a side effect, they'll round everybody up. . . . So I kind of go in with a sense of security that everybody's doing what they're supposed to do." Of course, the clinic's duty to disclose emergent risk information would not necessarily change the actual risk to participants, but for Arnel, it meant that risk protocols are followed, which made him feel safer.

In the context of commercial Phase I clinics that do not always inspire participants' trust, research oversight by IRBs can become even more critical to healthy volunteers. Consent forms include information about how to contact the IRB of record should participants feel as though their rights have been violated, and some have done so. Ross, an African American in his forties with 12 years of trial experience, personally contacted an IRB on one occasion. He had been enrolled in a study in which he was required to have a peripheral venous catheter, but the staff person gave Ross the distinct impression he did not know how to insert it properly. When Ross complained and asked for someone else to do the procedure, the staff member protested:

> [The staff member] insisted that, "Well, you gotta do it." I said, "I don't have to do it." He said, "Yes, you do," and he wrestled my arm for a minute. And I said, "No, I'm not gonna do it," . . . and so at 10:24, I left that night in the night. . . . [After, I] complained to their IRB, and you know, in general they [the clinic's staff] said that they, "Well, yeah, we recognize we did some things wrong." . . . Everyone offers you the consent form, saying we have the right to do this, [that] any time you want, you can stop, . . . but they fall apart if you call them on their behavior.

Because Ross had already been participating in clinical trials for years when this incident happened, not only did he feel confident about his rights but he also could see that the staff person—and the clinic by proxy—was in the wrong. Most participants, however, never take advantage of the IRB oversight in place, whether or not they have a legitimate complaint to make.[4] Ross's case illustrates how participants might exercise situational trust in the research enterprise, comparing their expectations for how the research process should be managed to their own positive and negative experiences in Phase I trials.[5]

Normalizing Phase I Risks

Healthy volunteers' status as model organisms is critical in shaping their perceptions of Phase I risks. Their engagement with the informed consent process demonstrates how they are calibrated to the risks of adverse events over time. Even as risks are normalized, healthy volunteers—as well as research staff—maintain some ambivalence about what harms could befall them. This is because the emphasis in the informed consent process on what *could* happen is often in conflict with people's actual study experiences. To negotiate the discrepancy between which risks are possible and which are likely, healthy volunteers seek evidence of risk that is experientially informed. While prior testing with an investigational drug does not guarantee the same results with new groups, it does offer a helpful guide for what adverse events might occur during a clinical trial. Moreover, serial participation facilitates risk desensitization because each time someone gets through a study without serious problems, it further confirms the safety of Phase I trials. Paradoxically, some participants' experiences of adverse events also contribute to the desensitization process, provided their symptoms subside relatively quickly. Hence, experiential risk information communicates that as model organisms, healthy volunteers will not be subjected to dangerous substances that could truly harm them.

Although research staff concede that most trials are perfectly safe, they simultaneously worry that healthy volunteers pay insufficient attention to the consent process, using as evidence the fact that people enroll even after being told the risks. For their part, healthy volunteers avow the importance of consent forms for their *own* participation, but they share the staff's belief that most participants do not take the process seriously enough. Both groups stigmatize typical healthy volunteers as individuals who are unable to comprehend the information or to appropriately weigh the study risks. Participants' financial need is always thought to overshadow their attention to risk. However, speaking with healthy volunteers demonstrates that most are neither apathetic nor "forced" by desperate circumstances to accept whatever harm could occur.[6]

Participants generally do believe they should stay alert to the risks by always reading the consent forms, but once they enroll in a study, they feel relatively certain they will not be harmed. This is also mirrored in the staff's view that temporary adverse events do not constitute harm as well as in the scholarly literature representing Phase I trials as low risk, notwithstanding that two-thirds of participants experience adverse events (Emanuel et al. 2015; Sibille et al. 1998). Additionally, rigorous study oversight helps to assuage any fear of harm healthy volunteers might have; they focus on how staff monitor participants and how outside organizations ensure participants' rights are protected. When healthy volunteers place their trust in the research process, it further contributes to risk desensitization. Rather than being discrete mechanisms, these forces work in tandem to construct Phase I trials as safe.

Desensitization and trust operate most powerfully for healthy volunteers when they evaluate the risks of the studies they have chosen to join. In other words, after consenting to participate in a given clinical trial, they are likely to downplay its risk and speak generally about studies as safe. Does this mean that once someone has chosen to enroll, the view that a clinical trial is risk free is a discursive device or a psychological defense mechanism? Or do healthy volunteers have criteria to determine which possible adverse events they are comfortable with and which are too much? The next chapter addresses these questions by illustrating how healthy volunteers make distinctions about studies to join or decline based on their perceptions of short- or long-term risks.

8

Constructing Risk Knowledge

At 6:00 AM, it was time for two healthy volunteers at Pharma Phase I to receive lumbar punctures. This procedure was part of an Alzheimer's disease trial that required a catheter placement for continuous cerebrospinal fluid (CSF) collection over a several-hour period. By the time Denise, the white nurse manager, had put me in a sterile gown and ushered me into the participants' room, the space was already buzzing. The clinic contracted out with local anesthesiologists to perform lumbar punctures, and Keith, one of the two hired for that morning, had already arrived. This white physician prepped Devon, an African American man and the first of the two healthy volunteers to receive the procedure. While Keith coated the lower segment of Devon's spine with iodine, Devon sat hunched over on the side of his bed. There also were multiple Pharma Phase I staff members in the room: Denise; Vince, a white physician-investigator; Josh, a white paramedic; and Carol, a white nurse.

As I found a place to stand in the crowded room, Keith adhered a fenestrated drape—a sterile paper sheet with a precut rectangular hole providing access to the correct vertebrae—to Devon's back. Keith asked Josh to secure "the patient" for the anesthesia, and Josh moved to the other side of the bed to face Devon and hold his shoulders from the front. Without speaking to Devon, Keith injected Devon's lower back with lidocaine, then turned to Vince to ask where Rich, the second anesthesiologist, was. Vince had not seen him yet, so he called him on his cell phone. Rich said he was pulling into the parking lot and would be there momentarily. With that, Denise dashed from the room to meet Rich and bring him into the secured clinic.

Keith looked at the large digital clock on the wall, perhaps thinking about the time-point for the procedure set by the study protocol, and wordlessly inserted the large, hollow needle between Devon's vertebrae. He asked Devon whether he felt any pain, and Devon shook his head mutely to indicate that he did not. The room was silent. Devon was still hunched over, now with a needle sticking out of his back, and Josh continued to hold his shoulders, though more loosely. There was evidently nothing to do but wait for Rich. I looked at the clock, and it was 6:11. As time passed and the room felt more and more awkward, Keith turned to me, wanting to know who I was. While we had a brief conversation about why I was visiting Pharma Phase I, my eyes kept returning to the needle in Devon's back.

Finally, at 6:22, Rich, an older white man, entered the room, gowned and full of apologies. Keith stepped out of his way, and Rich picked up the catheter from the tools spread out on the table. In a flash, he threaded the catheter through the lumbar needle, and CSF began flowing immediately. I was aghast and somewhat panicked to see that no one had thought to connect the catheter to a specimen tube, and Devon's fluid was steadily dripping onto the drape. Upon seeing this, Vince stumbled over to the table, grabbed a slender specimen container, and connected it the catheter, but not before the drape was quite wet from the fluid. No one verbally acknowledged what happened, but Rich's face communicated that somehow, he was the injured party. Vince then finished up the procedure by removing the specimen container and adding plastic tubing to act as a valve so the catheter could be used to collect additional CSF from Devon that day. Once this was done, Vince and Carol gently removed Devon's drape, and Carol secured the tubing to Devon's back with tape. She and Josh then helped Devon put on his pink Pharma Phase I t-shirt and laid him flat on his back. He had not said a word since I entered the room, and Rich spoke to him only after the catheter was secured.

As Keith and Vince started pulling open the second lumbar puncture kit, Josh left the room and returned seconds later with Manuel, a Puerto Rican man. He must have been waiting just outside the door. Now that everyone was present from the start, the morning's second lumbar puncture could proceed much more smoothly. Whether or not it was his responsibility, I noted Vince was already holding the specimen container and ready to place it by the time Rich inserted the catheter; this time not a single drop of CSF was lost. Unlike Devon, however, Manuel was vocal throughout the procedure. He was clearly nervous, especially when Keith injected him with the lidocaine and he reported that the anesthesia burned a lot. Throughout the procedure, Rich told corny jokes to make Manuel laugh, who complied half-heartedly, knowing the script he should follow. When Manuel was finally lying on his back in bed at the end of the procedure, he noticed me for the first time and grinned, saying, "I think we should get another Visa gift card for this. That was good stuff for you!" That comment finally roused Devon who laughed and agreed.

Lumbar punctures are rather rare in Phase I research, but they are one of the most feared and discussed procedures among healthy volunteers, who call them "spinal taps." The reason a protocol would include a lumbar puncture is to measure the degree to which an investigational drug crosses the blood-brain barrier, as evinced by its presence in cerebrospinal fluid.[1] The procedure is performed by a physician and carries the risk of intense spinal headaches due to a decreased pressure in the brain from CSF loss. In rare instances, lumbar punctures can cause bleeding or infection, longer-term back or leg pain, or brain herniation (Cavens and Ramael 2009).

A lumbar puncture's invasiveness as well as concerns about the remote chance of paralysis stand in sharp contrast to more typical Phase I trials. Whereas healthy volunteers might be thoroughly desensitized to the risks of taking an investigational drug and suffering through any short-term adverse events, they tend to consider spinal taps as too risky to undergo, regardless of their trust in the research enterprise. Importantly, their fear of participating comes from the possibility of *long-term* problems from the procedure more than worry about any adverse events the investigational drug might produce.[2] These concerns seemed quite justified on the morning of Devon's and Manuel's procedure.

Although Pharma Phase I prided itself on its rigorous standard operating procedures (SOPs) and highly trained staff, mistakes were made with Devon's lumbar puncture. Neither of the anesthesiologists were Pharma Phase I employees, but they were contracted to perform the procedure because of their expertise. Nonetheless, neither looked particularly professional that morning, when Keith started the procedure too soon and Rich inserted a catheter without a specimen container in place. To be honest, it was unclear who should have ensured the tube was ready. Vince's response could have either indicated culpability or shown quick reflexes. Perhaps the problem that morning was that three physicians were too many for a routine lumbar puncture.

The following day I checked on Devon and Manuel. They were both in great spirits but declared they would never do another spinal tap.[3] Manuel insisted the study did not pay enough for the procedure, and both agreed that lying around all day, especially the four hours they had to spend on their stomachs after the catheter was removed, had been like torture. Devon even suggested the United States should use this method against its enemies in Afghanistan. I asked them how much they had felt of the lumbar puncture itself. Manuel replied, "Didn't hurt much. . . . You ever seen *The Matrix*? Alright, you know when they pull out that big hose in the back of their skull? Alright, that's what it felt like. [Laughs.] Just like in *The Matrix*, it was like, [gasp] and then you're in. . . . It felt like that." In contrast, Devon reported he had not felt anything at all. Surprised, I mentioned how disconcerting it had been when the needle was sticking out of his back while we waited for the second anesthesiologist to show up. As his face changed to alarm, I realized he really had not known, and he stammered, "I somehow missed that." Suddenly grinning sheepishly, he confessed he had started to get really nervous when we were waiting for Rich because he was afraid the late doctor would be frazzled or hurry too much. He had kept thinking he wanted the guy to take a break before jumping into the procedure. He was absolutely right about this, but I opted not to tell him about the debacle with the CSF collection.

The events that transpired during Devon's lumbar puncture were disturbing not simply because of the procedure's risks or the mistakes Keith and Rich made. As medical errors go, the problems were fairly benign, given that Devon had not been unduly harmed by the needle or the lost CSF.[4] Instead, the procedure was unsettling because Devon was dehumanized. Like a laboratory animal in an experiment, Devon was a mere object of the procedure, providing the biological material that needed to be sampled without regard to informing him what was happening to his body. Devon had become just a back awaiting a procedure. Not only did Keith fail to tell Devon before inserting the needle, but also no one in the room verbally acknowledged that the needle was in Devon's back as we waited for Rich to appear. Devon's obvious fear had silenced him during the procedure, especially compared to Manuel, but it was the staff's lack of engagement with him as a person that was so objectifying.

Devon provides one view of what a model organism can look like in Phase I trials. He was the compliant participant who could be used as a medium for invasive data collection about an investigational drug. Even when problems occurred, he unflinchingly remained a reliable subject, ready for what needed to be done. This view of how model organisms operate, however, is an incomplete representation. Not all healthy volunteers are willing to consent to any clinical trial; they instead make choices about enrollment based on their perceptions of the differential risks of trials, and they actively avoid those they perceive as too risky. As *human* model organisms, serial participants leverage the knowledge and experience they gain from the informed consent process, their prior participation, and stories that circulate within the clinic to decide for themselves what drugs or procedures are acceptable risks. Unlike their nonhuman animal counterparts, healthy volunteers choose the experiment to which they are subjected. Indeed, unlike Devon and Manuel, many refuse to enroll in studies that require lumbar punctures, opting for far less invasive trials.

Whereas individual choice about study participation is an important part of the process, the more crucial underlying mechanism for decision-making is that healthy volunteers actively and *collectively* construct knowledge about Phase I risks. This shared knowledge can be thought of as *model organism epistemology*, or how healthy volunteers come to understand risk through "justified true belief" about their clinical trial options.[5] The need for this knowledge production is driven by participants' ambivalence about trial risks, described in the previous chapter as stemming from the gap between the consent process painting studies as risky and their personal experiences indicating they are safe. It is useful to extend that discussion by illustrating the distinctions healthy volunteers make among studies in order to keep themselves safe from harm.

Differentiating Study Risks

The longer individuals have been participating as healthy volunteers, the more likely it is they have memorable—and often negative or scary—personal experiences that become their Phase I trial "war stories." Such stories highlight multiple aspects of their trial histories, including incidents with specific investigational drugs or procedures. As I have already noted, Phase I trials' confinement structure enables the exchange of these stories because participants are brought together for days or weeks on end. While stories help pass the time, they also create an informal, shared knowledge base about the range of available Phase I trials and their risks. In this way, healthy volunteers provide potential warnings to newer healthy volunteers and reaffirm the higher risk of certain studies to more established serial participants. Additionally, the narrative process of differentiating among trial risks contributes to healthy volunteers becoming model organisms as well as savvy participants with shared perceptions about the science in which they are involved.

Although risk perceptions vary among healthy volunteers, storytelling functions to flag certain studies as ones to be avoided or joined cautiously. On the individual level, a healthy volunteer's personal experience of adverse events might shape her decision-making about her future participation. At the same time, personal and vicarious experiences accrete into what could be thought of as collective *risk filters*, especially when the same types of investigational drugs or clinical procedures continually star in healthy volunteers' stories. A risk filter acts as a preliminary basis for evaluating a *specific* Phase I study's risk by comparing it to the collective experience of the social network with *similar* clinical trials. Serial participants mobilize these filters when determining whether they are even willing to screen for an available study. When certain study types are prejudged as too risky, participants can decline without even having to read the consent form.[6] Moreover, risk filters create a gradient of risk that draws a line between acceptable and reckless study participation, and, in the face of financial temptation, this can remind healthy volunteers to protect themselves from harm. The primary risk filters created by healthy volunteers rule out studies with large doses of investigational drugs, substantial study compensation, specific types of drugs, and certain invasive procedures. Each of these filters illustrates how healthy volunteers acknowledge that Phase I trials can be a risky enterprise.

Drug Dose

Many of the stories circulating about terrible adverse events include a common element across types of Phase I trials: large doses of an investigational drug. Jay, an African American in his twenties, had participated in studies at several Northeast and Midwest clinics. Reflecting on the ones in which he had experienced adverse events, he identified the dose as the cause of the problem:

> I've ran into some medicines, some of these concoctions . . . I took something that really made me feel like, "Whoa, what is this?" . . . It depends on . . . how much is the dosage. . . . If they giving you something like, I mean, 5 milligrams? Oh yeah, that's nothing. But if they're talking about something like 900 milligrams or something, . . . that might have an effect on you, you know what I mean? You *gonna* feel that. I don't care, you know, you're gonna feel that regardless of what [type of drug] it is; you're gonna feel it.

As a result of these experiences, Jay not only avoided studies that administered a large dose, but he also declined those in which participants were dosed with the drug daily. Giving a hypothetical example, he asserted, "If they tell you, like, 'Oh yeah, we're dosing every single day at 500 milligrams of this,' then you're like, 'Oh, that's a red flag! . . . I think I'll pass even though the money's good.'" For participants who claimed the key to determining a trial's risk was the drug's dose, the consent process was essential because it was how they obtained that information and decided, irrespective of the compensation, whether to enroll.

This perspective on risk is quite intuitive: increasing the dose of an investigational drug increases the likelihood of adverse events. But what constitutes a "high" dose? Has it become too high at 50, 100, 500, 1000 milligrams? The category's flexibility works for healthy volunteers because it can become a gut feeling based on a specific trial or justification for why the money might be worth the risk after all. Beyond the indeterminacy of what counts as too high of a dose, this risk filter is also premised on a logical fallacy. Specifically, this perspective cannot account for the fact that some drugs are safe even at very high doses and that other drugs present severe risks even at minute doses. For example, healthy volunteers who were seriously injured in the 2006 Phase I trial in London had received the first—and therefore very low—dose of the investigational drug (Wood and Darbyshire 2006). Regardless, few participants recognized those anomalous cases as possibilities. In part, this is because risk filters act as heuristics, providing one source of information about how study risks might differ.

Study Compensation

Healthy volunteers hold a strong conviction that study compensation is based on each trial's risk.[7] A low- to moderate-paying study, in this view, is low to moderate risk whereas a high-paying study is high risk. Such evaluations of the pay either account for the overall compensation amount or the average daily pay. By these metrics, when one trial compensates significantly more than others at the same clinic, participants might feel concerned that such a study could be too dangerous to pursue. For many, this construction of risk stems not only from an instinct about how the payment structure must work but also from their own and others' experiences.

Participants' perceptions conflict with the ethical framework regulating human subjects research. Specifically, institutional review boards (IRBs) are charged with monitoring clinical trial compensation, and norms guiding these rates must be related to confinement length or travel reimbursement, not the drug type, procedures, or risks (Gelinas et al. 2018). This oversight limits how much money clinics can offer to participants so that payment does not act as an undue inducement, encouraging people to enroll against their better judgment (Largent et al. 2012). Many research staff explicitly acknowledged that it would be unethical to link compensation and risk. Charlotte, one of the physician-investigators at Pharma Phase I, got to the heart of the matter when she asserted, "We don't compensate for pain and suffering, at least not in the US, not in this [Phase I] facility, so we don't pay more for an invasive study. We only pay for [people's] time [in order] to avoid getting people that are more socially disadvantaged into more painful studies, obviously. So there is no consideration of that [paying more for riskier studies]." Charlotte's strong claim could make it seem as though healthy volunteers' perceptions of risk and payment are simply misinformed.

Nevertheless, over the course of my field work, I observed particular studies, such as those that included lumbar punctures, that could have been considered higher risk and paid much higher stipends. The clinics knew they must not compensate for risk, and this problem of payment rate emerged explicitly in a group interview with the Pharma Phase I recruiters. Erica somewhat defensively explained,

> My CSF [cerebrospinal fluid, or lumbar puncture] study, if you do the math on my study, my stipend is higher than what typically is an overnight-stay payment times however many nights it is. So, you'll get your volunteer be like, you know, "Hey, they're paying Joe Schmoe more because they're, you know, sticking him in the back a couple of times." Which is not actually the reason why we do it. We actually have an increase in stipend for certain types of studies where they can only do one of them a year. So, there's an allowance for that, but it has nothing to do with the type of procedure. [Hearing the contradiction:] It's, it is, it does in the sense that they can't do another CSF study for a year, so we make a compensation allowance for that, but not because, you know, his back is more important than your overall risk, you know what I mean?

Following this statement, Tanya, Yolanda, and Aaron, the other recruiters who were present, all murmured their agreement with Erica's explanation. In a nutshell, Pharma Phase I's position was that the extra compensation was not to offset the invasiveness of a lumbar puncture but to account for the restriction on how often participants could undergo this procedure. Yet, the reason why they would limit healthy volunteers' exposure to lumbar punctures was most certainly tied to its risk. Although the recruiters appeared sincere in their assertions about not compensating participants for risk, it was only through convoluted logic that they could disaggregate risk from higher payment. And ultimately, the bottom line was that a lumbar puncture study paid more than the going rate for Pharma Phase I's other studies that adhered to a per diem compensation scheme.

I describe the research staff's perspective here to provide some context for healthy volunteers' assumptions about the association between payment and risk. If there are contradictions in how staff describe the payment structure, then surely healthy volunteers' views cannot be dismissed outright. Contemplating clinics' official position on payment, John, a white man in his early thirties who had just completed his third study, struggled with the notion that payment was unconnected to risk. He remarked, "To be fair, the drug companies, if you take them at their word, they're compensating you for inconvenience; they're not compensating you for the drug necessarily. I mean, it seemed—, it's a little hard to kind of buy that at face value, but that seems to be what the drug companies will say: 'We pay you for your time. We don't pay you to take the risk.' That's weird. And that also just seems false to me, but I don't know." John believed that companies were universally disingenuous about this issue, but many participants described using the compensation amount instrumentally to gauge trial risks. For example, Joseph, an African American in his thirties who was participating in his fourth study, said, "If they're gonna give you 10,000 bucks for a study, there's a $10,000 risk associated with it, you know. . . . So I'm thinking like maybe, it may be more feasible to do a $1,200 one here, $1,500 one there. Maybe a $2,000. I'm starting to think anything over $4,000 is . . . a little more of a risk, at least from my experiences." It is striking to consider that even though Joseph and others were motivated by the compensation, some claimed to decline the highest-paying studies out of concern about the risks.

Participants' belief about the association between compensation and risk is further reinforced by their own and others' experiences with high-paying studies. Sharing these stories confirms that payment should serve as a risk filter, prompting them to exercise additional caution about studies that pay more. Tia, an African American serial participant in her early thirties, recounted in detail one of her own terrible experiences: "[It was] the first drug that I've ever had a really violent, horrible side effect from, and so did everyone in the study. I was at [commercial clinic], and it was an antibiotic, . . . [and] the side effects that were listed [in the consent form] or noted up until that point were minimal, and they [the research staff] kept saying, 'Oh, this is a breeze of a study.' I'm like, 'It pays a little bit too much for the time period that we're staying here.' But everyone insisted this is just an easy study." Despite staff reassurances, there was nothing easy about the trial. Tia continued her story, "We had *no* control of our bodily functions once we took this antibiotic. So, at the same time we were throwing up, everything else was releasing. The men couldn't make it to the restroom. I made it to the restroom every time, but we had to show them everything, so we had to catch it in these bags. And I would walk out [of] the bathroom with bag behind bag. . . . It was like a scene out of *Poltergeist*. It was just, it was horrible." Tia also recounted additional adverse events in that study, including a severe rash on her arms, thrush, and a vaginal yeast infection. She related the experience as a good storyteller, building suspense and drama as she detailed everything that happened. By the time she reached the moral, the listener would have arrived at the same conclusion: if the payment seems unusually high, prepare yourself for some serious adverse events.[8]

HIV/AIDS Clinical Trials

Compared to other elements of Phase I trials, healthy volunteers often focus less on the therapeutic area for which a drug is being developed. HIV/AIDS medications, however, prove an exception to this pattern, and many serial participants perceive this type of drug to be sufficiently risky to justify its own risk filter. Not many participants I met had personal experiences with HIV/AIDS studies, but it was common for people to discuss the importance of avoiding them. This was likely because of stories that circulate, such as the one told by Wesley, an African American in his early thirties with a long Phase I trial record. He described how all the participants had so much nausea and vomiting in the HIV study he was in that the clinic canceled the remainder of the trial out of concern for their safety. Other participants' perceptions are based on what they have witnessed first-hand while confined to a clinic that was conducting an HIV/AIDS study. Javier, a Latino serial participant in his mid-forties, averred, "I don't do AIDS medicines . . . because they will tear you up. Those medicines I've seen, been into studies that guys done AIDS tests [i.e., clinical trials] and I see them gettin' yellow, jaundice, and they didn't look too good. . . . I have seen [that] with my own eyes doing studies."

With information about the alleged prevalence of adverse events in HIV/AIDS trials, participants can become more fearful about the harm these studies might cause. Magnifying this perception is the rumor that healthy volunteers could contract HIV by participating, which would be a particularly traumatic adverse event. Although Troy, an African American in his mid-twenties, was a first-time participant when I met him, he had already been schooled by other participants about HIV trial risks. He emphatically told me he would never enroll in an HIV study: "Last week I was talking to this guy, he did an HIV study, . . . and they paid him $16,000 to do the research. . . . It's a huge risk he might catch the virus if he does the study. . . . But I guess it was worth it [to him] for $16,000. I don't wanna risk the chance of catching HIV and dying in a couple of years." This misperception of HIV trials is widespread and not just a mistake made by novices. Part of the difference between HIV and other Phase I trials is that the adverse event risked is not simply discomfort caused by short-term symptoms but the rumored risk of long-term infection and its consequences.

These participants' comments about HIV studies illustrate how a risk filter operates in healthy volunteers' decision-making. When a type of clinical trial is identified a priori as too risky, it effectively blocks the participants from finding out more about a study because they refuse to screen for one and, therefore, never read or hear the information contained in an official consent form. Thus, participants might never be disabused of the notion that they could become infected with HIV because their source of information is solely the stories that circulate among healthy volunteers. In this way, whether HIV trials always are riskier or more prone to adverse events is no longer relevant once this whole group of studies is filtered out.

Psychotropic Medications

Another dominant risk filter shaping Phase I trial participation focuses on psychotropic drugs. Often paired with HIV studies, the risk narrative around psychotropic medications shares similar features highlighting the risk of devastating short- and long-term adverse events. Malia, an African American participant in her twenties, encapsulated this succinctly when she said, "When you come here, if you talk to different people, you'll hear to stay away from AIDS studies because it makes you very sick. And you also hear to stay away from like the psycho studies that, you know, end up making you delusional or crazy permanent[ly]. So those is the ones that I stay away from." In other words, fear of psychotropic medications has the same underlying logic as HIV/AIDS drugs: healthy people risk being "infected" by the drugs and becoming mentally ill.

Some worries about psychotropic drugs are directly bolstered by individuals' personal experiences in these trials. Investigational drugs in this class are startling to healthy volunteers because they can and do produce mind-altering adverse events. For example, Kevin, an African American in his forties who had been participating full time in studies for four years, recounted one of his experiences:

> I did one [study] here called ADHD [attention deficit hyperactivity disorder]. It was like a horror movie. . . . I couldn't sleep. I was tossing and turning. . . . [When] I did get like a minimal of three hours of sleep, I had nightmares. . . . I woke up three o'clock in the morning, and the ice cooler in the kitchen, it sounded like some kind of monster. It was like making these noises like [makes growling sounds]. . . . I thought that I was going crazy. . . . I mean, I'm a horror movie buff myself, so I'm not afraid of things that creep and crawl through the night, but *that* night was creepy. . . . I be collecting myself the next morning, and I'm like, "Okay, I know who I am. I know what I'm doing here. It's all good. It was [just] the medication."

When I asked Kevin if it was possible that it had merely been the study he was in and not representative of all psychotropic drugs, he told me about another experience he had witnessed: "It was like last year. [Another group of healthy volunteers] was doing some schizophrenic study. I was doing cholesterol. I was good. I had no side effects. No AEs, no adverse events. . . . One guy, he was out of it for [only] four milligrams of schizophrenia medication. There was a point where they tried to stand him up, the nurses; they laid him on the floor and seven nurses were around him, and they couldn't wake him up. I think they stopped the study." Kevin's risk perception was heightened not only because he thought of psychotropic drugs as more dangerous, but also because the adverse event had been so severe with a small dose. Hence, if small doses are supposed to be safe, then when even a small dose of a schizophrenia drug could produce such dramatic events, these drugs should always be avoided.

Another example of a psychotropic clinical trial with major adverse events came from Stuart, a white serial participant in his early fifties. In that study, he experienced hallucinations, but the most worrisome part was that by the time his group was discharged from the study's first leg, he was still adversely affected by the investigational drug. Indeed, it took several days for his feeling high to dissipate. When he returned to the clinic for another dose of the investigational drug and confinement period, he felt a bit anxious about the risks:

> So I go in there, and I say to them, "Listen, I haven't taken the medication yet for the next group, but before I take it, I need to talk to you. . . . So," I said, "first question is: Is this gonna have any kind of deleterious effect on me? Like, taking it more than once, is there any chance of it having any kind of a long-term effect?" They said, "Oh, no, no, no, absolutely, it's not going to." . . . And I said [using a goofy voice], "Okay, they're the doctors." So, you know, it's the same thing when I took it again. It was the exact same thing! Nothing different. Same way [with hallucinations], and when I left, I was still high.

Stuart's worry about the long-term risks had not been eased by the staff assuring him he would be fine. Thinking both of that study and his future participation, he said, "I'm worried about my brain anyway, and I'm just really paranoid, and I don't wanna have anything [in a clinical trial] that's gonna hurt my brain, you know? . . . I think if one [a new study consent form] said, 'There's a possibility of hallucinating,' I probably would not take the study."

Experiences like Kevin's and Stuart's are especially compelling to other healthy volunteers because they are unfamiliar enough to intrigue and inspire a bit of fear. It is easy to imagine how stories about nightmares and hallucinations could make anyone think twice about enrolling in a psychotropic drug trial (see also Abadie 2010). Indeed, this fear is so pronounced that it creates a broad-based risk filter for many serial participants who claim to avoid all studies that could affect their brains, particularly in the long term, including drugs for schizophrenia, bipolar disorder, depression, anxiety, and attention deficit disorder.

Spinal Taps

More than any investigational drug, a lumbar puncture is one procedure that creates a nonnegotiable risk filter for many participants. While Devon and Manuel consented to such a study, most healthy volunteers perceive spinal taps as too risky. The image of a needle being inserted into one's spine could certainly suffice for someone to decline a lumbar puncture study, but many participants' stories further confirm for others that these studies are risky. While Devon's lumbar puncture illustrates that the procedure does not always go perfectly, participants' narratives about their own negative spinal tap experiences did not typically spotlight staff errors or incompetence. Instead, healthy volunteers described their *own* errors in judgment that created the bad experiences from the lumbar puncture. The procedure's most likely adverse event is a spinal headache, which occurs when there is a significant loss of cerebrospinal fluid (CSF) due to leakage at the puncture site. It is also a symptom that participants have some control over themselves. In order to avoid such headaches, staff caution healthy volunteers to lie flat in bed for several hours after the lumbar puncture to reduce their risk. Unfortunately for many participants, they do not always heed these warnings. For example, Wajid, a Pakistani immigrant in his forties, described his prior experience:

> I did a study here [at Pharma Phase I], and they did a spinal procedure on me, a spinal tap. I would encourage that on Satan. It's bad. . . . And then what happened is I thought I lay down enough, so I got up, went, took my shower, and apparently some of the spinal fluid, I guess, leaked out. . . . When it leaks out, it messes with your brain. . . . Imagine yourself having a headache as the most severe headache you've ever had. Well, the most severe, severe headache you've ever had, imagine it being a hundred times worse! It's awful. It's terrible! I mean, I cried because it hurt so bad.

Almost every healthy volunteer I interviewed who had participated in one of these studies had some explanation for why they could not stay in bed after their lumbar puncture: one wanted to get his iPod, another did not want to use a bedpan for a bowel movement, another got restless and went for a walk, and the list goes on. In one instance, Craig, an African American serial participant in his thirties, convinced the staff to release him from the study early so he could go home to attend his wife's Christmas party that evening. During the party, he became so sick that a research nurse had to come to his home to administer a "blood patch," in which she drew blood from his arm and injected it into his back at the spinal tap site to help form a clot and reduce the risk of further CSF leakage. Even though Wajid and Craig blamed themselves for their spinal headaches, implying the adverse event could have been avoided by following the staff's instructions, the pain was so extreme that they insisted they would never enroll in another lumbar puncture trial.

It should come as no surprise that healthy volunteers not only share their personal experiences undergoing lumbar punctures, but also tell elaborate stories that could be considered contemporary legends.[9] In these stories, unlike those in which they describe their personal experiences, the research staff are to blame for the spinal tap going awry. The shared tale has a simple storyline: a participant enters a clinical trial that requires a lumbar puncture, the physician makes a mistake inserting the needle, and the participant leaves the clinic in a wheelchair and is paralyzed for life. These stories are essential for placing spinal taps on many serial participants' list of risk filters because their fear of paralysis stems to a large degree from these legends rather than from the trial consent process or others' personal experiences. Kevin, the serial participant who had the bad experience in the ADHD study, had also undergone a spinal tap in a Phase I trial. He told me he had thought his head might "blow open" from the spinal headache. When I asked him whether he would do it again, he replied in a no-nonsense tone, "I would never do it again. It's a big risk." Instead of focusing on his own experience, however, he launched into a contemporary legend to prove the risk: "I seen one lady in here in a wheelchair. Her name's Judith. She was a pool shark. She was killing everybody on the pool table. Older lady. She was in one of these rooms. They pulled her out in a wheelchair. . . . She said, 'Yeah, I'd do it again.' I said, 'Judith, for real? You can't walk now. Are you serious?' I wish I had that on YouTube." This vicarious—and unlikely—experience of seeing Judith brazenly unshaken by being in a wheelchair was the justification Kevin gave for his decision never to participate in another spinal tap study. The spinal headache was ultimately temporary, so being paralyzed for life was Kevin's reason why the risk was too high. This was consistent with his mobilization of other risk filters, such as psychotropic drugs, to avoid long-term problems from clinical trials.

Because studies involving a spinal tap usually pay more for the time required, serial participants are often quite obsessed with talking about this procedure. Some healthy volunteers asserted that no compensation amount would get them to change their minds. Bennett, an African

American in his late twenties, was one such participant: "There's no amount of money, you know. And there've been guys that've walked in here for four days and left out with $5,000 [for a spinal tap study], and more power to you. I'll take the long walk through the park, and I'll do two weeks or three weeks and get the same amount of money, you know, and just do a cholesterol study." Bennett reframed his economic decision-making in terms of time rather than compensation alone, reasoning that he would earn the same amount as if he enrolled in a spinal tap study even if it took him longer to do so.

Compared to Bennett, others were not always as decisive. For Javier, the Latino participant who avoided HIV studies, it all boiled down to how much the study paid: "I never did a spinal tap. So, I don't, I don't think I would, and then again never say never. Because if it's like $12,000 or something like that and they want fluid from your body, wouldn't you do it? . . . To me, it would depend on the situation and how much money is at stake. If it's like one spinal tap and the money was right, I would probably do it." Assertions like Javier's are fascinating because healthy volunteers like him had never participated in a spinal tap study even though they actually did pay more. In a sense, their actions suggest that the risk filter against such studies was quite salient and they were not so heavily swayed by the money. Nonetheless, they often explicitly recited the idiom that "everyone has their price" because they imagined they might participate with sufficient financial incentive to do so.

Cardiac Arrest Studies

Typically risk filters are based on real-life studies. Yet, as I have suggested, fiction can enter into participants' accounts so that HIV studies and spinal taps include dangers that depart from the actual study risks. One story that circulates as a contemporary legend and acts as a risk filter for participants is fully fabricated. It describes a clinical trial in which participants allow the medical team to put them briefly in cardiac arrest then resuscitate them. The period of time varies from 60 seconds to several minutes, and as healthy volunteers retell this contemporary legend, they ruminate on how long the participant is "dead," implying that less time makes the study more legitimate and possibly worth doing. The circulation of this story reveals that participants believe there are very dangerous—and unethical—studies conducted on healthy volunteers.

After hearing stories about the cardiac arrest study, most healthy volunteers asserted unequivocally that they would never consent to such a study. For instance, Abbie, a white woman in her twenties who was participating in her third study, declared, "My friend once told me there was one like they temporarily stopped your heart somewhere like in North Dakota or something. I wouldn't want to do that!" Yet, healthy volunteers' own unwillingness to participate does not necessarily mean they are not intrigued by it. Given that the study is often said to pay anywhere from $25,000 to $100,000, participants' financial need can make this contemporary legend one worth contemplating.

Many healthy volunteers were quite conflicted about the veracity of stories about the cardiac arrest study. They knew how unlikely it was to be true but were unable to disregard it as fiction. For example, Trent, an African American serial participant in his thirties, commented, "I don't know if it's a myth going around or something that actually happened. I heard a story about the university that stops your heart for 60 seconds or whatever, and they pay you—I don't know—$50,000 or whatever. I don't know anybody that's ever done it. [Laughs.] I just hear everybody talking about it. Maybe nobody ever lived to come back and talk about it." Contemporary legends are analytically interesting because listeners know better than to believe the stories, but the narratives still resonate with them enough that they have trouble dismissing them outright (DiFonzo and Bordia 2007). Importantly, the moral of the story, which was also seen with the spinal tap studies, is that healthy volunteers must protect themselves from what can be serious, even life-threatening, risks.

The fascination with contemporary legends like these could be interpreted as a concrete illustration of healthy volunteers' fears about potential Phase I trial risks. Even when participants claim studies are low risk and voice their trust in the process, contemporary legends suggest that many retain some anxiety about the research enterprise—an anxiety they manage through tall tales and humor. The idea that researchers might put participants into cardiac arrest serves a double purpose in underscoring for participants that not all studies are without serious risks and that individuals' desperation can propel them to earn income in dangerous ways. Again, study payment becomes an important proxy for recognizing those risks as too extreme.

Mobilizing Risk Filters

Healthy volunteers actively construct knowledge about the risks of Phase I trials. Boundaries between acceptable and unacceptable risks are created through shared experiences and stories about prior studies. By naming specific types of clinical trials as those to avoid, participants filter their personal risk in relation to this collective knowledge base. Moreover, HIV and psychotropic drugs, lumbar punctures, and cardiac arrest are particularly powerful filters because they can operate in an abstract way. Individual participants do not need to know someone who actually enrolled in any of these clinical trials to feel strongly that they personally should avoid those studies altogether. These stories, rumors, and contemporary legends create fear and shape participants' risk perceptions. They also further confirm participants' deeper epistemological position that study compensation is tied to risk, especially risk of long-term harm. Importantly, the drawing of risk boundaries also helps to buttress participants' belief in the relative safety of most studies. As long as they mobilize collective risk filters, participants assume they are insulated from harm.

Thus, risk filters act as guides for healthy volunteers to protect themselves. This is particularly important in the face of decisions influenced by both economic incentives and perceptions of risk. A bottom-up epistemology by and for healthy volunteers aims to encourage good decision-making that is not clouded by money. This is evident in the advice Kevin, who, as we have seen, had done quite a few of these riskier studies, gave his friends:

> I'll tell some of my friends, "It's like when you call the recruiters, the only thing you hear is the compensation. Listen to what they're saying!" "Oh, we're paying $3,500 for this?" "We've got a schizophrenic [drug]." "We're gonna chop your head off." Or, "We're gonna put your feet in a basket." And people are quick to say, "Yeah [I'll do it]." [Laughs.] Next time I see Joe Schmoe, he has no head. "Where's your feet at, man?" People say yes to anything. It's all about listening to what they actually

tell you. The first thing you hear is [the compensation] . . . your heart is pounding: "God, let me see if I can get a $6,000 study."

Although Kevin adopted a joking tone, his point was a serious one: healthy volunteers must be cautious about what risks a study might have, even when the pay falls within a more average range, such as $3,500. Similarly, although Russell, an African American long-time serial participant in his forties, was unabashedly focused on the money, he insisted that there were limits as to what he would do: "[The decision to participate] all boils down to dollars and cents. . . . I normally read the consent form and pretty much do something I wanna do, so that's how I figure out what [drug] I wanna take. . . . 'Cause a study could pay you six grand, but they might wanna stop your heart beating or something. Nah, I don't think I'll do that, you know what I mean? So it's dollars and sense, have sense [laughs]." Russell cleverly played on the homonym of cents/sense that linked his desire to earn money from studies with his perception that they are not risk-free. Both Kevin and Russell explicitly used common risk filters as they advocated that participants be wary about studies rather than make foolish decisions driven by money. They also situated control of Phase I risks in participants' hands, emphasizing the need for wise choices about the risks to which researchers might expose healthy volunteers.

Appealing to the Protective Power of Health

For healthy volunteers, risks are epistemologically contingent not only on the studies offered but also on individual participants' health. This perspective engenders two complementary beliefs that merit further exploration. First, many believe their own good health ensures they cannot be harmed in a Phase I trial. Second, when someone else is harmed, it is taken as proof that this other person was really not as healthy as they seemed. In both instances, healthy volunteers see their individual risk as low.

The remarkable part of participants viewing their health as protective is that by definition all healthy volunteers equally share this attribute. Yet, many engaged in self-comparisons to judge themselves healthier than other participants. For them, this meant they were ultimately at less risk. Some participants even asserted explicitly that any serious adverse events were unlikely or impossible. For example, first-time participant Sasha, an African American in her late twenties, indicated, "I know I'm healthy. I used to run track and things like that, so I know physically I'm pretty healthy. So, hopefully, you know, I can be a person who won't suffer too many adverse side effects." In a variation on the theme, Troy, the first-time participant who spoke about HIV studies, highlighted how his age provided an advantage to his health and ensured his safety: "I think the best time to do it [participate in studies] is if you're young and your body has a better chance of repairing itself. When you are old, when it's just, you know, there's not much left in the tank, you know? So, I don't know, I think I'm in the right time of my life where I feel like I can fight off a lot of infections or I could recuperate from a lot of things." Of course, Sasha and Troy were cognizant of the risks associated with the studies in which they had enrolled, but they nevertheless assumed that they personally would not be harmed. Although they were most certainly aware that all participants must be healthy enough to qualify, they still saw themselves as more protected than others.

More experienced participants had even more firmly entrenched ideas about the protective power of their own health. Having just finished his third clinical trial, Drew, a white man in his mid-forties, described how his positive health behaviors made him unconcerned about study risks. He reflected, "It's kinda pretty general things that could go wrong [in studies] and whatnot. But I don't know, I just had a good feeling that, you know, that I'd be fine. I don't drink, . . . so my liver's not really damaged with anything. I don't use a lot of, like I say, any other kind of drugs or anything. I don't smoke, so I thought, well, I'm healthy and so there's not much that could really hurt me too bad here." Drew had never experienced any adverse events, but other participants who had had AEs attributed the short-term nature of their symptoms to how healthy they really were. Jake, a white man in his late thirties, colorfully demonstrated this phenomenon when he said, "The side effects [in this study] hit me really hard. I looked like death warmed over, and so I spent most of the day curled up in a ball, waiting for the day to go by. . . . [But] I know that by this time tomorrow, I will be right as rain. So whatever I go through now, you know, people say, 'Well, doesn't it suck?' Well, yeah, any job sucks. That's why they pay you to do it." Jake had nearly been disqualified from the study because his body-mass index (BMI) was high, but this did not affect his perception of his health or his supposition that he could bounce back from his adverse events very quickly.

Beyond general statements about their health, participants also noted how their status as "healthy" was constantly reinforced by the screening process. The physical examinations and laboratory tests technically assess whether individuals qualify for each clinical trial, but serial participants often take this information as essential proof that their study involvement has not had any negative, lasting effects on their health. Julius, an African American in his late thirties who had done eight studies, articulated this point explicitly: "And you have to be healthy [to participate]. That's the one thing that comforts me. At the end of each study, you have a physical, and then you go from a physical maybe to a screening [for a new study]. So you get checked out thoroughly—all your blood work, your lab work, your heart rate, EKGs, and blood pressure, everything—to make sure that you're healthy before the next study. So that means that you're okay. So that's comforting to me to know, there's a sense of having a physical [to tell you] like you're always healthy." In Julius's case, any lingering worries he might have had, due perhaps to some ambivalence he felt about the risk, were cast away each time he got a clean bill of health from a Phase I clinic. Obviously, the possibility that participants could be told they are not healthy is always present, but at the same time, it is not fully acknowledged because the assumption is that their good health will only be *confirmed* with each physical examination. This is then used as evidence that the clinical trials in which they have enrolled are safe.

The second way participants leverage their view of how health is protective against study risks explains *others'* experience of adverse events. Specifically, when something untoward happens to another participant, healthy volunteers typically assume the adverse event must be that person's fault. In the vein of "blaming the victim," many claimed adverse events happen to people who lied about their health and managed to trick the clinic into believing they were eligible to participate. As Vera, a Latina in her twenties participating in her second study, argued, "We have to be in good health [to participate]. Because many times people lie about their health, and they take risks and do the studies anyways without being in good health" (translated from Spanish). Trent, the participant who talked about the cardiac arrest study, determined that people's poor health behaviors jeopardized them in studies: "What I understand [is that] most adverse reactions are people that were probably doing something that they shouldn't have been doing before they got into the study, or [they're] on some type of medication that they didn't inform the doctors they were on, . . . and [so they] had an adverse reaction." In this framework, these other participants knowingly take risks, so it is their fault if they have an adverse reaction. Yet, this perspective creates a dilemma about how these individuals could pass their screening visits and qualify for the same study as people who are truly healthy.

Narratives that blame the victims of adverse events for what befalls them are important epistemological measures to make sense of Phase I risks. If health can truly be protective, then it cannot fail to safeguard participants from adverse events. Thus, the only explanation for why another healthy volunteer could be harmed is that they are not actually healthy. As we saw earlier, this approach to risk creates the possibility of simultaneously acknowledging and minimizing the risk of studies because whereas others might be harmed, one's own perfect health will see one through.

Model Organism Epistemology

Residential research clinics provide the context for collective knowledge production about Phase I study risks. Healthy volunteers have the opportunity to interact and tell stories about studies they have done or heard about. By adopting a shared understanding of trial risks, participants become further enmeshed in the research enterprise as model organisms. In developing their own epistemological approach to Phase I trials by cataloging and differentiating risks, healthy volunteers ultimately aim to exert some control over their risk exposure. This is particularly important when they are motivated to enroll for the financial compensation, which many healthy volunteers see as making them vulnerable to risks should they participate indiscriminately.

Risk filters are thereby one mechanism through which healthy volunteers actively acknowledge and avoid risk as part of their Phase I participation. These function to classify certain studies as ones to avoid completely, based on the amount and type of drug, procedures, compensation, and long-term risk. In some respects, what makes these studies unique is that serial participants do not have to investigate the specific risks of trials for which they have risk filters because they already have enough information—regardless of its technical or scientific accuracy—to make the decision to decline enrollment.

Likewise, just as all studies are not the same, neither are all healthy volunteers. By perceiving one's own good health as protective, participants can explain away adverse events they witness by assuming others are not as healthy as themselves, even to the point of deceiving the clinic about health conditions or compromising health behaviors. In this way, being healthy—including maintaining or even enhancing one's health—acts as a mechanism to control and diminish one's exposure to risk.

Of course, regardless of how well healthy volunteers assess the differential risks of Phase I trials, any control they assume they have is illusory. Choosing studies wisely might successfully diminish their risk, but they can still get hurt. Good health does not make participants immune to risks, and there are many clinical trials for which there is no collective risk filter. Yet, because Phase I trials are by and large very safe, healthy volunteers' view of risk and control is not commonly challenged. That is, participants are rarely confronted with counter-evidence to undermine their beliefs about risks. Indeed, participants' continued safety further confirms their collective knowledge base. In addition, protecting themselves from harm takes on further instrumental value, as the next chapter explores, because staying safe in studies preserves the longevity of their participation.

Speculating on Health

We have seen that as part of their management of risk, many healthy volunteers claim to be selective about their Phase I participation. I witnessed such selectivity in action at Academic Phase I. At the time of my visit, the clinic was conducting a dose-escalation trial of a hepatitis C investigational drug. The trial had been underway for several months, and as the dose increased in each new group of healthy volunteers, the adverse events had intensified, with a greater percentage of participants vomiting. My visit overlapped with recruitment and check-in for the final group, which was slated to receive 1,600 milligrams of the drug. To the research staff's credit, they did nothing during recruitment to downplay the expected adverse events. To the contrary, they informed prospective participants very clearly about what to anticipate, thereby providing experiential information as part of the consent process. Or, more to the point, Patty, the recruiter, warned in her down-to-earth way that participants should "plan on puking" during the study.

Although the trial paid well for the time commitment—$1,500 for four nights in the clinic plus an outpatient visit two weeks later—the clinic struggled to fill the eight-person cohort. Recall that many healthy volunteers use drug dose as a risk filter, so the combination of the high dose and Patty's candor led many prospective participants to decline after receiving the information. One of these participants was Jay, an experienced African American healthy volunteer in his twenties. He had arrived early for his screening appointment, so I interviewed him about his clinical trial experiences before Patty reviewed the study's consent packet with him. Explicitly referencing the risk filter, Jay asserted he would not enroll in studies with doses higher than 900 milligrams. He noted, however, that clinic recruiters provide such limited information by phone that it often necessitates a screening appointment to determine that the study falls outside his criteria. As Jay mentioned this, I wondered what he would think of the hepatitis C study's 1,600 milligram dose, but I asked instead whether the inconvenience of screening ever prompted him to join a study he would otherwise prefer to avoid. Jay considered this for a moment before replying, "I think most people go ahead and go through with the screening [tests], [to] see if they make it into the study, and then some people they screen somewhere else and find something else. . . . Most of the time, I would walk away from it." Thinking of the hepatitis C study as a test of Jay's adherence to his criteria, I avoided speaking about it during our interview. Later, Jay bee-lined to me after leaving Patty's office. He had declined the study because of the high dose, commenting, "She told me they're barfing in there . . . [so] I'm gonna pass." He also accused Academic Phase I of conducting more dangerous studies than other clinics he frequented, attributing this to its location in a hospital. Shaking his head, he concluded that the clinic must be taking advantage of first-time participants because they would not know any better but to enroll.

Over the next several days, prospective participants streamed into Academic Phase I to screen for the hepatitis C study. Yet, so difficult was it to get individuals' consent that Neil, the clinic director and physician-investigator, worried that the study would have to be postponed if more participants were not willing to enroll. With only two days to go before check-in, the clinic finally filled the eight-person cohort. (Contrary to Jay's belief, however, only one of the eight who signed up was a first-time participant.) This was hardly an unqualified success, however, given the staff were unable to identify additional healthy volunteers to serve as study alternates.

The problems intensified on the first day of the study. Only five of the eight participants checked in, and the inclusion-exclusion criteria for the trial had been modified. The sponsor now required healthy volunteers to have very low liver enzymes (i.e., healthier than typically "normal" levels) due to significant impairment in liver function in the previous cohort's participants.[1] The change in criteria created two new issues for the study. First, Neil voiced concern that some of the participants would become ineligible for the study, which would be determined by the routine lab work done as part of check-in procedures. Second, the clinic now had to re-obtain participants' consent after providing them with the updated risk information.

While the five healthy volunteers awaited their blood work results, Ellen, a white nurse manager, gathered them in Academic Phase I's tiny lounge. She explained that the clinic had received new study information, and she detailed how some of the participants in the prior group had experienced temporary but serious negative effects on their livers. Tony, a Hispanic African American man in his mid-forties, asked if there was a risk of permanent liver damage, and Ellen reassured them that all the "affected livers" had since returned to normal. Shirley, an African American in her thirties, followed up to ask how much time it took for their enzyme levels to rebound. Admitting she did not have all the facts, Ellen said she believed it was less than two weeks but that Neil could provide more information. No one asked any additional questions, and all five participants agreed to continue with the study and signed the updated consent form. The group then dispersed, and the participants went to find their assigned beds and settle into their rooms.

Within a few hours, the research team had the results from the participants' intake blood work and urinalysis, and two of the five did not meet the new liver-enzyme criteria. Neil telephoned his pharmaceutical company contact to verify that the company still wanted to exclude those participants given the small number remaining. His contact swiftly decided to postpone dosing, instructing Neil to send all five participants home and to recruit and reschedule a newly constituted cohort as soon as possible.

It was left to Ellen to break the news of the postponed study to the participants. She again gathered them in the clinic's lounge. They responded with disgruntlement to the loss of their expected $1,500. Sidney, an African American in his late forties who had done more than twenty studies almost exclusively at Academic Phase I, put Ellen on the spot asking her how he was supposed to pay his bills. She quickly offered everyone $200 on behalf of the clinic because they had showed up in "good faith" to complete the study. She also told them that whoever met all the inclusion-exclusion criteria could participate in the rescheduled study, and those who did not pass their labs would meet with a physician before being discharged. Ellen started to leave the room, but the group stopped her. A few participants blamed the clinic for the study's failure to start that day. They complained that the compensation had been set too low considering the drug's high dose, stating that this was obviously why three people had chosen not to check in that day. By this point, Ellen no longer hid her irritation, and in a tone that was not quite professional, she told them that no one was obligated to return for the rescheduled study.

After Ellen disentangled herself from the group, she fumed to the other research staff about the sponsor postponing the study and the participants' reaction to the news. Having followed her down the hallway, I inquired whether the missing three participants had contacted the clinic or simply failed to show up that day. Directing her frustration at my question, she said two had called with "pretty transparent excuses" but she had no doubt they had not come because "they didn't want to barf."[2] Ellen's callousness in this unguarded moment communicated clearly that she did not respect their decision to avoid a study that would (temporarily) make them sick.[3]

From the perspective of a healthy volunteer, however, declining participation in a study in which one *expects* adverse events like vomiting is quite rational. Participants could be seen as voting with their feet that the potential harm from the hepatitis C study was not worth the compensation, whether they chose to find another study or simply abandoned the idea of enrolling in one. Indeed, joining such a study almost compelled the healthy volunteers who had shown up that day to justify their choice. Prior to finding out the study was postponed, Shirley explicated, "Like the study that I'm in right now with the sixteen hundred [milligrams], it's . . . not necessarily something that I [normally] would jump at. But what did attract me to the study was the fact that it was so short. . . . I also made sure with Ellen . . . that with the last panel of fourteen hundred milligrams, that everybody bounced back and how quickly everybody bounced back with their labs and stuff like that. That was really important." Shirley later admitted she had been scrambling to find studies open to women of childbearing potential. With overdue bills weighing on her, she felt she could not afford to be as selective as she might otherwise have been. Even so, she rationalized her decision by minimalizing the risk: it was a large dose but previous healthy volunteers had recovered from the adverse events.

Shirley was an exception in this instance. Unlike dozens of other prospective participants, including Jay, she was one of the five people who actually checked in for the study. Her motivation for enrolling—a need for quick income to manage debt—was not unusual. The bigger surprise was that economic need would not make *others* compromise in their decision-making as well. Academic Phase I had failed to find enough willing healthy volunteers for the study to go forward. Was it simply that at $1,500, the study did not offer enough money for the high dose of the drug? This is a clearly plausible interpretation, one that would be supported by how the group reacted to the study's postponement. Yet, if—as we saw earlier—healthy volunteers are generally desensitized to Phase I risks and perceive adverse events as transient discomforts, why would something as banal as vomiting stop them from earning the income?

To explain why healthy volunteers might decline studies like this one, we need to situate Phase I participation in relation to the myriad studies and clinics available to healthy volunteers. If study options are limited, as Shirley's were, then individuals may have to consent to temporary adverse events. For most healthy volunteers, however, there are many studies to choose from.[4] In this context, why would they select a clinical trial they *know* would make them vomit and likely impair their liver function? This question is even more salient for serial participants who claim they never experience any adverse events at all when enrolled in studies.

As model organisms with the license to choose among Phase I trials, serial participants' risk framework is recalibrated. Healthy volunteers judge not only the potential for immediate discomfort in studies but also the possibility that those symptoms are indicative of harm that could affect their model organism status. In the context of serial enrollment, study risks are no longer restricted to each investigational drug or procedure but include an appraisal of how one study might affect their ability to qualify for subsequent studies. Thus, to understand serial participants' decision-making, risk cannot be viewed as if each trial exists in a vacuum; instead, risk is evaluated in terms of sustaining Phase I participation over time.

The primary risk that preoccupies serial participants is qualifying for and completing studies when they screen. Whether they rely solely on clinical trials for their income or enroll sporadically to help make ends meet, these participants are highly concerned about their ability to pass all the screening tests and qualify as healthy volunteers. Anxiety about qualifying stems from the near-universal experience of occasional screen failure as well as facing competition from other healthy volunteers to win a spot in each trial. To reduce the risk of ineligibility for clinical trials, most serial participants engage in a kind of somatic speculation on their future health. They invest energy and resources into maintaining or enhancing their health for continued Phase I participation. This includes reflecting on how their choices about studies and their everyday health behaviors affect measurable aspects of their bodily functions. Concretely, this means participating selectively, such as declining studies like the one at Academic Phase I, to minimize any toll on their bodies that could jeopardize their qualifying for the next study. It also involves the creation of explanatory frameworks for cultivating the best-suited body for clinical trials.[5] Whether it has to do with diet and exercise, avoiding recreational drugs and alcohol, or managing stress and sleep, serial participants postulate optimal routines to gain access to studies and for detoxifying their bodies after completing them. Participants construct such knowledge through a process of trial and error, observing which practices succeed for them, and by word of mouth, hearing what has worked for others. In triangulating multiple information sources and evaluating how behavioral changes seem to affect their physiology, they theorize the body with the goal of producing health. In short, they attempt to maximize their study participation by optimizing their bodies to the needs of the research enterprise. This is the true measure of becoming a model organism because these healthy volunteers allow Phase I trials to inform their everyday health behaviors and their broader orientation to health.

The Risk of *Not* Participating

Phase I participation requires finding available studies, passing all the screening tests, being selected by the clinics to enroll, and passing the same screening tests again on the day the study begins. Clinics commonly inform participants that no one is officially in a clinical trial until they receive the first dose of the investigational drug. Until that point, participants can be disqualified from or unneeded for the study, and then there is the possibility that the study will be postponed or canceled by the sponsor. The uncertainty of the process is perfectly represented by the hepatitis C study at Academic Phase I insofar as some participants were disqualified after check-in due to their lab work and the study was postponed, denying even those who remained eligible from continuing in it that day.

For serial participants, the unpredictability of making it to the point of dosing becomes recast as a risk. Carlos, a Latino in his thirties participating in his third study, explicitly articulated this: "It's kinda hard to get in because you have to come for the screening and . . . if you're not healthy, you not gonna pass. Even if you're healthy, . . . you never know, you know, maybe your blood pressure goes up or goes down and, like I say, [it] could be anything that you might not stay [after check-in]. 'Cause it's a risky thing: we come, maybe we stay [for the study or] maybe not." The real risk from this standpoint is that participants might not earn any money if they do not dose.

Because of the vicissitudes of the process, participants assume that the risk of rejection from each study they pursue will be high, regardless of how healthy they are. David, a white man in his forties who had participated in six studies, provided a vivid example: "I did one here [at Pharma Phase I] for like $12,000, and I came, I passed the screening, they invited me to come to do it. I was happy! When I come in [for the study check-in], they said my liver enzymes were up. That'll get you out. I was crying, literally. . . . I didn't know how to act. I was like, 'Oh man, I needed this one!'" Being excluded at the last minute can be especially stressful when participants have already counted on the income they expected to earn in a specific clinical trial. Bennett, an African American in his late twenties, bemoaned this aspect of studies: "The thing that the lab-rat thing lacks is consistency, you know. If my rent is due and I get into a study and the study gets canceled, my rent [check] gets canceled. If something happens like my muscle enzymes are up or something's off and I don't get into the study, I'm screwed. . . . It has its pros and it has its cons, and that's probably the biggest con for me is just that, you know, it's not guaranteed. Not only are you competing with yourself, your own body, you're competing with other people, you know?" Bennett's framing of competition highlights the risk associated with his economic dependence on Phase I trials. He must pass all the screening tests, but even when those tests come out well, someone else could be selected instead.

Competition from healthy people all vying to enroll in clinical trials was a common theme among serial participants. For example, Alexandra, a white transwoman who had participated in about a dozen studies, emphasized, "This is becoming competitive, too, like the job market. It's like applying for a job here [at the clinic]. That's how I look at it. And they pick the people that they think are gonna make the best candidates, you know, so it's not guaranteed. Nothing's guaranteed in this life." The competition creates additional stress to an already nerve-wracking process. Some clinics create first-come, first-served policies to make transparent which participants have priority for enrollment. Joseph, an African American in his thirties, reported, "You have to be one of the first people to call about the study, yeah, and then you have to be one of the first people to show up in the morning for the screening. So, oh, it may get to the point where people are sleeping out, like they're waiting for tickets to a concert. [Laughs hysterically.] You know what I'm saying?" This narrative underscores the urgency some participants might feel to improve their odds of qualifying in a competitive environment.

Getting into studies takes time and energy, and participants become significantly invested in a process that does not necessarily compensate them financially for their effort. The risk is even greater for individuals who must clear their work schedules for study confinement. If they are selected for the study but are discharged without dosing, they might not have the option of returning to work after having asked for the time off, thereby risking both chances of earning income. In one such case, Brad, a white man in his thirties who had signed up at Mega Phase I to participate in his first clinical trial, was told the day before his study check-in that the confinement schedule had changed and that he was needed for different dates. He had already taken the days off from his job at a home improvement store, however, and he could not get those shifts back. Contemplating this outcome, he said, "It's still a lot of money [for the study], but I guess it wouldn't have been cost effective for me to miss work." Situations like these, coupled with participants' economic dependence on Phase I trials, can quickly make them feel powerless. As a result, many seek ways to exert more control over their participation, chiefly through the screening process.

Experiencing Failure

Over the course of participating in clinical trials, healthy volunteers eventually fail a screening. There are many reasons for this, including an out-of-range BMI, elevated liver enzymes, and even evidence of illegal substance use, such as tetrahydrocannabinol (THC) (i.e., from marijuana use) in their urine. Whereas one might expect prospective participants to say that some reasons that disqualify them from studies are beyond their control, most people blame themselves instead. This is obvious for cases in which screen failures would appear to be more clearly linked to individuals' behaviors. For example, if someone indulged in too much alcohol or smoked tobacco before screening, these activities could be their own category of screen failure, one in which the prospective participant would be responsible for the negative outcome. However, participants also admonish themselves for screen failures due to out-of-range vital signs or blood work that have no immediate ties to behaviors. For instance, if someone had low red-blood-cell counts or high white-blood-cell counts, that person might be expected to think there was little to nothing he or she could have done to prevent the screen failure. Yet, the vast majority of serial participants routinely blame themselves for the whole range of disqualifications, believing that everything is within their control and that they can secure a place in studies with the right discipline and routine.

Serial participants often perceive the experience of screen failure as an opportunity for reflection and behavioral change. In short, they seek a cause for the unwanted effect. Many such participants conduct a postmortem of the events leading up to their screening to analyze what produced the putative problem with their body. In some instances, the causal pathways are more persuasive than others. For example, Albert, an African American serial participant in his mid-fifties, was a self-described "health nut" who loved to ride his bike, regularly did calisthenics, and used weight-training equipment at home. Despite the energy he spent maintaining his health, he confessed, "A couple of times I've had a little, slight battle with the BMI." After missing a few studies, Albert compensated for this risk by developing a new screening strategy: "I would have to make sure that I got myself underneath that [BMI threshold], and so there would be times they [the clinic staff] would say, 'Okay, well, we can set you up for a screening date. The first screening date is such and such and such and the last one is—,' and I would say, 'Give me the last one.' So [that way] I would have enough time to bring my BMI down." Albert would be at a disadvantage if that clinic selected participants on a first-come, first-served basis, but if his weight was too high, then he would have no chance of qualifying. Ironically, some healthy volunteers struggle with their weight because serial participation creates a sedentary lifestyle. While they are confined to a clinic, participants might eat high-fat diets and are restricted from exercise. Unless they combat this effect, many find they gain weight after months or years of pursuing clinical trials. Albert's strategy of working out between studies was also a compensatory measure to counterbalance the effects of the twelve studies he had done.

At the same time, exercise produces another case of clear cause and effect in screen failures. Strenuous exercise raises liver enzymes, so clinics instruct prospective participants to abstain from working out for 24 to 48 hours before screening. However, manual labor and housework can have the same effect on the body as recreational exercise. Arnel, a Filipino immigrant in his fifties, was enrolled in only his second study, but he had failed several screenings because of raised liver enzymes. The problem for Arnel was that he worked construction jobs. Initially, he had not realized his job was comparable to exercise, and he recalled, "It messed it up when I went to screen for a study, and I fail because of my work; I did some kind of workout, you know, [by lifting] heavy things." After realizing the problem, Arnel scheduled his screening visits on mornings following his day off from work. With both BMI and exercise, the simple cause and effect presents an obvious—but perhaps not always easy—solution to correct the problem before the next screening.

In many other instances, the causal pathway to explain screen failures requires more creativity on participants' part. For example, Bob, the man living out of his car who participated in studies throughout the country, confidently asserted an unusual reason for a prior disqualification: "I screened . . . and didn't get in because supposedly my body was trying to heal or fix something. They said my enzyme level and something was too high, and I attributed it to I dropped something on my toe. My toe was kinda messed up." Whether or not Bob's explanation was correct, it reveals how healthy volunteers theorize the body to make sense of disqualifying laboratory values.

The impetus to find a cause for screen failure is even stronger for participants who travel for studies. In these cases, the travel itself often becomes the culprit. When musing about screenings he had failed, Mikhail, a Russian immigrant in his forties with a long clinical trial history, said, "A lot of times a person . . . expends so much energy, so much effort to get to a location [to screen that it] can actually have their whole internal body working system so offset that it will actually show up in the labs and they will exclude you." Mikhail then described his exclusion from a recent study due to elevated liver enzymes. From his perspective, this happened because he had driven all night to make an eight-hour trip to screen. Mikhail concluded, "Actually, that was elevation of bilirubin, just part of the liver, and that happens—or can occur, I should say—to a person when they're exhausting themselves, simply by being awake and just stressing over something." For Mikhail, the association between driving so far for a screening appointment and being disqualified was both obvious and logical. Generally, the link between high liver enzymes and fatigue tracks in the other direction (i.e., the physiological state leads to the experience of fatigue), but Mikhail illustrates how serial participants' efforts to screen can potentially undermine their ability to qualify.

Thus, participants' accounts of their screen failures generally focus on something they did (or should have done). When it comes to explicating why *others* have been disqualified from studies, their blaming tends to be even more intense.[6] Specifically, participants frequently assume others consumed alcohol or illicit drugs prior to their screening. As an example of this, Robert, an African American in his twenties who had participated in a dozen studies, opined, "A lot of people I see them cry [about how] they didn't make it [i.e., qualify]. . . . Sometimes they'll drink before they come; why would you drink alcohol when you know you're coming [in]? . . . You have to be responsible and focused on what you're trying to do." Rather than expressing any empathy, Robert and many others distance themselves from these disqualified participants by accusing them of irresponsible behavior.

Whereas most patterns of blame are based on specific actions or inactions, participants can fault their own bodies directly when the screening involves an unusual test or the study requires very narrow inclusion-exclusion criteria. For instance, Dennis, an African American in his twenties, discovered he could not qualify for multiple cohorts of the same clinical trial. The screenings included measurements of participants' lung capacity using a spirometer. As Dennis recounted, it "involved inhaling and then breathing out for as long as possible, exhale.

And I guess I just don't have the wind power 'cause I wasn't able to do it. Every single time I screened for the study—I screened for it at least three times already—I wasn't able to, you know, meet the criteria that they wanted." Unlike other procedures, this atypical screening test became its own obstacle that was outside Dennis's control. After undergoing the test several times, Dennis ultimately decided that his body was incapable and he would never meet the criteria.[7]

Participants do recognize that pharmaceutical companies narrowly define "health," which means their physiology might exclude them from clinical trials from time to time. Yet, participants typically blame pharmaceutical companies for their screen failures only when they are told they are too healthy to qualify. This is, of course, unwelcome news when they have made the effort to go through the screening process. Pete, a white serial participant in his late fifties, wished the clinics gave more of the inclusion-exclusion information over the phone when he booked his screening appointments. He complained, "I have a very standard resting heart rate, a low [rate], which is good. They go, 'Well, my goodness, you know, you're very healthy for your age.' I go, 'Yeah, well, that doesn't matter when the client [i.e., sponsor] wants the heart rate above 50, and my EKG shows 48 or 49 and I'm excused from the study.' You know, I need to know that the client will take that heart rate *before* I show up [to screen]." Pete's knowledge of his heart rate and the criteria pharmaceutical companies use for Phase I trials exemplifies how healthy volunteers, as model organisms, can be quite savvy about which studies they are best suited for.

Examples like Pete's may be the exceptions that prove the rule, but they offer little insight into why participants typically overlook the variability in clinical trial criteria. If participants were to externalize the blame for their screen failures, they might be forced to perceive the inclusion-exclusion criteria as unfair, which would position them as powerless against those criteria. If instead participants believe they have control over the process, they are propelled to find not only explanations for screen failures but also tactics to improve their chances of qualifying in the future.

Selectivity about Studies

Serial participation introduces its own obstacles to qualifying for studies, especially for healthy volunteers who are keen to sign up for the next study as soon as they leave the last. This is because the most recent Phase I trial can create transient—or more rarely long-term—changes to participants' liver or kidney function and their red- and white-blood-cell counts, among other effects. To guard against this, some participants might "shop around" for the best study by screening at multiple clinics before deciding which study to do. The more clinical trials that are available at one time at one or multiple clinics, the more opportunity there is to be selective in these ways. The Academic Phase I hepatitis C study offers a concrete example of this. Participants who enrolled in that study would experience raised liver enzymes, and someone who wanted to screen for another clinical trial would have trouble qualifying until his or her levels returned to normal. In a situation like that, why settle on that clinical trial when there might be another available elsewhere with less impact on the body and possibly even more pay? This was exactly the logic that motivated Jay to walk away.

Even financial compensation must be evaluated in the context not of one single study but how that study might impact future Phase I income. Marcus, an African American in his forties with nearly 20 years of study participation, avoided all vaccine and intravenous drug-infusion studies regardless of how much they paid. He declared, "Now a pill? You can't catch nothing with a pill. When they inject you with something, [by comparison,] they telling you they giving you something. No, that's just ass stupid, 'cause what if they can't give you nothing for that [to counteract it] and can't get it outta you? That ain't gonna happen, captain. No, I don't need no money *that* bad." I could not resist asking, "So even if it was a really big stipend, you still wouldn't do that kind of study?" This pushed Marcus to give an example:

> Nah. Just because that actually—. Well, to me, that actually involves risk, you see what I'm saying? Because like we was in Texas one time, and a buddy of mine did one for the flu. They gave him the flu, and clearly there's no cure for the flu, and it messed him up so long with however they did it, he couldn't do a study for like four or five months. So, the thing about that is, yeah, you can go get [$]10,000 for a month [in a study], but if they inject you with something, with like a vaccine or something, then you know you shut down for quite a few months, so you actually *losing money*, you know what I mean?

Wanting to make sure I was following his point, I quickly asked, "So in his case, he couldn't screen to do a study?" Marcus laughed, "Yeah, he actually screened, but his labs were so messed up because of the vaccine and all that, the juice wasn't worth the squeeze." Marcus's concern about risk shifted away from the specific clinical trial to how potential adverse events could affect his future participation. He did not want exposure to vaccines or injected drugs to jeopardize his ability to qualify for subsequent trials. Wondering how he might have understood risks more generally, I followed up by asking, "What about short-term risks or side effects?" He replied, "As long as I know it's not a vaccine, I wanna do it. You know what I mean? I don't care if it's gonna have me seeing purple elephants or whatever, 'cause eventually it's gonna wear off, seriously." Marcus expected all adverse events to resolve eventually, so his decision-making rested more heavily on the question of how those bodily changes would impact his ability to qualify for new clinical trials.

Beyond the investigational drugs, the high volume of blood draws in Phase I trials might also affect healthy volunteers' future participation. Don, an African American in his late forties, had an interesting spin on the cost of blood collection. Seeing it in large part as racialized risk, Don commented, "That's one thing I try to stay away from, ones [studies] taking too much blood, because I'm a black male. A lot of black males have . . . some type of condition where your blood doesn't build back as fast, some type of genetic thing. And, plus, if you take too much blood, you could be tired for the next couple of weeks if your hemoglobin is low. So, if it's something [a clinical trial] that's taking a whole lot of blood, I gotta be compensated [better]." For Don, the study payment had to be commensurate with the blood draws' effect on his body, but his apprehension quickly expanded to qualifying for future trials. He added, "But it's like, in this study game you gotta be careful . . . 'cause you'll scar your veins up. . . . After a while if your veins is scarred up, they don't want you no more." Even though qualifying for new studies is generally perceived through the lens of passing screening tests, Don tapped into another important point about the longevity of healthy volunteers' Phase I participation. Specifically, as we saw earlier, clinics could refuse to accept serial participants for specific studies if their veins are unsuitable to the protocol. When this occurs repeatedly, it could be considered an instance of the model organism reaching the end of its utility for the

research enterprise due to its past overuse. Thus, to extend their participation, healthy volunteers need to keep their veins in good condition by
choosing studies with fewer blood draws.

A complementary worry about future participation is whether long-
term Phase I trial involvement could damage individuals' health. This
view of risk presumes each clinical trial is safe, but the cumulative effect
of serial participation might be harmful. In the short term, this drives
participants to detox their system by drinking a lot of water during studies and observing dietary regimens after they leave the clinic. Part of the
goal is to flush the investigational drugs out of their bodies as quickly
as possible. Kevin, an African American in his forties who had been
participating full time in studies for the prior four years, described his
efforts to protect himself from long-term health effects: "It's not really
a healthy thing to take medication. . . . I'm finding out it works on the
liver and the brain. . . . I know how to clean myself out [after studies];
that's the secret—herbs that keeps your liver clean. . . . As long as I stay
on top of the way I'm cleaning my body out, I'm good." Regardless of the
degree of risk actually associated with long-term participation,[8] these
concerns with "cleaning" their bodies shape healthy volunteers' orientation to Phase I trials. Their goal is to maintain their health, both to
remain eligible for studies into the future and to avoid any permanent
deleterious effects from investigational drugs.

Mastering the Screening Process

Part of becoming a model organism for Phase I trials is learning how to
maximize one's chances of qualifying. Being selective about enrollment
is only one component of this process. In addition, serial participants
develop health behaviors to meet the criteria pharmaceutical companies require of healthy volunteers. These behaviors can be highly
personalized—developed in response to their own screen failure—or
they might arise from more general tips that circulate among serial
participants. From blood pressure to enzymes, participants leverage
their collective expertise to try to exert mastery over the uncertainty of
screening.

A first step to prevailing in the screening process is recognizing how
anxiety about qualifying has physical manifestations. Some participants

even suggested they suffered from "White Coat Syndrome," which caused their blood pressure to rise at the mere sight of clinicians. Wesley, a study veteran with ten years of Phase I participation, reflected on this phenomenon: "If I get nervous [during a screening], sometimes I might not pass. It's like I get my nerves. . . . Like, my blood pressure or my heart rate might be high. . . . Your body has to be like in the mood to do this type of stuff. You know, you have to be like prepared for this mentally, physically." Mental preparation for Wesley and other serial participants included visualization and breathing exercises to reduce their stress.

Blood pressure is also a broader problem, with some participants identifying it as a real medical issue that always threatens to eliminate them from studies. For instance, Jeremy, a white man in his thirties, was in his sixth study but had been disqualified from many others due to "high" blood pressure. Unlike other participants, Jeremy did not perceive his results to be an artifact of screening; he suspected he had a real tendency toward hypertension. As long as he wanted to continue enrolling, medication was certainly not an option because he would then be disqualified for taking a pharmaceutical (and/or for officially being hypertensive). Hearing about many natural remedies from other participants, Jeremy excitedly told me about an "easy and effective" method with which he recently had success: "Funny enough is like somebody told me to eat some oranges and it lowers your blood pressure. And my blood pressure was testing out over 140/100 for like the last couple of studies I tried in the last couple of months. But I tested it out yesterday at 119/78, so I'm thinking oranges work." Wesley and Jeremy delineate how serial participants engage in multipronged tactics to improve their blood pressure results, from altering their diets to finding ways to relax during screening visits.

Although serial participants might select studies to limit the amount of blood collected from them, virtually all Phase I trials require their blood. As a result, many take behavioral measures to ensure one study does not adversely affect their chances of qualifying for the next. Jeffrey, an African American in his twenties who had screened for 100 studies in the past five years, had struggled to qualify. Because he routinely went from one study immediately to a screening visit, Jeffrey discovered that the blood collected in one study hampered his body's ability to qualify for the next: "I remember . . . [a study in 2007 that] literally drained most of the blood out of me. . . . So when I'm trying to go to study, study, study, I was getting turned down 'cause my hemoglobin was too low. . . . Mostly every place I went was like, 'Man, your hemoglobin's too low.' 'Your hemoglobin's too low.'" While the problem was clear to Jeffrey, the solution—other than participating in fewer studies—was more difficult to come by until he started focusing on his diet by "eating like a lot of raw vegetables and everything like that, so trying to get my blood up." He swore by this diet and subsequently developed a ritual of (and super-stition about) what he consumed when he finished a study so his body would be prepared for the next. That it appeared efficacious further con-firmed his interpretation of cause and effect, and he felt empowered by his intervention to continue enrolling just as frequently but with fewer screen failures.

As participants become more aware of their health, they acquire ex-pertise, and some even adopt technical ways of interpreting their bodily functions. While a few of the quotations above have already depicted participants' use of terms such as "bilirubin" (Mikhail) and "hemoglo-bin" (Don and Jeffrey), Eddie, an African American in his early forties, was a serial participant who effortlessly mobilized a medical lexicon. He expounded on his method for preparing his body for his next screening after having just finished participating in a study:

> Basically, I'm on like a vitamin regimen. So basically, we're putting back everything they took from us because it's vital, for one, to get into the next study. How much blood you gave and depending on how many studies you do on a yearly basis, you know, your hematocrit, your hemoglobin, all that stuff drops because they're taking the blood from you. So, you gotta make sure as soon as you get out of here, you've gotta say, "Okay, gotta take this blood builder. I've gotta drink this smoothie. I'm gonna eat this. I gotta make sure my cholesterol is right." So it's like we [study vet-erans] become like small pharmacists, dietitians, and we tell each other, "Oh man, take spirulina." . . . So yeah, we're more wise about our health now.[9]

I asked Eddie where his medical knowledge came from, curious how much was from interactions with research staff and how much was from participant social networks. He clarified, "Not from the research facilities, but actually from more just amongst us [study veterans] in this industry. We basically learn from each other, and like, 'Oh, that didn't work.' . . . 'Okay, take iron, but take [it with] orange juice 'cause the acidity will make it break down faster. Don't drink milk.' I mean, it's like we know so much now that it's crazy." To reduce their chances of screen failure, Eddie and others developed expertise in regulating their blood, enzymes, and other biological markers.

Although healthy volunteers would not describe themselves as model organisms per se, they do understand that their expertise and behavior are in the service of molding themselves into ideal, effective Phase I participants. If they are to maximize their utility for the industry, they must acquire health information from screening that can help them qualify. In this sense, screen failures are quite productive for generating knowledge about how to fine-tune oneself as a model organism. For example, Jay colorfully mused, "I've failed plenty of screenings. . . . That's how you find out how your body works when you fail a screening. . . . They tell you, 'Oh, you failed it because of that [factor].' And then you know it. . . . You're mad because that was maybe a $4,000 study, like you're upset, you're kicking yourself in the head, and it sucks, *sucks*. I mean you miss out on a lot of money because of something so stupid, you know what I mean? . . . I hate failing screenings!" Jay highlights the tension between the learning opportunity that screen failures can provide and the overwhelming frustration healthy volunteers experience from missing an opportunity to participate (and earn money) in a study. Jay detailed the changes he had made to his health behaviors based on these screen failures: "You learn what foods to eat that help your body, 'cause everybody body's different, you know what I mean? Like, they say African Americans, we have white-blood-cell counts that goes up and down sometimes, you know? So I have to do extra. . . . [I eat] a lot of green things that just strengthen my white-blood-cell count. And I'm like a natural anemic . . . so I have to eat more red meat [and] eat more greeny stuff and stuff like that." Jay demonstrates how Phase I screenings propel further engagement with one's health: screen failure prompts more research and increasingly sophisticated behavior change. However, complete mastery of the process is elusory.

Reappraising the Value of Health

When healthy volunteers' income depends on qualifying for new Phase I trials, their fixation on their health can become a critical part of their identities. Moreover, the choices they make about their diet, exercise, and use of tobacco, alcohol, and recreational drugs become routine parts of their life, not just as preparation for screening appointments. For example, contrasting her health behaviors to typical adult habits, Alexandra emphasized, "You can't really abuse your body in any way. You know, smoke and drink has to be very limited, . . . and you can't really live like other people. . . . 'Cause, you know, this is like a job, like a job that you have to be healthy for." Alexandra's orientation elucidates another facet of becoming a model organism: adopting a lifestyle informed by Phase I trials.

Some serial participants even believe they are healthier individuals *because of* Phase I trials, in particular from the knowledge and motivation they gain through their study involvement. The feedback loop from screenings makes participants more aware of how health behaviors impact their physiology positively and negatively, but in ways that would be impossible to notice without repeated routine medical testing. For example, Bennett professed, "You learn a lot about your body, you learn a lot about health, period, when doing these. The doctor [at the clinic] will tell you your blood pressure's a little high. So what does that mean? Well, maybe you're eating a little too much salt or too many greasy foods. . . . So, what do you do? You wanna get into the next study, so you cut down on it. Your blood pressure gets regulated, and you're healthier, *and* you're getting into more studies." Bennett also spoke proudly about the health improvements he achieved with his clinical trial lifestyle: "As far as a study career goes, I'm what you would consider an alpha male. My labs are always close to perfect. . . . I'm 27 years old, and I have perfect blood pressure. For a black male, that is very rare. . . . I'm healthier now than I was when I was 20, you know? My blood's better. My body's perfect. I couldn't ask to be anything else. I kinda owe that to the motivation of getting in the study." Bennett's comments also suggest a broader reevaluation of health that occurs in the process of adapting oneself to Phase I trials.

The indeterminacy of screening also encourages serial participants to give up habits they might not perceive as unhealthy but would disqualify them from studies. For anyone who expects to screen, engaging in behaviors like drinking alcohol, smoking tobacco, using illicit drugs, or even overindulging in junk food would be foolish. Abstaining from behaviors that could disqualify them from studies is all the more crucial for participants who travel to screen. With the expense of the journey to a far-off clinic, such participants are all the more likely to adhere strictly to a routine of health-promoting behaviors. Irrespective of where they participate, healthy volunteers are, in a sense, incentivized to always be screen-worthy, so the choices they make in their everyday lives are determined by and through the norms of trial participation. Reflecting on how he had changed accordingly, Don confided, "When I first started doin' studies, I was smokin' weed. And that's what got me to stop smokin' weed ten years ago. . . . [After a positive THC test at a Phase I clinic,] the guy said, 'I'm not gonna bar you this time, but don't ever do it again.' . . . Ever since then, I stopped smokin' weed. These studies got me off of smokin' weed because I got used to *not* getting high off of weed, and then eventually I just said, you know, I can live like this." I followed up to ask Don whether he had changed any of his other health behaviors. He pondered the question momentarily and, with some surprise in his voice, replied, "You know, another thing, I stopped drinkin' too 'cause your liver enzymes go up."

For many, the health education they receive through Phase I trials can be genuinely life-changing. Indeed, it can be a radical departure from the way they were raised or what their peers perceive as "normal" health behaviors. Tony, one of the people who checked in for the hepatitis C study, had been participating in Phase I trials for only about a year, but he marveled at how much he had changed his diet in that timeframe:

I cut down on the meat. I eat more vegetables, more greens, and I do a lot of chicken, . . . not fried chicken, [but] baked chicken, and broiled, and grilled with my salads. . . . [Being in studies] brought my awareness to my [blood] pressure and to maintain my BMI. . . . It's a conscious thing that you have to be aware of. . . . A lot of things you're gonna have to stop eating or . . . you're gonna have some really serious downfalls in health and you won't live a long life.

The combination of wanting to improve his health and be ready to screen for new studies even inspired Tony to purchase a blood-pressure cuff for everyday monitoring. His goal was to have more regular feedback about his diet's effects on his body. He explained, "I wanna know whether I ate wrong the day before, and it [the blood pressure reading] lets you know. You have a conscience too. When you eat something, you know, 'Wow, I hope that the pressure don't go high,' [then] when you check it, you see. It's gonna tell you automatically. So, that's what I do now. You know, I'm on top of myself." Tony was engaged almost in self-experimentation. He had taken to another level self-surveillance of his diet, catalyzed by his desire to map out the effects of his food selections. Importantly, this process further affirmed his commitment both to his health and to clinical trial participation.

Many serial participants also weigh the health benefits they gain from Phase I trials directly against the risks. For example, Eddie perceived the overall benefits to his health as far outstripping the risks. He contrasted others' views of Phase I risks to his own experiences:

> It's funny [that] a lot of people look at this industry and they, you know, they're scared about it. [They say,] "Oh, you're a guinea pig," or, you know, "You're risking your life." And I'm like, "But, actually, I'm more healthier than you are. I know what my labs look like, and I'm more healthier now doing clinical trials than I've ever been in my life." . . . I actually investigate the drug and what it does. So, I actually know things now. . . . I mean, I know what I'm getting into here. This is my field right now.

Eddie's assertion about his health and expertise became ammunition against the stigma of clinical trial participation. This orientation radically reimagines what it means to value one's health. Rather than a sign that serial participants prioritize money over health by willingly exposing themselves to study risks, this position asserts that health gets prioritized through the process of becoming a model organism for Phase I trials.

Health, Risk, and Qualifying

A major ethical worry about Phase I trials is that healthy people's financial need might overshadow their appropriate appraisal of the risks. As I have demonstrated, healthy volunteers typically perceive the trials in which they enroll as low risk. They also manage risk by avoiding actual and supposedly harmful studies that could produce long-term or permanent changes to the body. Yet, risk is multifaceted in the imaginaries of serial participants. We have seen that healthy volunteers' main risk narrative focuses largely on their ability to qualify for studies. In other words, the primary risk that preoccupies them is not the risk of experiencing adverse events but the risk of failing to get into new studies.[10] Thus, to counter the economic risk of not qualifying for studies, serial participants become *better* model organisms: they attempt to reduce their chance of future screen failure by selecting trials with the least toll on their bodies and by engaging in various behaviors to maximize their health.

Through Phase I trials, serial healthy volunteers engage in somatic speculation on their future health. Some participants develop coherent theories of the body as they increase their expertise in both biological processes and natural interventions to enhance their health. This is most striking when their identities are so deeply intertwined with their clinical trial participation that their investment in health becomes total. These participants are motivated to do what it takes to increase their chances of qualifying for studies while preserving their long-term eligibility for those trials. In the process, they start to see some of their "normal" health behaviors outside of clinical trials as risky. Even participants who merely cobble together information using trial and error to increase their chances of passing all the screening tests gain knowledge that potentially improves their general health. Not only does this focus on qualifying for studies encourage participants to become healthier individuals, but it also provides them with a sense of control given they are otherwise enmeshed in a system that leaves them powerless. They cannot dictate when studies are available, what those studies will be, or how much those studies pay, but they can promote their health through the choices they make.

Regardless of the time, energy, and money that serial participants put toward their health and qualifying for studies, their efforts are always speculative in the dual sense that they are unpredictable and that they are future-oriented. There are no guarantees—not for qualifying for studies or even remaining healthy. In both instances, health has instrumental value, securing entrance into clinical trials now and in the future. Yet, by speculating on their future health in these ways, participants also reveal their underlying fear about long-term Phase I trial risks. Serial participants are well aware that studies alter their bodies, if only through temporary adverse effects on their blood, which make it more difficult to game the system and ignore the washout period. Moreover, the possibility of making themselves ineligible for future studies by damaging their veins or bodies must be part of the enrollment decisions participants make to earn compensation today. Figuring out which studies are worthy of their time and bodies and which studies will not harm them is nonetheless always a gamble. Participants therefore direct their energy and resources toward becoming embodiments of the model organism the Phase I industry seeks. They enhance their health—and further track their progress through screening tests—to guard against illness, both those they believe could stem from clinical trials and those that are endemic to their communities, such as diabetes, hypertension, and so on. In many respects, this could mean serial participation, even with its attendant risks, has overall health benefits for volunteers. Many of my participants did or would make this claim.

Conclusion

The Social Inequality of Adverse Events

It should now be clear that there is a symbiotic relationship between the Phase I clinical trials industry and the profound economic insecurity in the United States. The pharmaceutical industry needs healthy bodies upon which it can test investigational drugs, and some healthy individuals are willing to consent to both the risks of those drugs and clinic confinement because Phase I trials offer substantial, lump-sum payments. This book has illustrated how experiences of imbricated stigma make clinical trial participation a particularly attractive option for earning income. When employment chances are limited by people's race, class, gender, education, incarceration history, and so on, enrolling in clinical trials seductively promises to ameliorate the material inequalities these people experience in their everyday lives. As we have seen, these social disadvantages can increase the allure of clinical trial participation, even with the stigma such an activity garners through its association with human guinea pigs or lab rats. That Phase I trials fail to transform people's lives ironically encourages some to enroll all the more frequently, providing them if not with a better life, then at least a different kind of lifestyle. Thus, not only does imbricated stigma propel individuals' choices to enroll in trials, but it also sustains the model organism itself by providing an endless supply of new humans who are willing to take a risk for the promise of the compensation.

By committing to longer-term Phase I participation, healthy volunteers restructure their lives and recalibrate their views of risk. They invest dramatically in their health by changing their behaviors and priming their bodies for trials, and they worry more about the risks of not participating than about the adverse drug events that might occur. Importantly, this preoccupation with the risk of not qualifying is in the context of myriad adverse study events, from rather banal headaches and gastrointestinal changes to cases of sleep paralysis, changes in liver function, and spinal headaches (to name just a few examples we have discussed). Even if healthy volunteers customarily underreport their adverse events, we have seen both the routine nature of bodily changes that occur to healthy volunteers and the unruffled responses that staff and participants normally display. These adverse *study* events just pale in comparison to the often-incessant adverse *life* events that befall healthy volunteers. For many, the risk and experience of adverse study events are a worthwhile trade-off for the immediate, even if short-lived, material advantages study income can provide, including helping to make ends meet, investing in their own or their children's futures, and engaging in conspicuous consumption. This money has symbolic value as well because it can be leveraged to reduce or deflect sources of stigma that people experience from un(der)employment and/or living in poverty.

Dismissing the physical risks of Phase I participation even further, serial healthy volunteers often claim they gain important health benefits. Although these participants indeed engage in more health-promoting behaviors and have measurable improvements in their blood pressure, cholesterol, and other bodily processes, these changes must also be understood in the context of social inequalities. That a certain segment of the population finds—and actively cultivates—health benefits from testing investigational pharmaceuticals might be better seen as a consolation prize for engaging in an otherwise risky activity that profits others. Indeed, healthy volunteers are expending significant financial and nontangible resources into improving their chances of qualifying for studies, not improving their health. If it were otherwise, they would stop enrolling. These health investments could temporarily make them better model organisms for the Phase I industry, but they deepen participants' commitment to an institution that has limited loyalty to them. Once they can no longer qualify due to age or health changes, there are no severance mechanisms to compensate them for their past contribution to the industry or to help them to transition away from their reliance on study income. Seen in this light, serial participants' investment in their health indicates all the more forcefully the kind of social disadvantages that would catalyze some participants' all-encompassing preoccupation with Phase I trials and maintaining their model organism status.

Moreover, the model organism approach to Phase I trials comes with a host of intrinsic and extrinsic validity problems that raise public health concerns. As pharmaceutical companies seek to control as many variables as possible in testing the safety and tolerability of their products, the clinical trials no longer resemble real-world conditions. For their part, healthy volunteers' adaptations to better fit (and thus qualify for) Phase I protocols further bias the data produced. Add to that the rule-breaking in which both healthy volunteers and research staff routinely engage, plus pharmaceutical companies' resistance to acknowledging that their drugs have caused adverse events, and the result is that the safety profile of FDA-approved drugs remains largely unknown. Despite the appearance that FDA-approved drugs have been proven safe, this perception is just a myth propagated by the pharmaceutical industry and supported by the regulatory system (Light, Lexchin, and Darrow 2013). The post-marketing data clearly indicate that adverse drug reactions mainly manifest only after patients take new pharmaceuticals as part of everyday treatment for their illnesses (Downing et al. 2017). Although clinical trials can never be expected to fully expose rare safety concerns (Strom 2006), the use of healthy volunteers in Phase I trials masks the whole spectrum of drug side effects, raising the question about whether healthy volunteers should be subjected to any risk of testing investigational drugs when the data generated have such limited scientific and public health value.

If the Phase I industry exploits social inequalities and generates specious data, why does all of this go virtually undetected? Where is the public controversy or scientific backlash to these research practices? To answer these questions, we must return to my initial framing of Phase I trials as a hidden world. This important feature of how healthy volunteer trials are conducted does not simply make Phase I studies a topic worth exploring, but also protects the industry from needed outside scrutiny.

The Dangers of Invisibility

The Phase I world is fundamentally an invisible one. It is a robust industry established throughout the United States (as well as in many other countries around the globe), yet few people are aware that residential facilities exist to test investigational drugs on healthy individuals who are paid for "volunteering" their time and bodies. For the uninitiated, it may seem like the stuff of science fiction rather than an ordinary part of the science of drug development (Cottingham and Fisher 2017; Fisher and Cottingham 2017). In many respects, that is what makes an exploration of the clinical trial facilities and the people who participate so fascinating. Indeed, healthy volunteers new to studies often narrate the experience as one in which a hidden realm revealed itself to them and they eagerly became its denizens.

The hidden nature of Phase I trials both adds to and mitigates the stigma of enrolling in studies. On one hand, the lack of information about these trials can make the public suspicious of them and, consequently, cast those who participate as being all the more desperate for exposing themselves to wild and/or unknown risks. On the other, healthy volunteers might be better able to hide their participation from others because the venipuncture marks on their arms or their long absences are not easily attributable to their trial enrollment. In other words, even with evidence of their participation in plain sight, healthy volunteers can nonetheless manage the stigma of the activity by choosing to whom, if anyone, they would like to disclose the truth. This helps to maintain study participation in the realm of "discreditable" rather than "discredited" stigma, to return to Goffman's (2009 [1963]) terms. Thus, no one is automatically stigmatized or loses face from their participation. For those seeking the economic benefits of clinical trials, that the stigma is the discreditable form can be positive because it can mask not only how they earned that money but also how dire their financial situation might be.

Yet, the invisibility of these clinical trials protects the interests of the pharmaceutical and Phase I industries while making healthy volunteers more vulnerable to exploitation. A situation in which there is little outside scrutiny of how these trials are conducted creates the conditions for companies to devise studies that have questionable external validity and for clinics to put their own profits over the comfort and safety of participants. If few are aware of these residential facilities, then situating them in cramped spaces with poorly trained staff is unlikely to raise any backlash from the public (e.g., Evans, Smith, and Willen 2005). Not all Phase I facilities engage in these practices, but there is little to hinder existing or future clinics from doing so (Fisher and Walker 2019). Similarly, there is no incentive for companies to pay more than the market will bear for studies, which means that in tough economic climates, compensation for studies could diminish even while expectations for what is involved, such as confinement time or number of return visits, increase. Finally, the harms that come to participants from taking investigational drugs are downplayed as temporary and inconsequential (Emanuel et al. 2015). The implication is that healthy volunteers are appropriately compensated for any adverse study events they experience, and so these inconveniences are simply the basis for that payment. By making adverse events unremarkable in this way, they too are rendered invisible, neutralizing any questions about how much healthy volunteers should be expected to undergo and what compensation might be fair and reasonable for any sickness or distress they experience. Instead, the focus remains on preventing "undue inducement," or keeping compensation low enough that it cannot compel people to participate in studies they would otherwise rationally refuse to do (Dickert and Grady 1999; Largent et al. 2012; VanderWalde and Kurzban 2011). Yet, rationally any healthy person should refuse to enroll without a compelling financial or altruistic motivation for doing so. All of these factors advantage the companies that pay for or conduct Phase I trials and set the conditions for exploiting the most impoverished members of society.

There is at least one more danger associated with the invisibility of the Phase I industry. By operating in shadows in the United States, it occludes the social inequalities that allow it to prosper in this country just as well if not better than it could in less affluent nations. The fiction of American prosperity so easily allows many to imagine that the conditions that would compel healthy people to enroll in medical research exist somewhere else, such as India or China (Cooper and Waldby 2014; Rajan 2007), rather than in their own backyards. This means that for those who are less affected by imbricated patterns of social and economic stigmas, the effects of such "spoiled identities" (Goffman 2009 [1963]) do not require much consideration. Whether or not Phase I trials are risky or safe, the adverse *life* events that make them the best choice for some individuals to earn income are unfairly distributed. Making Phase I trials visible is one small step toward confronting inequalities in society.

ACKNOWLEDGMENTS

This book has taken a decade to come to fruition. It began with exciting and often challenging ethnographic field work, and it ended with a scramble for time to write and re-write. On better days, I have felt like this project is a rewarding calling to give voice to people who are often invisible and ignored. On harder days, this book has seemed like an albatross around my neck. I've been fortunate to have an incredible network of friends, colleagues, and the institutional support of the Department of Social Medicine and the Center for Bioethics at the University of North Carolina at Chapel Hill (UNC).

In particular, I would like to thank those who were instrumental to this research. First and foremost, a project like this would not have been possible without grant funding from the National Cancer Institute (NCI), US National Institutes of Health (NIH) through grant number 1R21CA131880. Of course, the research and this book do not necessarily represent the official views of NCI or NIH. Second, I am so appreciative of the six organizations that gave me access to their Phase I clinics and the people who taught me all about these types of clinical trials. To protect my informants' confidentiality, I can say only how grateful I am that so many individuals were willing to participate in my research and trusted me enough to share their experiences as research staff and healthy volunteers. In addition, Dulce Medina and Irma Beatriz Vega de Luna provided tremendous help by conducting Spanish-language interviews with healthy volunteers. Behind the scenes, Denise Lillard at Vanderbilt University ensured that the grant was administered properly and I got reimbursed for all my travel expenses and payments to research participants.

This book was also supported by the invitations I received to give talks on my research. Having the opportunity to present early thoughts and to get feedback was essential for this book to coalesce around the themes in the way that it has. These events included the 2010 "Human

Sciences, Human Subjects" workshop held at the University of Chicago, co-sponsored by the Max Planck Institute and organized by Lorraine Daston, Alison Winter, and Robert Richards; the 2011 "When the Subject Speaks" workshop held at Wesleyan University, organized by Jill Morawski and funded by a Sawyer-Mellon grant; the 2012 "Clinical Labour and the New Labour Studies" workshop held at the University of Sydney and organized by Melinda Cooper and Catherine Waldby; the 2013 "Ethics, Labour and Boundaries: Examining the Work and Position of Frontline Workers" workshop held at the Ethox Centre of the University of Oxford and organized by Patricia Kingori; the 2015 "Journée Scientifique en Sciences Humaines et Sociales" workshop held at the Université Paris Est Créteil, organized by Caroline Ollivier-Yaniv and Mathilde Couderc and sponsored by the l'Institut de Recherche sur le Vaccin (VRI); and the 2017 "Taming the Pharmakon" workshop held at the Notre Dame Global Gateway–Rome and organized by Philip Mirowski. I also benefited from giving talks to the Medical Humanities and Bioethics Program at Northwestern University; the Department of Gender Studies at Indiana University–Bloomington; the Department of Social and Behavioral Sciences at the University of California–San Francisco; the School of History, Technology, and Society at the Georgia Institute of Technology; the Medical Humanities Interest Group at the Massachusetts College of Pharmacy and Health Science; the Center for Bioethics and Social Sciences in Medicine at the University of Michigan; and the Leslie Dan Faculty of Pharmacy at the University of Toronto. Thank you to Tod Chambers, Stephanie Sanders, Shari Dworkin, Jennifer Singh, Dien Ho and Kenneth Richman, Raymond De Vries, and Elise Paradis for the respective invitations and for hosting my visits. Thanks are also owed to my colleagues at UNC for engaging the multiple talks on healthy volunteers that I have given over the years. (Sorry to say that those are not over quite yet!) Medical students in my annual "Pharmaceuticals, Politics, and Culture" course have routinely asked excellent questions about the Phase I world.

I have also had the benefit of colleagues reading draft chapters as I worked on this book. My biggest debt of gratitude is owed to Torin Monahan, who provided feedback on each chapter and then read the entire book after I had made major revisions. Two anonymous reviewers also offered excellent suggestions for improving (and shortening) this book.

The UNC Center for Bioethics also hosted an Intramural Faculty Workshop in 2017 wherein I benefited from feedback on a chapter from UNC faculty Mara Buchbinder, Arlene Davis, Eric Juengst, Douglas MacKay, Stuart Rennie, and Rebecca Walker, as well as our guests for the event, Carl Elliott, Maria Merritt, and Christian Simon. In addition to those already named, other friends and colleagues offered insights, assistance, and/or moral support that helped with this project over the years, including John Abraham, Leslie Alexander, Jeffrey Bishop, Lauren Brinkley-Rubinstein, Jean Cadigan, Nancy Campbell, Larry Churchill, Ellen Clayton, Giselle Corbie-Smith, Mariana Craciun, Daniel Dohan, Steven Epstein, Sue Estroff, Joseph Fanning, Jennifer Fishman, Mary Margaret Fonow, Elise Giroudon, Jeremy Greene, LaDawn Haglund, Adam Hedgecoe, Carol Heimer, Elizabeth Heitman, Gail Henderson, David Hess, Ana Iltis, Corey Kalbaugh, Nicholas King, Barbara Koenig, Rebecca Lave, Susan Lederer, Trudo Lemmens, Donald Light, Anne Drapkin Lyerly, Velma McBride Murry, Jonathan Metzl, Jennifer Mokos, Kelly Moore, Daniel Mosely, Daniel Nelson, Nicole Nelson, Raúl Necochea, Jonathan Oberlander, JuLeigh Petty, David Resnik, Michele Rivkin-Fish, Noelle Robertson, Mary Romero, Salla Sariola, Barry Saunders, David Schenck, Janet Shim, Sergio Sismondo, Jeffrey Sonis, Laura Stark, Stefan Timmermans, Sarah Wadmann, Matthew Weinstein, and Rose Weitz. This can hardly be a complete list, and my sincere apologies to anyone I have forgotten.

Some of the material used in chapters 5 and 7 was previously published in a very different form in "Feeding and bleeding: The institutional banalization of risk to healthy volunteers in phase I pharmaceutical clinical trials," *Science, Technology, and Human Values* 40 (2):199–226, and is used by permission of SAGE. This article was part of a special issue, and I received helpful feedback on drafts from Jennifer Croissant (guest editor), Harry Perlstadt, Anne Pollock, Jennifer Singh, Laurel Smith-Doerr, and Itai Vardi. Chapter 8 also draws upon material previously published in "Stopped hearts, amputated toes, and NASA: Contemporary legends among healthy volunteers in US phase I clinical trials," *Sociology of Health and Illness* 37 (1):127–142, and is used by permission of Wiley.

While I was writing this book, I also led a follow-up longitudinal study of healthy volunteers. The HealthyVOICES team provided outstanding assistance on the demanding data collection required for that research. I am grateful to Julianne Kalbaugh, Marci Cottingham, Chandler Batchelor, Katelyn Chiang, Rebecca de Guzman, Heather Edelblute, Maral Erol, Rebecca Forcier, Luis Gonzalez, Nupur Jain, Karla Jimenez, Lauren Martin, Lisa McManus, Alex Nusbickel, Elena Pinzon, Lucía Stavig, Teresa Swezey, Arianna Taboada, Margaret Waltz, Quintin Williams, and Megan Wood. Although this book does not include the HealthyVOICES participants' stories, these individuals also continued to deepen my understanding of the adverse events that happen to people in their everyday lives and while participating in Phase I trials. This book would likely be a different one if I hadn't been speaking with those individuals while writing, so while this book is not literally about them, they have informed and enriched it. On that front, a grant from the National Institute of General Medical Sciences (NIGMS) (grant number R01GM099952) and the enthusiastic support of my NIH program officer Donna Krasnewich made that research possible. HealthyVOICES has more recently morphed into an ethics and policy-focused project, and I am thrilled to be able to continue to develop the concept of healthy volunteers as a model organism with my stellar colleague Rebecca Walker.

Finally, this book could not have been completed without sacrifice. There were many times I would have rather spent the holidays with family or not worked on this manuscript during a vacation, and I am thankful that my family understood that this book had to take priority in order for me to ever finish it. The Fishers, Rinaldis, and Monahans have been incredibly supportive of my work, and this means so much to me. And Torin, what could I possibly say? You make this crazy academic life worthwhile. I have found in you the perfect life partner, friend, and collaborator. Thank you for making me a better scholar and being there through everything that life has thrown at us.

NOTES

INTRODUCTION

1   The clinical trial I describe here is a composite of several Phase I studies that were being conducted during my ethnographic research.

2   In the US regulatory framework, research ethics boards are not supposed to weigh financial benefits of participation against the study's risks when evaluating trial protocols (US Food and Drug Administration [FDA] 1998; US National Institutes of Health [NIH] 2005). Nonetheless, prospective healthy volunteers typically perceive the financial compensation as a benefit and factor it into their decision-making. This raises many issues about the ethics of paying people to enroll in research (see, for example, Iltis 2009; Largent et al. 2012; Phillips 2011; Wilkinson and Moore 1997).

3   The pharmaceutical industry has been regulated in the United States since the 1906 passage of the US Pure Food and Drug Act. However, the system of FDA preapproval to market drugs was put into effect for safety only in 1938 and for efficacy only in 1962 (Donohue 2006; Hilts 2003). Phased clinical trials are a post-1962 FDA mandate designed to standardize how companies obtain and report evidence of investigational new drugs' safety and efficacy (Carpenter 2010).

4   Efficacy is often determined by demonstrating either a drug's superiority to a placebo, which is an inactive sugar pill, or its "non-inferiority" to a product that is already on the market. The low bar for pharmaceutical companies to "prove" the value of their investigational drugs has received well-deserved critical attention (e.g., Angell 2004; Light, Lexchin, and Darrow 2013).

5   The clinical trials industry is global. Phase I trials are concentrated in North America, Western Europe, and Asia. Despite critical media and scholarly attention to trials in the developing world (e.g., Cooper 2008; Prasad 2009; Rajan 2007; Sariola et al. 2019; Shah 2006), the United States remains the dominant site of all clinical trials worldwide at every phase of development (Fisher 2009; Petryna 2009; Redfearn 2015). There is surprisingly little documentation of the number and location of clinical trials conducted each year, but it is believed to be in the tens of thousands (Petryna 2009).

6   There are now robust anthropological and sociological literatures exploring clinical trials on the ground. These scholarly investigations have focused on both pharmaceutical industry and publicly funded medical research around the world (e.g., Adams et al. 2005; Corrigan 2003; Davis et al. 2002; Hayden 2003; Jain 2013;

Joseph and Dohan 2012; Kaufman 2015; Kingori 2015; Lakoff 2007; Montoya 2011; Peterson 2014; Petryna 2009; Petty and Heimer 2011; Pollock 2012; Rajan 2017; Timmermans and McKay 2009; True, Alexander, and Richman 2011; Wadmann and Hoeyer 2014; Weinstein 2010; Wentzell 2013; Whitmarsh 2008; Will and Moreira 2016). My previous book on clinical trials examined the whole spectrum of clinical development, and it had a primary focus on Phase III and IV trials conducted on affected patients in the United States (Fisher 2009).

7 Phase I clinics could be thought of as a type of total institution. Goffman (1961) described places like prisons and mental institutions using this term in order to highlight the closed nature of places in which the residents are cut off from the wider society. Elsewhere, Quintin Williams and I (2018) analyze the Phase I clinic as a "temporal total institution," focusing in particular on healthy volunteers' comparison of their experience in studies to prison and drawing upon Susie Scott's (2010) work on the "reinventive" institution.

8 Since I completed the ethnographic research for this book, two for-profit companies that act as participant registries have been established. These are Verified Clinical Trials and clinicalRSVP. However, they track participants only within their network of clinic subscribers, which leaves considerable gaps in information about participants because neither system has been widely adopted. In that same time period, there has also been increased interest among Phase I researchers and bioethicists in advocating for registries (Kupetsky-Rincon and Kraft 2012; Resnik and Koski 2011).

9 In his ethnographic work on healthy volunteers, Roberto Abadie (2010) lived among a small, predominantly white anarchist group in Philadelphia and observed their day-to-day lives outside of the Phase I clinic. I observed and interviewed participants around the country while they were in the clinics and did not follow them once they left a study. Together our research details aspects of at least some of these healthy volunteers' lives, finding similar themes in how they perceive Phase I trials. Because my focus was inside the clinic, I was able to observe and learn from more diverse healthy volunteers, those from many different areas of the country, with different racial and ethnic backgrounds, and radically different perspectives on their study participation's importance to their identities and their economic well-being. As we will see, white anarchist "guinea pigs" of the kind Abadie studied were indeed present in some of the clinics I visited, but these individuals were a numerical minority relative to the population of healthy volunteers. However, their cultural message critiquing capitalism and agitating for change was more pervasive and inflected many healthy volunteers' view of the research enterprise.

10 Readers familiar with intersectional theory might wonder why I have chosen to develop the concept of "imbricated stigma" rather than "intersectional stigma." Feminist and critical race scholars use intersectionality to analyze how multiple forms of disadvantage accrue to oppress certain members of society (see Collins 2009 [1990]; Crenshaw 1991; Grzanka 2014). For example, class, race, and gender

are not just discrete characteristics, but for those who do not have membership in the privileged ranks of these social groups (think poor black women versus affluent white men), their intersectional position can be thought of as imposing particular, compounding stigmatized identities. The image of the "welfare queen" is one such stigmatized identity that dominant US culture uses to disregard the structural inequalities that disadvantage low-income minority women. By examining the combined effects of class, race, and gender, scholars can more aptly interrogate social hierarchies.

Michele Berger (2006) developed the concept of intersectional stigma in her research on HIV-positive women of color to show how these women received substandard medical care because of how they were perceived. Intersectional stigma is an appealing concept because it has the power to show the extent of marginalization of some individuals due to their membership in multiple op-pressed groups. Berger also found that their experiences often catalyzed these women to become politically active—and thus to cross conventional barriers to political participation by stigmatized individuals.

While my thinking is deeply influenced by intersectional theory, I concen-trate in this book on imbrication instead. This choice is in part influenced by the diversity of individuals who are Phase I healthy volunteers. They vary dra-matically in terms of race, ethnicity, legal status, age, educational attainment, employment status, and even income level. Intersectionality as a concept was never intended to include partially privileged groups, and I wanted a concept that had the flexibility to be inclusive of the most disadvantaged *and* most privileged participants in my sample. Additionally, I did not want to include re-search participation as a de facto node within the "matrix of domination" (Col-lins 2009 [1990]) because I situate it as a form of discreditable stigma (Goffman 2009 [1963]), meaning that it is a stigma that can be hidden or managed, unlike many others that healthy volunteers may face. This notion of concealment and selective information-sharing departs from how social categories are typically treated in intersectional theory. In sum, imbrication provides the analytic flexibility to account for healthy volunteers' different backgrounds as well as their relative control over disclosure of the stigmatized activity of Phase I trial participation.

11 Paul Leonardi (2012) develops the concept of sociomaterial imbrication in his study of automotive engineers' design of car-crash simulation models. He il-lustrates not only how organizations are resistant to change but also how "new" modalities are always predicated on and shaped by previous imbrications. In addition, he demonstrates how an imbricated system is highly interdependent despite its unique component parts.

12 Devah Pager's (2008) empirical research on individuals' difficulty in securing work post-incarceration, which shows that white individuals who have a criminal record are offered more jobs than blacks, demonstrates the degree to which race mediates opportunities.

13 I have previously analyzed this phenomenon in terms of *structural coercion*, arguing that social inequalities are forms of structural violence that compel individuals to enroll in clinical trials as a form of healthcare for those who are ill patients
or as a source of income for those who are healthy volunteers (Fisher 2013). This
concept applies here as well. However, I am more interested throughout this book
in examining how healthy volunteers respond to those social inequalities through
their active involvement in Phase I trials, and the lens of imbricated stigma is a
useful one for exploring the experiential aspects of clinical trial participation.

14 While women are underrepresented more generally in Phase I trials, there were
only five women in my sample who had participated in more than 10 clinical
trials; all of these women were minorities. Only one woman had participated in
more than 25 studies.

15 My sample included 72 first-time participants, 33 of whom were white (46 percent
of first-timers and 38 percent of white healthy volunteers), 24 of whom were
black (33 percent of first-timers and 29 percent of black healthy volunteers), and
8 of whom were Hispanic (11 percent of first-timers and 16 percent of Hispanic
healthy volunteers). One particular Phase I clinic contributed disproportionately
to the number of first-time participants in my sample. Although 36 percent of the
first-time healthy volunteers were recruited there, that clinic had an overall higher
percentage of black participants than whites (53 percent and 44 percent, respectively), so sampling from that clinic does not appear to have created a confound-
ing effect with respect to race.

16 Key works on theorizing model organisms, especially within a constructivist
framework, include Ankeny and Leonelli (2011); Birke (2012); Birke, Arluke, and
Michael (2007); Davies (2012); Leonelli (2012); Lewis et al. (2012); Nelson (2013);
and Rader (2004).

17 Within drug development, there is mounting concern that current animal models
have very poor predictive validity, especially for drug efficacy in humans (Garner
et al. 2017; McGonigle and Ruggeri 2014). Further, Lynda Birke (2012) has noted
that in spite of the biological standardization of laboratory animals, the local
conditions of each laboratory greatly affect the outcome of research. Departing
from the biomedical term "translation," Friese and Clarke (2012) use the concept
of "transposition" to analyze how knowledge moves across animal models in the
case of reproductive sciences, including developments in human medicine and
assisted reproduction in endangered species.

18 This book's aim is not to evaluate the ethics of nonhuman animal research. For
excellent resources on the history of animal use in research, see Guerrini (2003),
Lederer (1995), Campbell (2007), and Rader (2004). For a nuanced discussion of
the ethical and moral concerns of nonhuman animal research compared to human
research, see Rebecca L. Walker's (2006, 2007, 2016) philosophical work on the
topic (see also Biller-Andorno, Grimm, and Walker 2015). More broadly, the field
of animal studies has produced critically important research on the role of nonhuman animals in society (see Daston and Mitman 2005; DeMello 2012; Weil 2012).

19 A therapeutic misconception occurs when participants mistakenly believe that they will benefit medically from enrolling in a clinical trial (Appelbaum, Lidz, and Grisso 2004; Dresser 2002; Henderson et al. 2007; Lidz et al. 2004). This phenomenon is particularly troubling in the case of Phase I trials on affected patients (e.g., Anderson and Kimmelman 2014; Kimmelman and Palmour 2005; Kimmelman 2012). With the notable exception of Nancy Burke's (2014) scholarship, there has, however, been a dearth of research on how therapeutic misconceptions operate in the context of social inequalities.

20 In the language of science studies, this could be thought of as a kind of "boundary object" (Star and Griesemer 1989).

21 Many scholars in science and technology studies (STS) have analyzed science as an institution (see Hess 1997). Their research highlights how science is shaped by the interests of its practitioners, the economic and political climate, and various cultures that define fields or subfields (e.g., Barnes 1977; Clarke 1998; Fisher 2011; Fujimura 2006; Harding 1998; Knorr-Cetina 1999; Latour and Woolgar 1979; Murphy 2012; Restivo 1994; Sarewitz 1996; Shostak 2013; Traweek 1988).

22 Cruciferous vegetables include leafy greens (e.g., kale, collard greens, and cabbage), broccoli, and cauliflower. They are restricted in some clinical trials because of their tendency to promote the expression of the CYP1A2 liver enzyme. For more technical information on how food could affect the action of drugs, see Won, Oberlies, and Paine (2012).

23 Prior experience works in both directions. Based on the business principle that past performance is the best predictor of future behavior, research staff rely on their observations of healthy volunteers to determine if they should be allowed to participate in future studies. This means that if someone seems to have difficulty with the confinement or leaves the trial before it is complete, the staff might officially or unofficially place that person on a "Do Not Use" list or restrict their access to certain clinical trials.

24 Rebecca Dresser (2013) coined the phrase "subversive subjects" to describe how serial participants lie and cheat as part of their enrollment in clinical trials. The field of bioethics has been particularly focused on this type of rule-breaking in part out of concern about the validity of clinical trial results and the safety of participants (Devine et al. 2013; Dickert 2013; Resnik and Koski 2011; Resnik and McCann 2015).

25 When focusing on the quotidian nature of Phase I trials, it can be difficult to make connections between what happens on the ground with the important critiques of the pharmaceutical industry that have proliferated. For example, Marcia Angell (2004) has persuasively demonstrated the extent to which pharmaceutical companies make economic choices that do not necessarily lead to better drugs being available on the market. Pharmaceutical companies have also developed highly sophisticated techniques to get physicians and patients to support the companies' aim of generating profits (e.g., Abraham 2010; Bell and Figert 2012;

Brody 2008; Busfield 2006; Dumit 2012; Ecks 2013; Greene 2007; Healy 2004; Kassirer 2005; Lakoff 2005; Williams, Martin, and Gabe 2011). Works by Donald Light and colleagues have been particularly insightful at demonstrating that new drugs are not only typically a lot more expensive than older drugs but also much more harmful (Light 2010; Light and Lexchin 2012; Light, Lexchin, and Darrow 2013; Light and Warburton 2011). For an introduction to the interdisciplinary subfield of "pharmaceutical studies," see Sismondo and Greene (2015). These types of criticisms are most salient to my later analysis of the validity concerns than emerge in Phase I trials on healthy volunteers.

CHAPTER 1. ENTERING THE CLINIC

1 All names of clinics, staff, and healthy volunteers used in this book are pseudonyms.

2 This quotation is based on field notes; as with other exchanges I heard during my observations rather than in interviews, quotation faithfully captures the sentiment of what was said, but it might not be the exact words.

3 One could compare the stunts in *Jackass* to Phase I trial participation, and I found it ironic that this was the television show volunteers had chosen to watch.

4 Historical scholarship on medical research has extensively documented past abuses of human subjects. Many such abuses have targeted racial and ethnic minorities or vulnerable institutionalized populations. Much has been written about the infamous US Public Health Service Syphilis Study, commonly known as the Tuskegee experiment (see Jones 1981; Reverby 2000, 2009); other books have examined prison experiments (e.g., Hornblum 1998), research on institutionalized children (e.g., Rothman and Rothman 1984), and exploitation of colonized peoples (e.g., Briggs 2002; Graboyes 2015; Smith 2005). More broadly, medical research has long inspired angst about the possibility of nefarious researchers (Fisher 2015b; Lederer 1995), and as a result, contemporary research clinics are often very concerned about public relations (Fisher and Cottingham 2017; Getz 2013).

5 It has been a long process from conducting field work to finishing this manuscript. Although the data for this book come strictly from the ethnographic research I conducted in 2009 and 2010, I have remained deeply involved in research on US Phase I trials through my subsequent longitudinal study of healthy volunteers (2012–2017). I reference this latter study in endnotes where it can offer additional insights.

6 The Vanderbilt University Institutional Review Board reviewed and approved this research.

7 Phase I research staff are typically white with an overrepresentation of women, especially in the study nurse and recruitment roles. Specifically, of the 33 research staff I interviewed, 21 were women (12 were men), and 25 were non-Hispanic whites (there were also 5 African Americans, 1 Asian American, 1 Hispanic, and 1 Native American).

8 While I conducted the majority of interviews, two bilingual graduate students conducted 28 interviews with healthy volunteers in Spanish.

9 The shortest interview was with a participant who had to wait his turn when I interviewed several people who had screened for the same study. After I obtained his informed consent and we began the interview, he realized he would miss his long-distance bus if he did not leave the clinic immediately.

10 Healthy volunteers in their fifties, sixties, and seventies made up 10 percent, 8.5 percent, and 1 percent of my sample respectively.

11 Tourism studies has investigated the phenomenon of social relations that manifest during group travel (e.g., Brown 2005; Pearce 2005; White and White 2009). Bonding among healthy volunteers is similar in that it is meaningful to participants during their time together but does not normally continue beyond the activity that brought them together. For example, David Cashman (2017) describes music-festival cruise ships as "social containers." He illustrates how the contained space enables the formation of a "ship fam," or intensely intimate family-like relationships, during the cruise. Relationships are rarely maintained off of the ship, but many look forward to reprising these friendships by doing the activity again.

12 Typically, participants are weighed and measured, have their blood drawn and vital signs checked, and are hooked up to ECGs in front of other participants. They are generally given privacy to collect urine or fecal samples and for any physical examinations conducted by a physician. Phase I trials also have parallels with other highly corporeal experiences. For example, Marcelle Dawson (2017) has described the cult-like bonding that occurs in the CrossFit exercise community because of the fitness regimen's intensity and strenuousness.

13 Large-scale sociological evidence indicates that Americans in the past decades have markedly fewer friends or intimates with whom to share their concerns and feelings (McPherson, Smith-Lovin, and Brashears 2006).

14 Research staff find women to be more difficult participants and see them as prone to irritability, both with each other and with the staff. Donna, a white recruiter at CRO Phase I, contrasted men's and women's behavior in a single clinical trial: "The females were very difficult to work with. . . . You know: 'We want more to do. We don't like the food. We are bored. And we want a masseuse to come in.' And, yeah, now, the men were just sitting over there watching their sports, and . . . no problem whatsoever. [Laughs.] . . . [CRO Phase I] actually brought a masseuse in for 'em [the women], . . . so they were happy then." For Donna, that the study was exactly the same for the two groups proved that the difference in behavior had been due to participants' gender and not the trial protocol. Amazingly, the women's complaints were rewarded with professional massages!

CHAPTER 2. "DOING THE LAB RAT THING"

1 Valdez (2011) briefly mentions these entrepreneurs, but her book focuses primarily on more classic conceptions of entrepreneurialism by comparing Latinx, white, and black restaurant owners in Houston, Texas.

2 The hustler lens can also be productively applied directly to healthy volunteers (see Monahan and Fisher 2015a).

3 Despite negative perceptions of many "dead-end" jobs, people who take them may, in the long term, be more likely to complete their education or secure better employment, especially if they use such jobs as a stepping stone for achieving those goals (Newman 2006).

4 For example, Algorithme Pharma used the tagline, "1 Weekend for 1 Hefty Down Payment," on its website and depicted a happy young Latina taking a selfie as an older white man placed car keys in her hand (https://www.fargostudies.com, last accessed August 13, 2018).

5 Clinic staff protested the idea that their research facilities might take advantage of certain segments of the population. For example, Charlotte, a white physician-investigator at Pharma Phase I, asserted, "I'm very skeptical about all that, you know, jargon about exploiting, you know, poor people and minorities. People choose this as opposed to an hour[ly] job. I mean, there are so many other jobs that are, you know, equally low paying, [laughs] so I don't see this as any different." In other words, Phase I trial participation cannot be exploitative in Charlotte's view because it is no different than other jobs that poorly compensate workers. This logic relies on the belief that adherence to the status quo in an unjust system provides moral justification for an unjust action.

6 Clinical trials have a tense relationship with work (Elliott and Abadie 2008; Johnson 2016; Lemmens and Elliott 1999, 2001). The term "volunteer" is clearly inaccurate given that healthy participants are paid. For income tax purposes, however, they are technically independent contractors, not clinic employees. Melinda Cooper and Catherine Waldby (2014) incisively analyze research participation as "clinical labor," mobilizing Marx's labor theory of value and attending both to historical developments and the current neoliberal, postindustrial labor context.

7 Data from my longitudinal research on healthy volunteers' actual trial participation indicate that only 4–8 percent earned more than $20,000 in a single year, and they typically had to participate in five or more Phase I trials to do so. Those participants who enrolled in at least one trial per year made an average of $8,720 (median = $5,685) annually during the three years of research. For an overview of that study see Edelblute and Fisher (2015). Likewise, Abadie (2010) found that the "professional guinea pigs" in his study earned only between $15,000 and $20,000 in "exceptionally good years" (5).

8 For an overview of identity work, see Brown (2015).

9 Indeed, the money gained through studies can even become addictive. Joseph jocularly illustrated this: "I mean, doing the studies gets addictive, 'cause you're doing nothing. You're just sitting around, chilling; somebody's giving you something to eat; somebody's wiping your butt; somebody's doing whatever. Whatever they've gotta do, they're doing it for you. You know what I mean? . . . So I just wanna

do one more. I just need to do one nice size—. [Laughs.] I sound like an addict already: 'Just one more. Just one more hit. Just one more study and I'll be—' [laughs]." When he stopped short, I asked for clarification, "You mean one more *after* this one?" And Joseph affably replied, "Yeah, one more after this one. Right. [Laughs.] One more after this one, and I'll be good, but oh geez, I don't know. That's my story and I'm sticking to it."

10 Some US states make people who are released on parole from prison subsidize the cost of their own supervision (Katzenstein and Nagrecha 2011).

11 While rare, altruism is an impetus for some healthy volunteers to enroll in clinical trials. More often, certain diseases, such as Alzheimer's, cancer, or multiple sclerosis (MS), inspire participants to see their clinical trial involvement as contributing to science. Apart from the possibility of helping family members or friends afflicted with those diseases, some healthy volunteers also articulated a not-so-altruistic sentiment about helping a future *self*. In that narrative, they imagined they might someday need the drug currently being tested. For more on how healthy volunteers perceive the nonfinancial benefits of their clinical trial participation, see Fisher et al. (2018b).

12 In social identity theory, comparisons with others become the basis for one's sense of self, influencing one's self-esteem and subjective well-being (Suls and Wheeler 2000).

CHAPTER 3. A TALE OF THREE CULTURES

1 For precise demographic details, see tables 1.1a, 1.1b, and 1.1c, which provide information about the participants at each of the six clinics I visited.

2 I cannot give accurate counts for these groups because I did not systematically collect demographic data on educational attainment or incarceration. It was striking, however, that these social factors emerged unprompted in interviews with many East Coast participants.

3 Alan Wertheimer (1999) proposes the concept of "mutually advantageous exploitation" to describe circumstances when research participants benefit even while being exploited. He argues that it is more ethically permissible to allow exploitation in these cases compared to when the exploited receive nothing in return. Many healthy volunteers would likely agree with this view, but the arrangement is problematic in that it supports the status quo in these unequal power relations.

4 Midwestern participants rarely discussed pharmaceutical companies. When they did, they typically perceived them in a positive light. For example, Annie, a white woman in her thirties and second-time participant, said, "I'm surprised that they have to run this kind of study. So, you learn . . . 'Oh, is that why medicine is so expensive?' Because they're paying us so much money to be volunteers. . . . So it's all of this along the way that then creates the big picture like, 'Aha! Okay, now I get it.'" For Annie, being in clinical trials did not reveal the workings of capitalist value extraction, but it instead justified the high cost

of drugs; ironically, one could argue, participating in drug-testing made Annie *less* knowledgeable about how pharmaceutical companies set drug prices.

5 To do so, the clinics must hire bilingual staff and provide IRB-approved informed consent forms and other documentation in Spanish.

6 Brian and Louis avoided me to an almost comical degree at Mega Phase I, probably out of unnecessary concern that I would tell clinic staff they had lied about their washout period. Also at Mega Phase I, I reconnected with Stuart, a participant I had met at Pharma Phase I nearly a year earlier. So as not to double-count him in my sample, I opted not to interview him again, but I talked with him informally about his trial participation since I had last seen him.

7 Although Honesto was mistaken about the details from the news report he had seen about the government infecting people with HIV, he was referring to the US government's real involvement in penicillin studies in Guatemala. In the 1940s, American researchers intentionally infected several hundred prisoners, soldiers, and others with sexually transmitted diseases, including syphilis and gonorrhea, in order to test penicillin's efficacy in curing these infections (Reverby 2011). This scandal was in the news in October 2010, the time of my visit to the West Coast clinics. It is less clear what news reports about Mafia involvement with clinical trials he might have seen on television.

CHAPTER 4. THE COMMERCIALIZATION OF PHASE I TRIALS

1 In addition to reflecting broader trends in outsourcing, neoliberal legislation in the 1980s contributed to the formation and success of the clinical trials industry. Specifically, the 1980 Patent and Trademark Law Amendments Act—or the Bayh-Dole Act, the combined names of the bill's co-sponsors—aimed to spur innovation by allowing individuals and universities to hold patents and profit from inventions that resulted from federally funded contracts and grants (Goozner 2005). Additionally, Congress passed the 1984 Drug Price Competition and Patent Term Restoration Act, more commonly referred to as "Hatch-Waxman." The goal of this latter legislation was, in part, to modernize the FDA review of generic drugs. In brief, the law stipulated that to have generic drugs approved for the market, manufacturers needed simply to demonstrate that in healthy volunteers their products were "bioequivalent" to the original brand-name drug (Carpenter and Tobbell 2011; Greene 2014).

2 The early history of Phase I trials also included the widespread use of prisoners as healthy participants (Harkness 1996). Pharmaceutical companies found that many prisons were eager to partner with them, cooperating to the point of offering prisoners reduced prison sentences, better food, more comfortable living conditions, and modest compensation (Hornblum 1998). For their part, pharmaceutical companies received large populations of motivated research participants in a highly controlled environment, helping to establish Phase I trials as "confinement" studies. By 1976, 85 percent of all Phase I trials occurred in

prisons (Bonham and Moreno 2008). However, fallout from the US Public Health Service's 40-year Syphilis Study in Tuskegee, Alabama, drew national attention to unethical human subjects research (Jones 1981; Reverby 2009), and prisoners' participation in nontherapeutic research also became the subject of congressional scrutiny (Mitford 1973). Prisoners came to be identified as a vulnerable population (National Commission 1976, 1979), and subsequent federal regulations restricted the use of prisoners in research, requiring that the research would benefit the prisoners themselves or provide important information about crime, corrections, and recidivism that could benefit society. With these regulations in place, Phase I trials were effectively banned from prisons. More recently, there has been concern that the federal regulations have been too restrictive and should be relaxed to allow more research to occur in prisons and with prisoners (Institute of Medicine 2007).

3 In her research on the clinical trials industry, Adriana Petryna (2009) refers to these research clinics as "floater sites" that underbid on contracts from the pharmaceutical industry and have subpar operations compared to more legitimate contract research organizations.

4 Investing in this way in its testing facility could have been particularly important to Pharma Phase I given that the largest pharmaceutical companies have been criticized for not being the source of innovation in the industry (e.g., Angell 2004; Goozner 2002). The most profitable companies often wait for smaller companies to develop promising products, which they then acquire and test in Phase III clinical trials (Fisher, Cottingham, and Kalbaugh 2015).

5 In my earlier research on clinical trials, some of the research coordinators also vilified Eunice Rivers for her role as an African American woman who helped to recruit and retain African American men in the Public Health Service Tuskegee Syphilis Study (Fisher 2009: 92–93).

6 Six Sigma is a method for creating more efficiency in organizations and is generally directed at increasing companies' profits (https://www.6sigma.us, last accessed June 18, 2018). The training and certification process has levels that borrow from martial arts, with colored belts indicating someone's proficiency in the method. To earn certification, individuals must pay for and enroll in online or in-person seminars. The cost of these seminars increases dramatically to earn higher-level "belts."

7 Kyle's use of the word "seeds" in this quotation is likely slang for testicles, with the more common idiom being "to have the balls" to do something risky.

8 It is unclear whether healthy volunteers would have criticized these same pharmaceutical company clinics had I interviewed them five or ten years earlier. It is quite possible that participants remembered them better than they had been or that they looked good only compared to worse clinics in operation. An important component of nostalgia is that individuals are often missing a past that was never as happy as the memories convey. Regardless, nostalgia importantly reveals how people wish things to be now.

CHAPTER 5. A LABORATORY FOR HUMAN ANIMALS

1 Of the clinics I visited, five included such a procedure area. As the smallest clinic, Academic Phase I was the exception. The participants there remained in bed for their procedures, and the research staff would go room by room to accomplish their tasks.

2 The implication for the clinic was that it likely had to replace those participants and run the protocol for the smaller number of participants. Ultimately, the choice would be the sponsoring pharmaceutical company's to make.

3 Elsewhere (Fisher 2015a), I have written about Phase I clinics as having "Fordist" qualities. This is because the spaces are often designed for maximum efficiency. For example, Local Phase I's procedure area was not unlike an assembly line, with the difference being that it was the research staff who had to move to the next participant, rather than the participants moving in sync with an automated system.

4 When they have safety concerns about the drug, the sponsor or an ethics review board might impose a lengthier minimum interval between dosing each participant. By conservatively pacing dosing, investigators have the opportunity to stop the protocol should severe adverse effects occur. In first-in-human trials, the protocols occasionally utilize double-blind "sentinel dosing," which dictates that one participant will randomly receive the experimental drug and another a placebo twenty-four hours before the rest of the group doses. This design—increasingly being required in Europe—limits the majority of healthy volunteers' exposure to the investigational drug until after there is preliminary human safety data from a single participant (van Gerven and Bonelli 2018). Although some observers might prudently argue for a period of hours or days between dosing healthy volunteers in any Phase I trial, investigators and ethics review boards typically view this as impractical, especially given how rare it is for serious harm to occur (Hedgecoe 2014).

5 The comparison between nonhuman animal research and Phase I trials is obviously not absolute. Unlike nonhuman animals, healthy volunteers are allowed a nonresearch life outside of a protocol's scope. They can choose how and when they participate, and their lives are not intentionally "sacrificed" at the study's end (Birke 2012). Nonetheless, the concept of the healthy volunteer as a model organism gives analytic traction for understanding the dynamic of what it means to qualify for a Phase I trial, be confined to a research facility, and be subjected to a study protocol's rules and obligations.

6 These studies were originally called "first-in-man" clinical trials, but the industry has largely abandoned that term for the gender-neutral alternative since 1993, when the FDA lifted its ban on the enrollment of "women of childbearing potential" in early-phase trials (Corrigan 2002; Fisher and Ronald 2010). Of course, despite the regulatory change and the new term, these trials are almost exclusively filled with male volunteers.

7 Specifically, to market their products in Japan, pharmaceutical companies must complete small-scale clinical trials using ethnic Japanese participants to confirm

that Japanese bodies exposed to traditional Japanese diets metabolize the drugs similarly to the original trial subjects' bodies (Kelly and Nichter 2012). For more on generics, see Carpenter and Tobbell (2011).

8 It is noteworthy that a critical word is absent from this phrase. Without administering the investigational drug, staff would have little reason to feed participants or collect blood from them. The more appropriate phrase would be "dose 'em and bleed 'em," or better yet, "drug 'em and drain 'em," especially for those days when volunteers could expect frequent blood draws following the dose. Obviously, what makes the industry's phrase work is its cadence and rhyme, but it also occludes the single most important procedure conveying the risk of harm to participants.

9 Healthy volunteers similarly understood that, as humans, their important contribution to Phase I trials was through self-reporting adverse events. For example, Jake, a white man in his thirties, said of his role in research, "I'm a human petri dish: you know, you give me a shot, I tell you how it feels later. That's all they're asking [of me]."

10 Paul's rather heroic scientific narrative is also highly gendered. It reflects a more traditional masculine approach to science with its roots in the Scientific Revolution in which brave men had to unflinchingly explore the dangers and mysteries of nature (see also Merchant 1990).

11 Laura Stark documents the fascinating history of the "normal controls" residential research program at the National Institutes of Health (NIH), wherein healthy volunteers were "procured" for NIH researchers beginning in the 1950s through contracts with religious organizations (Stark 2018, forthcoming). These early "normal" volunteers were more broadly representative of the general healthy population than are today's Phase I healthy volunteers.

12 In my first book, *Medical Research for Hire* (2009), I describe screening for a Phase I trial as part of my research. I was summarily dismissed when the research staff member evaluated my veins and deemed them to be so poor that she did not even bother drawing my blood. Healthy women volunteers often feel they are at a disadvantage when research staff evaluate their veins (Jain, Cottingham, and Fisher in press).

13 Similarly, in her analysis of athletes as model organisms, Andi Johnson (2013) found that researchers in studies of fatigue and human performance valued athletes for their "big veins."

14 Research staff's constructions of ideal veins also inflected how healthy volunteers saw themselves. Even though Adam was a first-time participant when I met him, he recounted a story about a man who had been at the screening visit and was sent home because of his veins. Adam boasted about his own: "They don't even have to tie mine off; they can hit mine, I mean. Mine are perfect." The real testament to embodying the role of ideal research subject is when serial participants gain enough expertise about phlebotomy and their own bodies to aid the research staff. Brian, a study veteran who traveled the entire country to enroll in Phase I trials, proclaimed, "When they teach you how to do this [draw blood], they make this based on a clock. And then, you know, it's one o'clock, six o'clock, twelve

o'clock, whatever the time is. . . . I used to tell people, I said, 'Look, you need to go into me like 1:30, and the more sticks I have, the deeper you need to go.' 'Cause a lot of times they're afraid to go deep, so you need to know your body, particularly for the blood draws." Not all research staff appreciate instruction from participants, but these participants' embodied expertise highlights how they become model organisms for Phase I trials.

15 It should not be forgotten that participants can withdraw from a clinical trial at any time for any reason; that is a right granted to them by US federal protections of research subjects. For the sake of the study data and their contracts with the sponsors, research staff attempt to select participants who are unlikely to do so.

16 The Phase I clinic is routinely a locked space, and the women staff were highly aware of being locked into that space with healthy volunteers who were predominantly men. While they were not afraid of the participants per se, some expressed anxiety about what *could* happen. For example, Roxanne, an African American nurse at Academic Phase I who said that the clinic reminded her of a locked psych ward, confessed her anxiety that someday a study participant would become violent. Painting a vivid—and rather cinematic—scenario of what might happen, she pictured herself being attacked and strangled. Pausing to consider further what might happen, she added that she trusted another participant would overpower her attacker and prevent him from killing her. For her part, Kristen, a white phlebotomist at Cottage Phase I, experienced a threatening incident in which a participant had "some sort of psychotic break and was convinced I was trying to kill him!" In a bizarre coincidence, Kristen's story shared a detail with Roxanne's fear-triggered scenario: a healthy volunteer who was a trained "Ultimate Fighter" was there to help protect her and together they safely got the threatening participant out of the clinic and called the police. Reflecting on the dangerous man's mental state, Kristen hypothesized, "I bet people do go off their meds to get into studies. I'm sure he wasn't the only one. He's the only one who just lost it. Some people probably can hold it together for three to five days." She shuddered, "Well, I don't want to know about that."

17 One might expect that if research staff were vigilant about screening out participants who might prove a danger to those in the clinic, then someone with a criminal record would have trouble qualifying for a study. This is not the case. Instead, participants with a history of incarceration are actually deemed well suited to confinement studies. Because Phase I trials are very structured and invasive, participants have to be comfortable with losing some control over their schedules, actions, and bodies during a study. Thus, from the staff's perspective, good participants are comfortable being told what to do and when to do it. The presumed advantage of those who have been incarcerated is that they can be seen as more predictable in a confined or institutionalized setting than those who have never experienced that type of loss of freedom before. However, even when participants agreed that clinical trials can be positive for someone struggling to find a job because of a criminal record, they often expressed concern about being

in studies with former inmates. Many believed that former criminals would have no qualms about stealing other participants' belongings or robbing them of their compensation at a study's end. Indeed, rumors of such occurrences abounded.

18 I have to admit that Pharma Phase I's docking system was also a huge source of stress for me because I did not want to cost participants a portion of their study compensation. Whenever I conducted an interview with a healthy volunteer there, I found out when that participant's next procedure was so I could help watch the clock. If the interview was not complete when it was time for the event, we simply paused the recorder while the participant went to the procedure and then picked back up where we had left off.

19 No one wants to walk out of a Phase I trial with less money than was promised. Nonetheless, a remarkable thing about Pharma Phase I's structure is that many participants voiced appreciation for how clinical trials there ran. Larry, a white man in his late fifties, explicitly condemned clinics that either did not have rules or failed to enforce them: "I think a lot of these studies could be run a little smoother. A lot of times the inmates take over and, you know, kind of run the place themself instead of being specific, you know, as to what should be done when."

More profoundly, Charles, an African American man in his late thirties, made it seem like Pharma Phase I's structure and clinical trials more generally had been transformative for his life. He had participated in about a dozen studies in so many years, and he said of his Phase I trial experience, "So, there's a science to it, being involved in science. I mean I've gotten that as a tool, you know, from being a participant in a study and knowing how a study operates is disciplining me in that sense and gives me a different outlook in how to approach things [outside of studies] to make them run smooth."

CHAPTER 6. THE DARK SIDE OF THE MODEL

1 Extrinsic validity threats could also be analyzed as "organizational deviance" (Vaughan 1996). Adam Hedgecoe (2014) used this concept to explain how Phase I trials can go awry when no one person or group has technically done anything wrong. Investigating the life-threatening adverse events in a first-in-human trial in London, Hedgecoe argues that organizational cultures normalize deviance because they facilitate clinical trials' speed and efficiency. Likewise, the validity problems I present here are pervasive in Phase I research, but they can be seen as undermining the purported safety mission of clinical trials and drug development more broadly.

2 STS scholars have written about the politics of "undone science" (Frickel et al. 2010) and "strategic ignorance" (Heimer 2012; McGoey 2009, 2012b). These are helpful concepts for understanding how science operates in the pharmaceutical industry. Specifically, the testing required for pharmaceuticals to come to market leaves many clinical blind spots about these products. For example, drugs are rarely tested for long-term use, either to assess their safety or efficacy, yet patients

often take such products for months, years, or even decades. As a result of this "undone science," the pharmaceutical industry can leverage "strategic ignorance" that typically makes their products appear safer and more efficacious than they really are.

3 The literature and national debate focus on "women" rather than "females," which conflates sex and gender. Technically, the scientific concern is about sex (i.e., female versus male participants), but the social justice concerns are largely about gender (i.e., opportunities for women to participate equally in clinical trials).

4 Although most staff desired greater inclusion of women in Phase I trials, they also agreed that excluding women of childbearing potential was prudent. Roxanne, an Academic Phase I study nurse, provided an example: "We don't really do childbearing women [studies], which I'm probably, actually, a little happy about because the whole pregnancy thing, that would be a nightmare to deal with. . . . It's like if they get pregnant, yikes! It's, it's a bigger yikes for us, I think." Because the clinic and sponsor would have to follow the woman throughout her pregnancy, Roxanne believed the fallout for the clinic was greater than it was for a participant who became pregnant. Of course, collecting additional data on adverse fetal outcomes would likely be stressful for any woman who chose to continue the pregnancy instead of seeking an abortion. Moreover, as-yet unpublished data from my longitudinal study of healthy volunteers indicate that women do get pregnant while enrolled in Phase I trials, typically when they are not confined to the clinic and have additional follow-up visits to complete. Even in my modest sample of 47 women, two became pregnant in clinical trials during the three years of my study. Both women had abortions, but they knew other women in similar situations who had chosen to continue their pregnancies. Cases like these are important obstacles to changing norms around women's Phase I trial inclusion.

5 Robust social science scholarship delves into the politics of genetics and race (e.g., Bliss 2012, 2018; Koenig, Lee, and Richardson 2008; Nelson 2011; Reardon 2009; Whitmarsh and Jones 2010).

6 Tanya held the view that biological differences are the cause of health disparities in the etiology and treatment of cardiovascular disease. This is a contested view in medicine and the social sciences, which tend to attribute at least some differences to social factors, such as differing access to and type of healthcare received. Even differences that are assumed to be biological are often thought to stem from the environment, such as the impact on the body of the stress caused by racism and social inequalities. A more theoretical treatment of the history of racial differences in the science and treatment of heart disease can be found in Anne Pollock's (2012) book on the topic. While her goal is not to sort out the messy interaction between biological and social factors' impact on health and disease, she illustrates the persistence of beliefs about racial differences even when existing epidemiological data could and should challenge such views. This indicates the degree to which, in Pollock's terms, race will remain a "durable preoccupation" in medicine.

Additionally, Jonathan Kahn (2012) and Janet Shim (2014) also astutely explore heart disease, race, and social inequalities in their scholarship.

7 The quintessential example of such corporate decision-making can be found in the case of the Ford "Pinto" automobile. Ford opted not to add to each Pinto an $11 part that would prevent gas tank ruptures and fire when the car was rear-ended. Part of the reason for not doing so derived from company estimates of how much Ford would have to pay in lawsuits for not fixing the problem, which was calculated at a lower overall cost than adding the part to each car produced (see Dowie 1977).

8 Later-phase trials are typically not conducted as confinement studies, so some might argue that these validity concerns are sorted out once patients are taking investigational drugs in their "natural" environments. This certainly improves the knowledge generated about pharmaceuticals, but safety and tolerability studies on healthy volunteers are premised on the idea that it is important to distinguish between bodily changes that could be caused by the investigational drug and those caused by the disease. Safety concerns that emerge later are more likely to be attributed to the illness rather than the drug, and typically no data are collected in later trials on patients about how food, caffeine, exercise, and so on might affect the action of the drug. More importantly, large-scale Phase III clinical trials have also been criticized for lacking real-world protocols that would better mirror the conditions in which patients seek treatment and manage illness (see, for example, Light and Maturo 2015; Montgomery 2017; Tunis, Stryer, and Clancy 2003).

9 It is possible for healthy volunteers to enroll simultaneously in two studies. This can be done if a trial has a relatively long period of outpatient visits following the confinement period and a participant begins a new study before those visits are concluded. Another, more difficult to execute scenario is when a trial has multiple confinement periods that are separated by enough days out of the clinic that someone could join a short trial before returning to the first study.

10 Of course, not all serial participants break the rules. In fact, some found it baffling that their peers would risk getting kicked out or banned from studies by engaging in such behavior. For instance, Joseph, the African American participant who spoke about the inclusion-exclusion criteria making drugs seem safer than they are, was critical of people who break the rules: "There're guys sneaking in candies and stuff. . . . Come on, give me a break. You know? You're just doing it because you just wanna buck the system. You just wanna thumb up your nose at authority or something. I don't know. . . . I mean, you're not supposed to be doing exercise. Some people will close their curtain [around their bed] and just do push-ups and stuff like that. What?! Why? Just relax. You know? Geez. You're getting paid to relax."

11 There are clear cultural prohibitions against snitching when it comes to criminal activity (Morris 2010; Natapoff 2009), and these codes of conduct also seem to apply to the Phase I clinic. Individuals prefer to mind their own business and keep out of trouble rather than informing the staff about someone else's wrongdoing.

12 In her book on the clinical trials industry, Adriana Petryna (2009) describes in detail the institutional structures that promote wide-scale underreporting of harms caused by pharmaceuticals while they are being tested. The data here support the points she has made, particularly in terms of the economic incentives and disincentives surrounding adverse event reporting.

13 Unfortunately, I did not have the opportunity to observe any meetings between investigators and sponsors when they adjudicated adverse events. This would be a fruitful area for future research, notwithstanding the likely obstacles to gaining access to these conversations.

14 Interestingly, healthy volunteers were the only ones to articulate validity concerns about this aspect of the trial process. Even though this does not change disincentives to reporting, evidence suggests that it could prompt some individuals to report their symptoms out of concern about providing accurate data for future patients (see also McManus and Fisher 2018). In contrast, the research staff did not explicitly link their active negotiations with sponsors around AE coding as a validity threat. Perhaps this was because they self-censored when talking to me or there was enough ambiguity in determining causation that they had confidence that the process did not unduly affect trial outcomes.

CHAPTER 7. CONSENTING TO ADVERSE EVENTS

1 In my sample, a staff member at Academic Phase I and CRO Phase I typically did one-on-one consent sessions with healthy volunteers. Because of the lower volume of participants screening at these clinics, individual appointments rather than en-masse screening appeared to make their workflow more efficient.

2 Participants are given a copy of the consent form to take home, so it is quite possible they read through the information more carefully after their screening visit.

3 This also mirrors what I described earlier when I illustrated how staff almost never consider short-term symptoms as "harm" to participants.

4 Participants rarely talked explicitly about IRBs. In one instance, Tia, an African American in her early thirties who had participated in more than 35 studies, described her decision *not* to contact the IRB even after a staff member broke a catheter off in her arm. She was concerned that if the IRB closed down the clinic, it would take away an important economic opportunity for people. However, other participants might have thought Tia was naive in her view of the power IRBs have over clinics. Eddie, an African American long-time participant in his early forties, derided IRBs: "When I first came into the industry, I thought they were a government agency and they regulated everything, and now I know that they're independent and they're commercial. And pretty much, even though they're independent, it really is a conflict of interest because they're hired by whatever company they work for." Eddie was tapped into major concerns about the current IRB system, which does allow commercial—though normally referred to as "centralized"—IRBs to oversee and manage clinical trials.

His criticism demonstrates that knowledge about IRBs does not unilaterally enhance participants' trust in the research enterprise. For scholarly criticisms of commercial IRBs, see Emanuel, Lemmens, and Elliot (2006) and Lemmens and Freedman (2000).

5 Recall that earlier Ross related several stories of research misconduct he had witnessed.

6 I have opted here not to engage the question of how people's financial situations shape their view of risk. Of course, people weigh the risk of not earning income through clinical trials against the risk of enrolling in these studies, and I have shown elsewhere how this dynamic is central to healthy volunteers' risk perceptions (Cottingham and Fisher 2016). The problem with this approach to risk perception is that it implies that clinical trials are a de facto risky activity to pursue. I find it more fruitful to focus on how, given the fact that Phase I trials are relatively low risk, healthy volunteers manage that risk to the best of their ability.

CHAPTER 8. CONSTRUCTING RISK KNOWLEDGE

1 In most cases, the companies testing CSF have designed their drugs to cross the blood-brain barrier in order to treat central nervous system conditions. Much drug development for Alzheimer's disease is premised on the idea that for the treatment to be effective, high concentrations of the drug must be present in the brain (Pardridge 2009).

2 This is perhaps a misplaced fear as drugs that successfully cross the blood-brain barrier might increase participants' risk, exposing them to the possibility of seizures or cognitive impairment (Upadhyay 2014).

3 This stance was notably in contrast to the participants who had experienced sleep paralysis during their study at Academic Phase I. Once the adverse event had passed, those participants were unconcerned about the experience. In this case, Devon and Manuel were adamant they would not do another lumbar puncture study even though they had gotten through it relatively unscathed.

4 I do not mean to imply that Devon might not have been harmed by these errors. It is possible that if he moved while the needle was sticking out of his back, he could have injured a nerve or worse. Additionally, the loss of additional CSF beyond that which was collected for the study could have contributed to a severe spinal headache.

5 This expression, which dates back to Plato, refers to the longstanding problem of defining knowledge (Fine 2003). Kirstin Borgerson (2014) also uses this expression in her description of social epistemology, which focuses on how the creation and maintenance of knowledge is a social, not individual, enterprise.

6 Despite healthy volunteers' assertions about avoiding particular types of Phase I trials, research staff did not identify these same trials as recruitment challenges. It is possible that newcomers are more likely to enroll in less desirable studies than are serial participants, but it remains a bit of a mystery how so many healthy

volunteers could claim to avoid these studies without affecting clinics' enrollment for such trials. At least in Devon's case, he was a first-time participant, but Manuel was in his fourth study.

7 Cryder at al. (2010) also found that participants believe compensation amounts are tied to risk.

8 This experience was harrowing for Tia not only because the drug had such an unexpectedly virulent effect on the participants' bodies, but also because she believed the clinic had failed to put their safety above the interests of their client, the pharmaceutical company: "I'm shocked that they kept the study going because the doctor himself told me this is the worst study ever. . . . [I told them,] 'I'm sick. You should've stopped this study.' They said the sponsor [the pharmaceutical company] would not agree. *Would not.* I thought the doctors had the right to pull the study if they felt that it was not safe."

9 Contemporary legends—or more colloquially, urban legends or myths—are stories with longevity that circulate widely and are told as true events that occurred to someone within the teller's social network but who is not directly known to the teller. Using elements of humor as well as horror, contemporary legends tend to contain a moral, often communicating a warning to the listener (DiFonzo and Bordia 2007). For example, Joel Best and Gerald Horiuchi (1985) analyzed the 1970s emergence of contemporary legends about Halloween sadists, individuals who were adulterating candy to kill or harm children. There are also contemporary legends about the medical profession, especially those focused on black market organ theft, wherein the poor and unsuspecting are targets (Campion-Vincent 2002; Dingwall 2001). Risk, vulnerability, and distrust are common features of the tales (Fine 1992; Turner 1993). I have developed the theme of Phase I contemporary legends, including additional stories, more fully in a separate publication (see Fisher 2015b).

CHAPTER 9. SPECULATING ON HEALTH

1 This is a further example of the issue discussed earlier of how pharmaceutical companies create strict inclusion-exclusion criteria to either keep participants safe in the trial and/or make their drugs appear safer than they might actually be.

2 Ellen's job responsibilities also included business administration functions, so a generous reading of this series of events could attribute her reaction that day to the stress associated with the clinic's lost income from the postponed study. Concerns about the clinic's financial stability were part of the broader context of how the research staff discussed their work there. For this particular clinical trial, Academic Phase I gambled that they would have a sufficient number of healthy volunteers to conduct it (and illuminated why clinics typically want alternates to check in for each trial). In this instance, they lost, just as did the participants who showed up that day for the trial.

3 Individuals do, of course, have the right to decline enrollment or to end their research participation at any time for any reason. Failing to show up is one way

of exercising this right, but it creates difficulties for the clinics because staff are unaware they need to continue recruitment. For this reason, some clinics blacklist healthy volunteers who fail to check in after agreeing to participate. Academic Phase I did not have this policy, but being "no-shows" could have affected those individuals' future participation if the staff selected others for a new study instead.

4 Typically, men expressed more freedom to adhere to the criteria they set for their participation because studies for healthy males are generally abundant. In contrast, women have fewer study choices (Jain, Cottingham, and Fisher, in press), so Shirley and others often prioritized the money offered in otherwise unappealing Phase I trials. Tia, an African American in her early thirties who relied solely on clinical trial income, articulated the dilemma women face: "Sometimes for women it's really hard to find a study, so you kinda compromise yourself. When you find something that's there, you take it." Earlier, Tia also talked about the limited number of studies available to women as a reason not to observe the washout period.

5 Determining how to condition one's body for clinical trials is also an epistemological process, comparable to what we saw earlier when participants constructed collective understandings about risk. However, risk perceptions were generally more consistent across participants than were their health-promoting behaviors.

6 This, of course, also mirrors previous discussions about healthy volunteers' tendency to blame the victim of adverse events.

7 Dennis did not flag this aspect of the problem, but spirometry might create a larger hurdle for African American participants to meet inclusion-exclusion criteria for "normal" lung capacity. In her historical study of the spirometer, Lundy Braun (2014) illustrates how racial "differences" have been constructed in biomedicine in ways that affirm social and political hierarchies of health that mirror racist views held about African Americans. Based on the specious assumption that African Americans have a "naturally" higher lung capacity than whites, the technology demands that the race of the patient/participant be identified and entered into the machine. African Americans' measurements are automatically reduced by 15 percent, purportedly to normalize their results. For Braun, the importance of these "race corrections" is that African Americans need to have a higher threshold of lung damage to qualify for workman's compensation in employment sectors that pose such a risk (e.g., asbestos workers). Depending on how spirometers are used in Phase I trials, African Americans might be disadvantaged by having their lung capacity automatically lowered compared to white participants who would be given their unadjusted results.

8 There are no published studies about the long-term harms—if there are any—of enrolling serially in Phase I trials. Meta-analyses of Phase I adverse events instead evaluate the risk of participating in single clinical trials (Emanuel et al. 2015; Kumagai et al. 2006; Sibille et al. 1998, 2006).

9 Eddie repeatedly referred to experienced serial participants as "veterans" during his interview. To clarify his use of the words "us" and "we," I inserted "study veterans" in brackets.

10 Similarly, in a study of healthy volunteers' experiences participating in Phase I trials, Kass et al. (2007) found that they rarely mentioned risk.

BIBLIOGRAPHY

Abadie, Roberto. 2010. *The professional guinea pig: Big pharma and the risky world of human subjects*. Durham, NC: Duke University Press.

Abraham, John. 2010. "Pharmaceuticalization of society in context: Theoretical, empirical and health dimensions." *Sociology* 44 (4):603–622.

Abraham, John, and Courtney Davis. 2005. "A comparative analysis of drug safety withdrawals in the UK and the US (1971–1992): Implications for current regulatory thinking and policy." *Social Science and Medicine* 61 (5):881–892.

Adams, Vincanne, Suellen Miller, Sienna Craig, Nyima, Sonam, Droyoung, Lhakpen, and Michael Varner. 2005. "The challenge of cross-cultural clinical trials research: Case report from the Tibetan Autonomous Region, People's Republic of China." *Medical Anthropology Quarterly* 19 (3):267–289.

Almeida, Luis, Benedita Azevedo, Teresa Nunes, Manuel Vaz-da-Silva, and Patricio Soares-da-Silva. 2007. "Why healthy subjects volunteer for phase I studies and how they perceive their participation?" *European Journal of Clinical Pharmacology* 63 (11):1085–1094.

Anderson, James A., and Jonathan Kimmelman. 2014. "Are phase 1 trials therapeutic? Risk, ethics, and division of labor." *Bioethics* 28 (3):138–146.

Angell, Marcia. 2004. *The truth about the drug companies: How they deceive us and what to do about it*. New York: Random House.

Ankeny, Rachel A., and Sabina Leonelli. 2011. "What's so special about model organisms?" *Studies in History and Philosophy of Science* 42 (2):313–323.

Appelbaum, Paul S., Charles W. Lidz, and Thomas Grisso. 2004. "Therapeutic misconception in clinical research: Frequency and risk factors." *IRB: Ethics and Human Research* 26 (2):1–8.

Arnold, Kathleen R. 2007. *America's new working class: Race, gender, and ethnicity in a biopolitical age*. University Park: Pennsylvania State University Press.

Badenhausen, Kurt. 2009. "The world's highest-paid athletes." *Forbes*, June 17, 2009. https://www.forbes.com.

Banerjee, Subhabrata Bobby. 2008. "Corporate social responsibility: The good, the bad and the ugly." *Critical Sociology* 34 (1):51–79.

Barnes, Barry. 1977. *Interests and the growth of knowledge*. London: Routledge.

Battelle. 2015. Biopharmaceutical industry-sponsored clinical trials: Impact on state economies. Washington, DC: Pharmaceutical Research and Manufacturers of America (PhRMA). http://phrma-docs.phrma.org.

Bell, Susan E., and Anne E. Figert. 2012. "Medicalization and pharmaceuticalization at the intersections: Looking backward, sideways and forward." *Social Science and Medicine* 75 (5):775–83.

Berger, Michele T. 2006. *Workable sisterhood: The political journey of stigmatized women with HIV/AIDS*. Princeton, NJ: Princeton University Press.

Bertrand, Marianne, and Sendhil Mullainathan. 2004. "Are Emily and Greg more employable than Lakisha and Jamal? A field experiment on labor market discrimination." *American Economic Review* 94 (4):991–1013.

Best, Joel, and Gerald T. Horiuchi. 1985. "The razor blade in the apple: The social construction of urban legends." *Social Problems* 32 (5):488–499.

Biddle, Justin. 2007. "Lessons from the Vioxx debacle: What the privatization of science can teach us about social epistemology." *Social Epistemology* 21 (1):21–39.

Biller-Andorno, Nikola, Herwig Grimm, and Rebecca L. Walker. 2015. "Professionalism and ethics in animal research." *Nature biotechnology* 33 (10):1027–1028.

Birke, Lynda. 2012. "Animal bodies in the production of scientific knowledge: Modelling medicine." *Body and Society* 18 (3–4):156–178.

Birke, Lynda, Arnold Arluke, and Mike Michael. 2007. *The sacrifice: How scientific experiments transform animals and people*. West Lafayette, IN: Purdue University Press.

Bliss, Catherine. 2012. *Race decoded: The genomic fight for social justice*. Stanford, CA: Stanford University Press.

Bliss, Catherine. 2018. *Social by nature: The promise and peril of sociogenomics*. Stanford, CA: Stanford University Press.

Bonham, Valerie H., and Jonathan D. Moreno. 2008. "Research with captive populations: Prisoners, students, and soldiers." In *The Oxford textbook of clinical research ethics*, edited by Ezekiel J. Emanuel, Christine Grady, Robert A. Crouch, Reidar K. Lie, Franklin G. Miller, and David Wendler, 461–474. New York: Oxford University Press.

Bonilla-Silva, Eduardo. 1997. "Rethinking racism: Toward a structural interpretation." *American Sociological Review* 62 (3):465–480.

Borfitz, Deborah. 2013. "R&D cuts by sponsors spur more collaboration, innovation." *CenterWatch Monthly* 20 (5):1, 16–18, 20.

Borgerson, Kirstin. 2014. "Redundant, secretive, and isolated: When are clinical trials scientifically valid?" *Kennedy Institute of Ethics Journal* 24 (4):385–411.

Bourgois, Philippe. 1995. *In search of respect: Selling crack in el barrio*. New York: Cambridge University Press.

Braun, Lundy. 2014. *Breathing race into the machine: The surprising career of the spirometer from plantation to genetics*. Minneapolis: University of Minnesota Press.

Briggs, Laura. 2002. *Reproducing empire: Race, sex, science, and U.S. Imperialism in Puerto Rico*. Berkeley: University of California Press.

Brody, Howard. 2008. *Hooked: Ethics, the medical profession, and the pharmaceutical industry*. New York: Rowman and Littlefield.

Brown, Andrew D. 2015. "Identities and identity work in organizations." *International Journal of Management Reviews* 17 (1):20–40.

Brown, Donathan. 2013. "Manufacturing fear, creating the threat: The state of American immigration policy." *Journal of Latino/Latin American Studies* 5 (1):57–67.

Brown, Sally. 2005. "Travelling with a purpose: Understanding the motives and benefits of volunteer vacationers." *Current Issues in Tourism* 8 (6):479–496.

Burke, Nancy J. 2014. "Rethinking the therapeutic misconception: Social justice, patient advocacy, and cancer clinical trial recruitment in the US safety net." *BMC Medical Ethics* 15 (1):68.

Busfield, Joan. 2006. "Pills, power, people: Sociological understandings of the pharmaceutical industry." *Sociology* 40 (2):297–314.

Campbell, Nancy D. 2007. *Discovering addiction: The science and politics of substance abuse research*. Ann Arbor: University of Michigan Press.

Campion-Vincent, Véronique. 2002. "Organ theft narratives as medical and social critique." *Journal of Folklore Research* 39 (1):33–50.

Carpenter, Daniel. 2010. *Reputation and power: Organizational image and pharmaceutical regulation at the FDA*. Princeton, NJ: Princeton University Press.

Carpenter, Daniel, and Dominique A. Tobbell. 2011. "Bioequivalence: The regulatory career of a pharmaceutical concept." *Bulletin of the History of Medicine* 85 (1):93–131.

Cashman, David. 2017. "'The most atypical experience of my life': The experience of popular music festivals on cruise ships." *Tourist Studies* 17 (3):245–262.

Cavens, Luc, and Steven Ramael. 2009. "Cerebrospinal fluid sampling in phase 1 clinical trials: Mind over matter?" *SGS Life Science | Technical Bulletin* (30):1–5.

CenterWatch. 2007. "FDA tells sponsors to review MDS Pharma Services' pharmacokinetic data." *CenterWatch Weekly* 11 (3):1, 3.

Chapman, Audrey R. 2011. "Addressing the ethical challenges of first-in-human trials." *Journal of Clinical Research and Bioethics* 2 (4):113.

Chen, Alice, Hilary Wright, Hawi Itana, Merina Elahi, Ayomide Igun, Guoxing Soon, Anne R. Pariser, and Emmanuel O. Fadiran. 2018. "Representation of women and minorities in clinical trials for new molecular entities and original therapeutic biologics approved by FDA CDER from 2013 to 2015." *Journal of Women's Health* 27 (4):418–429.

Clarke, Adele E. 1998. *Disciplining reproduction: Modernity, American life sciences, and "the problems of sex."* Berkeley: University of California Press.

Clayton, Janine A., and Francis S. Collins. 2014. "NIH to balance sex in cell and animal studies." *Nature* 509 (7500):282–283.

Cohn, Samuel, and Mark Fossett. 1995. "Why racial employment inequality is greater in northern labor markets: Regional differences in white-black employment differentials." *Social Forces* 74 (2):511–542.

Collins, Patricia Hill. 2009 [1990]. *Black feminist thought: Knowledge, consciousness, and the politics of empowerment*. New York: Routledge.

Cooper, Melinda. 2008. "Experimental labour: Offshoring clinical trials to China." *East Asian Science, Technology and Society: An International Journal* 2 (1):73–92.

Cooper, Melinda, and Catherine Waldby. 2014. *Clinical labor: Tissue donors and research subjects in the global bioeconomy*. Durham, NC: Duke University Press.

Corbie-Smith, Giselle M. 2004. "Minority recruitment and participation in health research." *North Carolina Medical Journal* 65 (6):385–387.

Corbie-Smith, Giselle, Stephen B. Thomas, and Diane Marie M. St. George. 2002. "Distrust, race, and research." *Archives of Internal Medicine* 162:2458–2463.

Corbie-Smith, Giselle, Stephen B. Thomas, Mark V. Williams, and Sandra Moody-Ayers. 1999. "Attitudes and beliefs of African Americans toward participation in medical research." *Journal of General Internal Medicine* 14:537–546.

Corrigan, Oonagh P. 2002. "'First in man': The politics and ethics of women in clinical drug trials." *Feminist Review* 72:40–52.

Corrigan, Oonagh. 2003. "Empty ethics: The problem with informed consent." *Sociology of Health and Illness* 25 (3):768–792.

Cottingham, Marci D., and Jill A. Fisher. 2016. "Risk and emotion among healthy volunteers in clinical trials." *Social Psychology Quarterly* 79 (3):222–42.

Cottingham, Marci D., and Jill A. Fisher. 2017. "From fantasy to reality: Managing biomedical risk emotions in and through fictional media." *Health, Risk and Society* 19 (5–6):284–300.

Crenshaw, Kimberlé W. 1991. "Mapping the margins: Intersectionality, identity politics, and violence against women of color." *Stanford Law Review* 43 (6):1241–1299.

Cryder, Cynthia E., Alex John London, Kevin G. Volpp, and George Loewenstein. 2010. "Informative inducement: Study payment as a signal of risk." *Social Science and Medicine* 70 (3):455–464.

Daston, Lorraine, and Gregg Mitman, eds. 2005. *Thinking with animals: New perspectives on anthropomorphism.* New York: Columbia University Press.

Davies, Gail. 2012. "What is a humanized mouse? Remaking the species and spaces of translational medicine." *Body and Society* 18 (3–4):126–155.

Davis, Arlene M., Sara Chandros Hull, Christine Grady, Benjamin S. Wilfond, and Gail E. Henderson. 2002. "The invisible hand in clinical research: The study coordinator's critical role in human subjects protection." *Journal of Law, Medicine and Ethics* 30 (3):411–419.

Dawson, Marcelle C. 2017. "CrossFit: Fitness cult or reinventive institution?" *International Review for the Sociology of Sport* 52 (3):361–379.

DeMello, Margo. 2012. *Animals and society: An introduction to human-animal studies.* New York: Columbia University Press.

Derendorf, Hartmut, Lawrence J. Lesko, Philip Chaikin, Wayne A. Colburn, Peter Lee, Raymond Miller, Robert Powell, Gerald Rhodes, Donald Stanski, and Jurgen Venitz. 2000. "Pharmacokinetic/pharmacodynamic modeling in drug research and development." *Journal of Clinical Pharmacology* 40 (12):1399–1418.

Devine, Eric G., Megan E. Waters, Megan Putnam, Caitlin Surprise, Katie O'Malley, Courtney Richambault, Rachel L. Fishman, Clifford M. Knapp, Elissa H. Patterson, Ofra Sarid-Segal, Chris Streeter, Laurie Colanari, and Domenic A. Ciraulo. 2013. "Concealment and fabrication by experienced research subjects." *Clinical Trials* 10 (6):935–948.

Dickert, Neal, and Christine Grady. 1999. "What's the price of a research subject? Approaches to payment for research participation." *New England Journal of Medicine* 341 (3):198–203.

Dickert, Neal W. 2013. "Concealment and fabrication: The hidden price of payment for research participation?" *Clinical Trials* 10 (6):840–841.

DiFonzo, Nicholas, and Prashant Bordia. 2007. "Rumor, gossip and urban legends." *Diogenes* 54 (1):19–35.

Dingwall, Robert. 2001. "Contemporary legends, rumours, and collective behaviour: Some neglected resources for medical sociology?" *Sociology of Health and Illness* 23 (2):180–202.

Dohan, Daniel. 2003. *The price of poverty: Money, work, and culture in the Mexican American barrio*. Berkeley: University of California Press.

Donohue, Julie. 2006. "A history of drug advertising: The evolving roles of consumers and consumer protection." *Milbank Quarterly* 84 (4):659–699.

Dowie, Mark. 1977. "Pinto madness." *Mother Jones* September/October. www.motherjones.com.

Downing, Nicholas S., Nilay D. Shah, Jenerius A. Aminawung, Alison M. Pease, Jean-David Zeitoun, Harlan M. Krumholz, and Joseph S. Ross. 2017. "Postmarket safety events among novel therapeutics approved by the US Food and Drug Administration between 2001 and 2010." *JAMA* 317 (18):1854–1863.

Dresser, Rebecca. 2002. "The ubiquity and utility of the therapeutic misconception." *Social Philosophy and Policy* 19 (2):271–294.

Dresser, Rebecca. 2013. "Subversive subjects: Rule-breaking and deception in clinical trials." *Journal of Law, Medicine and Ethics* 41 (4):829–840.

Dumit, Joseph. 2012. *Drugs for life: How pharmaceutical companies define our health*. Durham, NC: Duke University Press.

Ecks, Stefan. 2013. *Eating drugs: Psychopharmaceutical pluralism in India*. New York: New York University Press.

Edelblute, Heather B., and Jill A. Fisher. 2015. "Using 'clinical trial diaries' to track patterns of participation for serial healthy volunteers in U.S. Phase I studies." *Journal of Empirical Research on Human Research Ethics* 10 (1):65–75.

Edin, Kathryn, and Timothy J. Nelson. 2013. *Doing the best I can: Fatherhood in the inner city*. Berkeley: University of California Press.

Elliott, Carl. 2008. "Guinea-pigging: Healthy human subjects for drug-safety trials are in demand. But is it a living?" *New Yorker*, January 7, 36–41.

Elliott, Carl. 2017. "Commentary on Grady et al.: Using poor, uninsured minorities to test the safety of experimental drugs." *Clinical Trials* 14 (5):547–550.

Elliott, Carl, and Roberto Abadie. 2008. "Exploiting a research underclass in phase 1 clinical trials." *New England Journal of Medicine* 358 (22):2316–2317.

Ellis, Mark, Richard Wright, Matthew Townley, and Kristy Copeland. 2014. "The migration response to the Legal Arizona Workers Act." *Political Geography* 42:46–56.

Emanuel, Ezekiel J., Gabriella Bedarida, Kristy Macci, Nicole B. Gabler, Annette Rid, and David Wendler. 2015. "Quantifying the risks of non-oncology phase I research in healthy volunteers: Meta-analysis of phase I studies." *British Medical Journal* 350:h3271.

Emanuel, Ezekiel J., Trudo Lemmens, and Carl Elliot. 2006. "Should society allow research ethics boards to be run as for-profit enterprises?" *PLOS Medicine* 3 (7):e309.

Epstein, Steven. 2007. *Inclusion: The politics of difference in medical research.* Chicago: University of Chicago Press.

Evans, David, Michael Smith, and Liz Willen. 2005. "Big pharma's shameful secret." *Bloomberg Markets,* December.

Evelyn, B., T. Toigo, D. Banks, D. Pohl, K. Gray, B. Robins, and J. Ernat. 2001. "Participation of racial/ethnic groups in clinical trials and race-related labeling: A review of new molecular entities approved 1995–1999." *Journal of the National Medical Association* 93 (12, Suppl):18S-24S.

Faden, Ruth R., and Tom L. Beauchamp. 1986. *A history and theory of informed consent.* New York: Oxford University Press.

Fine, Gail. 2003. *Plato on knowledge and forms: Selected essays.* New York: Oxford University Press.

Fine, Gary Alan. 1992. *Manufacturing tales: Sex and money in contemporary legends.* Knoxville: University of Tennessee Press.

Fisher, Jill A. 2007. "'Ready-to-recruit' or 'ready-to-consent' populations?: Informed consent and the limits of subject autonomy." *Qualitative Inquiry* 13 (6):875–894.

Fisher, Jill A. 2009. *Medical research for hire: The political economy of pharmaceutical clinical trials.* New Brunswick, NJ: Rutgers University Press.

Fisher, Jill A. 2011. *Gender and the science of difference: Cultural politics of contemporary science and medicine.* New Brunswick, NJ: Rutgers University Press.

Fisher, Jill A. 2013. "Expanding the frame of 'voluntariness' in informed consent: Structural coercion and the power of social and economic context." *Kennedy Institute of Ethics Journal* 23 (4):355–379.

Fisher, Jill A. 2015a. "Feeding and bleeding: The institutional banalization of risk to healthy volunteers in phase I pharmaceutical clinical trials." *Science, Technology, and Human Values* 40 (2):199–226.

Fisher, Jill A. 2015b. "Stopped hearts, amputated toes, and NASA: Contemporary legends among healthy volunteers in US phase I clinical trials." *Sociology of Health and Illness* 37 (1):127–142.

Fisher, Jill A., and Marci D. Cottingham. 2017. "This isn't going to end well: Fictional representations of medical research in television and film." *Public Understanding of Science* 26 (5):564–578.

Fisher, Jill A., Marci D. Cottingham, and Corey A. Kalbaugh. 2015. "Peering into the pharmaceutical 'pipeline': Investigational drugs, clinical trials, and industry priorities." *Social Science and Medicine* 131:322–330.

Fisher, Jill A., and Corey A. Kalbaugh. 2011. "Challenging assumptions about minority participation in U.S. clinical research." *American Journal of Public Health* 101 (12):2217–2222.

Fisher, Jill A., Lisa McManus, Marci D. Cottingham, Julianne M. Kalbaugh, Megan M. Wood, Torin Monahan, and Rebecca L. Walker. 2018a. "Healthy volunteers' perceptions of risk in US phase I clinical trials: A mixed-methods study." *PLOS Medicine* 15 (11):e1002698.

Fisher, Jill A., Lisa McManus, Megan M. Wood, Marci D. Cottingham, Julianne M. Kalbaugh, Torin Monahan, and Rebecca L. Walker. 2018b. "Healthy volunteers' perceptions of the benefits of their participation in phase I clinical trials." *Journal of Empirical Research on Human Research Ethics* 13 (5):494–510.

Fisher, Jill A., and Lorna M. Ronald. 2010. "Sex, gender, and pharmaceutical politics: From drug development to marketing." *Gender Medicine* 7 (4):357–370.

Fisher, Jill A., and Rebecca L. Walker. 2019. "Advancing ethics and policy for healthy-volunteer research through a model-organism framework." *Ethics and Human Research* 41 (1):4–14.

Florida, Richard. 2009. "How the crash will reshape America." *Atlantic* 303 (2):44–56.

Frickel, Scott, Sahra Gibbon, Jeff Howard, Joanna Kempner, Gwen Ottinger, and David J. Hess. 2010. "Undone science: Charting social movement and civil society challenges to research agenda setting." *Science, Technology, and Human Values* 35 (4):444–473.

Friedman, Gerald. 2014. "Workers without employers: Shadow corporations and the rise of the gig economy." *Review of Keynesian Economics* 2 (2):171–188.

Friese, Carrie, and Adele E. Clarke. 2012. "Transposing bodies of knowledge and technique: Animal models at work in reproductive sciences." *Social Studies of Science* 42 (1):31–52.

Fujimura, Joan. 2006. "Sex genes: A critical sociomaterial approach to the politics and molecular genetics of sex determination." *Signs* 32 (1):49–82.

Garner, Joseph P., Brianna N. Gaskill, Elin M. Weber, Jamie Ahloy-Dallaire, and Kathleen R. Pritchett-Corning. 2017. "Introducing therioepistemology: The study of how knowledge is gained from animal research." *Nature* 46 (4):103–113.

Gelinas, Luke, Emily A. Largent, I. Glenn Cohen, Susan Kornetsky, Barbara E. Bierer, and Holly Fernandez Lynch. 2018. "A framework for ethical payment to research participants." *New England Journal of Medicine* 378 (8):766–771.

George, Sheba, Nelida Duran, and Keith Norris. 2014. "A systematic review of barriers and facilitators to minority research participation among African Americans, Latinos, Asian Americans, and Pacific Islanders." *American Journal of Public Health* 104 (2):E16–E31.

Getz, Kenneth A. 2013. "Public perceptions are turning the corner." *Applied Clinical Trials* 22 (5):22–23.

Gieryn, Thomas F. 2018. *Truth-spots: How places make people believe.* Chicago: University of Chicago Press.

Gilroy, Paul. 2010. *Darker than blue: On the moral economies of Black Atlantic culture.* Cambridge, MA: Belknap Press of Harvard University Press.

Goffman, Erving. 1961. *Asylums: Essays on the social situation of mental patients and other inmates.* New York: Anchor.

Goffman, Erving. 2009 [1963]. *Stigma: Notes on the management of spoiled identity*. New York: Simon and Schuster.

Goozner, Merrill. 2002. "The price isn't right." *American Prospect*, November 30. https://prospect.org.

Goozner, Merrill. 2005. *The $800 million pill: The truth behind the cost of new drugs*. Berkeley: University of California Press.

Graboyes, Melissa. 2015. *The experiment must continue: Medical research and ethics in East Africa*. Athens: Ohio University Press.

Grady, Christine, Gabriella Bedarida, Ninet Sinaii, Mark Anthony Gregorio, and Ezekiel J. Emanuel. 2017. "Motivations, enrollment decisions, and socio-demographic characteristics of healthy volunteers in phase 1 research." *Clinical Trials* 14 (5):526–536.

Greene, Jeremy A. 2007. *Prescribing by numbers: Drugs and the definition of disease*. Baltimore, MD: Johns Hopkins University Press.

Greene, Jeremy A. 2014. *Generic: The unbranding of modern medicine*. Baltimore, MD: Johns Hopkins University Press.

Grzanka, Patrick, ed. 2014. *Intersectionality: A foundations and frontiers reader*. Boulder, CO: Westview Press.

Guerrini, Anita. 2003. *Experimenting with humans and animals: From Galen to animal rights*. Baltimore, MD: Johns Hopkins University Press.

Hacker, Jacob S. 2006. *The great risk shift: The new economic insecurity and the decline of the American dream*. New York: Oxford University Press.

Halpern-Meekin, Sarah, Kathryn Edin, Laura Tach, and Jennifer Sykes. 2015. *It's not like I'm poor: How working families make ends meet in a post-welfare world*. Berkeley: University of California Press.

Haraway, Donna. 2001. "Situated knowledges: The science question in feminism and the privilege of partial perspective." In *The gender and science reader*, edited by Muriel Lederman and Ingrid Bartsch, 169–188. New York: Routledge.

Harding, David J. 2003. "Jean Valjean's dilemma: The management of ex-convict identity in the search for employment." *Deviant Behavior* 24 (6):571–595.

Harding, Sandra. 1991. *Whose science? Whose knowledge?: Thinking from women's lives*. Ithaca, NY: Cornell University Press.

Harding, Sandra. 1998. *Is science multi-cultural?: Postcolonialisms, feminisms, and epistemologies*. Bloomington: Indiana University Press.

Harkness, Jon H. 1996. "Research behind bars: A history of nontherapeutic research on American prisoners." PhD diss., University of Wisconsin–Madison.

Harris, Gardiner. 2004. "Student, 19, in trial of new antidepressant commits suicide." *New York Times*, February 12, A30.

Hawkes, Nigel. 2016. "French drug trial had three major failings, says initial report." *British Medical Journal* 352:i784.

Hayden, Cori. 2003. *When nature goes public: The making and unmaking of bioprospecting in Mexico*. Princeton, NJ: Princeton University Press.

Healy, David. 2004. *Let them eat Prozac: The unhealthy relationship between the pharmaceutical industry and depression*. New York: New York University Press.

Hedgecoe, Adam. 2014. "A deviation from standard design? Clinical trials, research ethics committees, and the regulatory co-construction of organizational deviance." *Social Studies of Science* 44 (1):59–81.

Heimer, Carol A. 2012. "Inert facts and the illusion of knowledge: Strategic uses of ignorance in HIV clinics." *Economy and Society* 41 (1):17–41.

Henderson, Gail E., Larry R. Churchill, Arlene M. Davis, Michele M. Easter, Christine Grady, Steven Joffe, Nancy Kass, Nancy M. P. King, Charles W. Lidz, Franklin G. Miller, Daniel K. Nelson, Jeffrey Peppercorn, Barbra Bluestone Rothschild, Pamela Sankar, Benjamin S. Wilfond, and Catherine R. Zimmer. 2007. "Clinical trials and medical care: Defining the therapeutic misconception." *PLOS Medicine* 4 (11):1735–1738.

Henwood, Flis, Sally Wyatt, Angie Hart, and Julie Smith. 2003. "'Ignorance is bliss sometimes': Constraints on the emergence of the 'informed patient' in the changing landscapes of health information." *Sociology of Health and Illness* 25 (6):589–607.

Hess, David J. 1997. *Science studies: An advanced introduction.* New York: New York University Press.

Hilts, Philip J. 2003. *Protecting America's health: The FDA, business, and one hundred years of regulation.* New York: Knopf.

Holder, Michelle. 2016. *African American men and the labor market during the Great Recession.* New York: Palgrave Macmillan.

Hornblum, Allen M. 1998. *Acres of skin: Human experiments at Holmesburg Prison.* New York: Routledge.

Hussain-Gambles, Mahvash. 2003. "Ethnic minority under-representation in clinical trials: Whose responsibility is it anyway?" *Journal of Health Organization and Management* 17 (2):138–143.

Iltis, Ana S. 2009. "Payments to normal healthy volunteers in phase 1 trials: Avoiding undue influence while distributing fairly the burdens of research participation." *Journal of Medicine and Philosophy* 34 (1):68–90.

Institute of Medicine. 2007. *Ethical considerations for research involving prisoners.* Edited by Committee on Ethical Considerations for Revisions to DHHS Regulations for Protection of Prisoners Involved in Research. Washington, DC: National Academies Press.

Iversen, Roberta Rehner, and Annie Laurie Armstrong. 2006. *Jobs aren't enough: Toward a new economic mobility for low-income families.* Philadelphia: Temple University Press.

Jain, Nupur, Marci D. Cottingham, and Jill A. Fisher. In press. "Disadvantaged, outnumbered, and discouraged: Women's experiences as healthy volunteers in U.S. Phase I trials." *Critical Public Health.*

Jain, S. Lochlann. 2013. *Malignant: How cancer becomes us.* Berkeley: University of California Press.

Johnson, Andi. 2013. "The athlete as model organism: The everyday practice of the science of human performance." *Social Studies of Science* 43 (6):878–904.

Johnson, J. A. 2000. "Predictability of the effects of race or ethnicity on pharmacokinetics of drugs." *International Journal of Clinical Pharmacology and Therapeutics* 38 (2):53–60.

Johnson, Rebecca A. 2016. "From altruists to workers: What claims should healthy participants in phase I trials have against trial employers?" In *Ethics and governance of biomedical research: Theory and practice*, edited by Daniel Strech and Marcel Mertz, 29–45. New York: Springer.

Johnson, Rebecca A., Annette Rid, Ezekiel Emanuel, and David Wendler. 2016. "Risks of phase I research with healthy participants: A systematic review." *Clinical Trials* 13 (2):149–160.

Jones, James H. 1981. *Bad blood: The Tuskegee syphilis experiment*. New York: Free Press.

Joseph, Galen, and Daniel Dohan. 2012. "Recruitment practices and the politics of inclusion in cancer clinical trials." *Medical Anthropology Quarterly* 26 (3):338–360.

Kahn, Jonathan. 2012. *Race in a bottle: The story of BiDil and racialized medicine in a post-genomic age*. New York: Columbia University Press.

Kalleberg, Arne L. 2011. *Good jobs, bad jobs: The rise of polarized and precarious employment systems in the United States, 1970s–2000s*. New York: Russell Sage Foundation.

Kass, N. E., R. Myers, E. J. Fuchs, K. A. Carson, and C. Flexner. 2007. "Balancing justice and autonomy in clinical research with healthy volunteers." *Clinical Pharmacology and Therapeutics* 82 (2):219–227.

Kassirer, Jerome P. 2005. *On the take: How America's complicity with big business can endanger your health*. New York: Oxford University Press.

Katz, Michael B. 2013. *The undeserving poor: America's enduring confrontation with poverty*, 2nd edition. New York: Oxford University Press.

Katzenstein, Mary Fainsod, and Mitali Nagrecha. 2011. "A new punishment regime." *Criminology and Public Policy* 10 (3):555–568.

Kaufman, Sharon R. 2015. *Ordinary medicine: Extraordinary treatments, longer lives, and where to draw the line*. Durham, NC: Duke University Press.

Kelly, Kimberly, and Mark Nichter. 2012. "The politics of local biology in transnational drug testing: Creating (bio)identities and reproducing (bio)nationalism through Japanese 'ethnobridging' studies." *East Asian Science, Technology and Society* 6 (3):379–399.

Kimmelman, J., and N. Palmour. 2005. "Therapeutic optimism in the consent forms of phase 1 gene transfer trials: An empirical analysis." *Journal of Medical Ethics* 31 (4):209–214.

Kimmelman, Jonathan. 2012. "A theoretical framework for early human studies: Uncertainty, intervention ensembles, and boundaries." *Trials* 13 (1):173.

Kingori, Patricia. 2015. "The 'empty choice': A sociological examination of choosing medical research participation in resource-limited sub-Saharan Africa." *Current Sociology* 63 (5):763–778.

Kirby, David A. 2002. "Are we not men? The horror of eugenics in *The Island of Dr. Moreau.*" *Paradoxa: Studies in World Literary Genres* 17:93–108.

Knorr-Cetina, Karin. 1999. *Epistemic cultures: How the sciences make knowledge.* Cambridge, MA: Harvard University Press.

Koenig, Barbara A., Sandra Soo-Jin Lee, and Sarah S. Richardson. 2008. *Revisiting race in a genomic age.* New Brunswick, NJ: Rutgers University Press.

Kolata, Gina. 2001a. "Johns Hopkins admits fault in fatal experiment." *New York Times,* July 17, A16.

Kolata, Gina. 2001b. "Johns Hopkins death brings halt to U.S.-financed human studies." *New York Times,* July 20, A1, A18.

Korieth, Karyn, and Steve Zisson. 2007. "Phase I market consolidates." *CenterWatch Monthly* 14 (1):1, 6–9.

Kumagai, Y., I. Fukazawa, T. Momma, H. Iijima, H. Takayanagi, N. Takemoto, and Y. Kikuchi. 2006. "A nationwide survey on serious adverse events in healthy volunteer studies in Japan." *Clinical Pharmacology and Therapeutics* 79 (2):P71–P71.

Kupetsky-Rincon, E. A., and W. K. Kraft. 2012. "Healthy volunteer registries and ethical research principles." *Clinical Pharmacology and Therapeutics* 91 (6):965–968.

Kwon, Jong Bum, and Carrie M. Lane, eds. 2016. *Anthropologies of unemployment: New perspectives on work and its absence.* Ithaca, NY: Cornell University Press.

Lacy, Karyn R. 2007. *Blue-chip black: Race, class, and status in the new black middle class.* Berkeley: University of California Press.

Lakoff, Andrew. 2005. *Pharmaceutical reason: Knowledge and value in global psychiatry.* New York: Cambridge University Press.

Lakoff, Andrew. 2007. "The right patients for the drug: Managing the placebo effect in antidepressant trials." *BioSocieties* 2 (1):57–71.

Lamont, Michèle, and Virág Molnár. 2001. "How blacks use consumption to shape their collective identity." *Journal of Consumer Culture* 1 (1):31–45.

Lamont, Michèle, Graziella Moraes Silva, Jessica Welburn, Joshua Guetzkow, Nissim Mizrachi, Hanna Herzog, and Elisa Reis. 2016. *Getting respect: Responding to stigma and discrimination in the United States, Brazil, and Israel.* Princeton, NJ: Princeton University Press.

Largent, Emily A., Christine Grady, Franklin G. Miller, and Alan Wertheimer. 2012. "Money, coercion, and undue inducement: Attitudes about payments to research participants." *IRB: Ethics and Human Research* 34 (1):1–8.

Latour, Bruno, and Steve Woolgar. 1979. *Laboratory life: The construction of scientific facts.* Princeton, NJ: Princeton University Press.

Lederer, Susan E. 1995. *Subjected to science: Human experimentation in America before the Second World War.* Baltimore, MD: Johns Hopkins University Press.

Lemmens, Trudo, and Carl Elliott. 1999. "Guinea pigs on the payroll: The ethics of paying research subjects." *Accountability in Research* 7 (1):3–20.

Lemmens, Trudo, and Carl Elliott. 2001. "Justice for the professional guinea pig." *American Journal of Bioethics* 1 (2):51–53.

Lemmens, Trudo, and Benjamin Freedman. 2000. "Ethics review for sale? Conflict of interest and commercial research review boards." *Milbank Quarterly* 78 (4):547–584.

Leonardi, Paul. 2012. *Car crashes without cars: Lessons about simulation technology and organizational change from automotive design.* Cambridge, MA: MIT Press.

Leonelli, Sabina. 2012. "When humans are the exception: Cross-species databases at the interface of biological and clinical research." *Social Studies of Science* 42 (2):214–236.

Lerman, Amy E. 2013. *The modern prison paradox: Politics, punishment, and social community.* New York: Cambridge University Press.

Lewis, Jamie, Paul Atkinson, Jean Harrington, and Katie Featherstone. 2012. "Representation and practical accomplishment in the laboratory: When is an animal model good-enough?" *Sociology* 47 (4):776–792.

Lidz, Charles W., Paul S. Appelbaum, Thomas Grisso, and Michelle Renaud. 2004. "Therapeutic misconception and the appreciation of risks in clinical trials." *Social Science and Medicine* 58 (9):1689–1697.

Light, Donald, ed. 2010. *The risks of prescription drugs.* New York: Columbia University Press.

Light, Donald, and Joel Lexchin. 2012. "Pharmaceutical R&D: What do we get for all that money?" *British Medical Journal* 345:e4348.

Light, Donald W., Joel Lexchin, and Jonathan J. Darrow. 2013. "Institutional corruption of pharmaceuticals and the myth of safe and effective drugs." *Journal of Law, Medicine and Ethics* 41 (3):590–600.

Light, Donald W., and Antonio F. Maturo. 2015. *Good pharma: The public-health model of the Mario Negri Institute.* New York: Palgrave Macmillan.

Light, Donald W., and Rebecca Warburton. 2011. "Demythologizing the high costs of pharmaceutical research." *BioSocieties* 6 (1):34–50.

Longino, Helen E. 1994. "In search of feminist epistemology." *Monist* 77 (4):472–485.

Lury, Celia. 2011. *Consumer culture*, 2nd edition. Malden, MA: Polity.

Marchevsky, Alejandra, and Jeanne Theoharis. 2006. *Not working: Latina immigrants, low-wage jobs, and the failure of welfare reform.* New York: New York University Press.

Marks, Jonathan. 2013. "The nature/culture of genetic facts." *Annual Review of Anthropology* 42:247–267.

Matory, J. Lorand. 2015. *Stigma and culture: Last-place anxiety in black America.* Chicago: University of Chicago Press.

Mazure, Carolyn M., and Daniel P. Jones. 2015. "Twenty years and still counting: Including women as participants and studying sex and gender in biomedical research." *BMC Women's Health* 15 (1):94.

McGoey, Linsey. 2009. "Pharmaceutical controversies and the performative value of uncertainty." *Science as Culture* 18 (2):151–164.

McGoey, Linsey. 2012a. "The logic of strategic ignorance." *British Journal of Sociology* 63 (3):553–76.

McGoey, Linsey. 2012b. "Strategic unknowns: Towards a sociology of ignorance." *Economy and Society* 41 (1):1–16.

McGonigle, Paul, and Bruce Ruggeri. 2014. "Animal models of human disease: Challenges in enabling translation." *Biochemical Pharmacology* 87 (1):162–171.

McManus, Lisa, Arlene M. Davis, Rebecca L. Forcier, and Jill A. Fisher. 2019. "Appraising harm in phase I trials: Healthy volunteers' accounts of adverse events." *Journal of Law, Medicine and Ethics* 47 (2):323–333.

McManus, Lisa, and Jill A. Fisher. 2018. "To report or not to report: Exploring healthy volunteers' rationales for disclosing adverse events in phase I drug trials." *AJOB Empirical Bioethics* 9 (2):82–90.

McPherson, Miller, Lynn Smith-Lovin, and Matthew E. Brashears. 2006. "Social isolation in America: Changes in core discussion networks over two decades." *American Sociological Review* 71 (3):353–375.

Meibohm, Bernd, Ingrid Beierle, and Hartmut Derendorf. 2002. "How important are gender differences in pharmacokinetics?" *Clinical Pharmacokinetics* 41 (5):329–342.

Merchant, Carolyn. 1990. *The death of nature: Women, ecology, and the Scientific Revolution*. San Francisco: Harper and Row.

Miller, Franklin G. 2003. "Ethical issues in research with healthy volunteers: Risk-benefit assessment." *Clinical Pharmacology and Therapeutics* 74 (6):513–515.

Miller, Margaret Ann. 2001. "Gender-based differences in the toxicity of pharmaceuticals: The Food and Drug Administration's perspective." *International Journal of Toxicology* 20 (3):149–152.

Mirowski, Philip. 2011. *Science-mart: Privatizing American science*. Cambridge, MA: Harvard University Press.

Mitford, Jessica. 1973. *Kind and usual punishment: The prison business*. New York: Knopf.

Monahan, Torin, and Jill A. Fisher. 2010. "Benefits of 'observer effects': Lessons from the field." *Qualitative Research* 10 (3):357–376.

Monahan, Torin, and Jill A. Fisher. 2015a. "'I'm still a hustler': Entrepreneurial responses to precarity by participants in phase I clinical trials." *Economy and Society* 44 (4):545–566.

Monahan, Torin, and Jill A. Fisher. 2015b. "Strategies for obtaining access to secretive or guarded organizations." *Journal of Contemporary Ethnography* 44 (6):709–736.

Montgomery, Catherine M. 2017. "Clinical trials and the drive to material standardisation." *Science and Technology Studies* 30 (4):30–44.

Montoya, Michael J. 2011. *Making the Mexican diabetic: Race, science, and the genetics of inequality*. Berkeley: University of California Press.

Morris, Edward W. 2010. "'Snitches end up in ditches' and other cautionary tales." *Journal of Contemporary Criminal Justice* 26 (3):254–272.

Murphy, Michelle. 2012. *Seizing the means of reproduction: Entanglements of feminism, health, and technoscience*. Durham, NC: Duke University Press.

Mwaria, Cheryl. 2005. "From conspiracy theories to clinical trials: Questioning the role of race and culture versus racism and poverty in medical decision making." In *Gender, race, class, and health: Intersectional approaches*, edited by Amy J. Schulz and Leith Mullings, 289–312. San Francisco: Jossey-Bass.

Natapoff, Alexandra. 2009. *Snitching: Criminal informants and the erosion of American justice*. New York: New York University Press.

National Commission. 1976. *Research involving prisoners: Report and recommendations*. Edited by National Commission for the Protection of Human Subjects of Biomedical and Behavioral Research. Washington, DC.

National Commission. 1979. *The Belmont report: Ethical principles and guidelines for the protection of human subjects of research*. Edited by National Commission for the Protection of Human Subjects of Biomedical and Behavioral Research. Washington, DC.

Nelson, Alondra. 2011. *Body and soul: The Black Panther Party and the fight against medical discrimination*. Minneapolis: University of Minnesota Press.

Nelson, Nicole C. 2013. "Modeling mouse, human, and discipline: Epistemic scaffolds in animal behavior genetics." *Social Studies of Science* 43 (1):3–29.

Newman, Katherine S. 2006. *Chutes and ladders: Navigating the low-wage labor market*. New York: Russell Sage Foundation and Harvard University Press.

Newman, Katherine S. 2009. *No shame in my game: The working poor in the inner city*. New York: Vintage.

NIH Office of Research on Women's Health. 2017. *Report of the NIH Advisory Committee on Research on Women's Health, fiscal years 2015–2016*. Bethesda, MD: US Department of Health and Human Services, Public Health Service, National Institutes of Health.

O'Neill, Robert D. 2006. "'Frankenstein to futurism': Representations of organ donation and transplantation in popular culture." *Transplantation Reviews* 20 (4):222–230.

Osterberg, Lars, and Terrence Blaschke. 2005. "Adherence to medication." *New England Journal of Medicine* 353 (5):487–497.

Paap, Kris. 2006. *Working construction: Why white working-class men put themselves—and the labor movement—in harm's way*. Ithaca, NY: Cornell University Press.

Pager, Devah. 2008. *Marked: Race, crime, and finding work in an era of mass incarceration*. Chicago: University of Chicago Press.

Pardridge, William M. 2009. "Alzheimer's disease drug development and the problem of the blood-brain barrier." *Alzheimer's and Dementia* 5 (5):427–432.

Pearce, Philip L. 2005. "The role of relationships in the tourist experience." In *Global Tourism*, 3rd edition, edited by William F. Theobald, 103–122. New York: Elsevier.

Peterson, Kristin. 2014. *Speculative markets: Drug circuits and derivative life in Nigeria*. Durham, NC: Duke University Press.

Petryna, Adriana. 2009. *When experiments travel: Clinical trials and the global search for human subjects*. Princeton, NJ: Princeton University Press.

Petty, JuLeigh, and Carol A. Heimer. 2011. "Extending the rails: How research reshapes clinics." *Social Studies of Science* 41 (3):337–360.

Phillips, Trisha. 2011. "Exploitation in payments to research subjects." *Bioethics* 25 (4):209–219.

PhRMA. 2016. 2016 profile: Biopharmaceutical research industry. Washington, DC. http://phrma-docs.phrma.org.

Pollock, Anne. 2012. *Medicating race: Heart disease and durable preoccupations with difference*. Durham, NC: Duke University Press.

Prasad, Amit. 2009. "Capitalizing disease: Biopolitics of drug trials in India." *Theory, Culture and Society* 26 (5):1–29.

Prescott, Heather Munro. 2002. "Using the student body: College and university students as research subjects in the United States during the twentieth century." *Journal of the History of Medicine* 57 (1):3–38.

Pugh, Allison J. 2015. *The tumbleweed society: Working and caring in an age of insecurity*. New York: Oxford University Press.

Rademaker, Marius. 2001. "Do women have more adverse drug reactions?" *American Journal of Clinical Dermatology* 2 (6):349–351.

Rader, Karen Ann. 2004. *Making mice: Standardizing animals for American biomedical research, 1900–1955*. Princeton, NJ: Princeton University Press.

Rajan, Kaushik Sunder. 2007. "Experimental values: Indian clinical trials and surplus health." *New Left Review* 45 (May–June):67–88.

Rajan, Kaushik Sunder. 2017. *Pharmocracy: Value, politics, and knowledge in global biomedicine*. Durham, NC: Duke University Press.

Reardon, Jenny. 2009. *Race to the finish: Identity and governance in an age of genomics*. Princeton, NJ: Princeton University Press.

Redfearn, Suz. 2012. "Cetero CEO: Sale is forthcoming—until then it's business as usual despite bankruptcy filing." *CenterWatch Weekly* 16 (13):1, 4.

Redfearn, Suz. 2013. "PRACS Institute closes doors abruptly, locking out employees; chapter 7 imminent." *CenterWatch Weekly* 17 (12):1, 4.

Redfearn, Suz. 2015. "Global clinical trials: Calling the hype to task." *CenterWatch Weekly* 22 (9):1, 8–13.

Redstone Akresh, Ilana. 2006. "Occupational mobility among legal immigrants to the United States." *International Migration Review* 40 (4):854–884.

Resnik, David B., and Greg Koski. 2011. "A national registry for healthy volunteers in phase 1 clinical trials." *JAMA* 305 (12):1236–1237.

Resnik, David B., and David J. McCann. 2015. "Deception by research participants." *New England Journal of Medicine* 373 (13):1192–1193.

Restivo, Sal. 1994. *Science, society, and values: Toward a sociology of objectivity*. Allentown, PA: Lehigh University Press.

Reverby, Susan M. 2009. *Examining Tuskegee: The infamous syphilis study and its legacy*. Chapel Hill: University of North Carolina Press.

Reverby, Susan M. 2011. "'Normal exposure' and inoculation syphilis: A PHS 'Tuskegee' doctor in Guatemala, 1946–1948." *Journal of Policy History* 23 (1):6–28.

Reverby, Susan M., ed. 2000. *Tuskegee's truths: Rethinking the Tuskegee syphilis study*. Chapel Hill: University of North Carolina Press.

Ribas, Vanessa. 2015. *On the line: Slaughterhouse lives and the making of the New South*. Berkeley: University of California Press.

Rosen, Christine. 2006. "Are we worthy of our kitchens?" *New Atlantis* 11 (Winter):75–86.

Rothman, David J., and Sheila M. Rothman. 1984. *The Willowbrook wars*. New York: Harper-Collins.

Salami, Bukola, and Sioban Nelson. 2014. "The downward occupational mobility of internationally educated nurses to domestic workers." *Nursing Inquiry* 21 (2):153–161.

Sandıkcı, Özlem, and Güliz Ger. 2013. "Stigma, identity, and consumption." In *The Routledge companion to identity and consumption*, edited by Ayalla Ruvio and Russell W. Belk, 111–118. New York: Routledge.

Sarewitz, Daniel R. 1996. *Frontiers of illusion: Science, technology, and the politics of progress*. Philadelphia: Temple University Press.

Sariola, Salla, Roger Jeffery, Amar Jesani, and Gerard Porter. 2019. "How civil society organisations changed the regulation of clinical trials in India." *Science as Culture* 28 (2):200–222.

Schor, Juliet B. 1999. *The overspent American: Why we want what we don't need*. New York: HarperCollins.

Schor, Juliet B. 2017. "Does the sharing economy increase inequality within the eighty percent?: Findings from a qualitative study of platform providers." *Cambridge Journal of Regions, Economy and Society* 10 (2):263–279.

Scott, Susie. 2010. "Revisiting the total institution: Performative regulation in the reinventive institution." *Sociology* 44 (2):213–231.

Shah, Sonia. 2006. *The body hunters: How the drug industry tests its products on the world's poorest patients*. New York: The New Press.

Shamir, Ronen. 2005. "Corporate responsibility and the South African drug wars: Outline of a new frontier for cause lawyers." In *The worlds cause lawyers make: Structure and agency in legal practice*, edited by Austin Sarat and Stuart A. Scheingold, 37–62. Stanford, CA: Stanford University Press.

Shavers-Hornaday, Vickie L., Charles F. Lynch, Leon F. Burmeister, and James C. Torner. 1997. "Why are African Americans under-represented in medical research studies? Impediments to participation." *Ethnicity and Health* 2 (1–2):31–45.

Shim, Janet K. 2014. *Heart-sick: The politics of risk, inequality, and heart disease*. New York: New York University Press.

Shostak, Sara. 2013. *Exposed science: Genes, the environment, and the politics of population health*. Berkeley: University of California Press.

Sibille, M., N. Deigat, A. Janin, S. Kirkesseli, and D. Vital Durand. 1998. "Adverse events in phase-I studies: A report in 1015 healthy volunteers." *European Journal of Clinical Pharmacology* 54:13–20.

Sibille, Michel, Yves Donazzolo, Franck Lecoz, and Emmanuel Krupka. 2006. "After the London tragedy, is it still possible to consider phase I is safe?" *British Journal of Clinical Pharmacology* 62 (4):502–3.

Silva, Jennifer M. 2013. *Coming up short: Working-class adulthood in an age of uncertainty*. New York: Oxford University Press.

Sismondo, Sergio, and Jeremy A. Greene, eds. 2015. *The pharmaceutical studies reader*. Malden, MA: Wiley Blackwell.

Slade, Giles. 2006. *Made to break: Technology and obsolescence in America*. Cambridge, MA: Harvard University Press.

Smith, Andrea. 2005. *Conquest: Sexual violence and American Indian genocide*. Cambridge, MA: South End Press.

Standing, Guy. 2011. *The precariat: The new dangerous class*. New York: Bloomsbury Publishing.

Star, Susan Leigh, and James R. Griesemer. 1989. "Institutional ecology, 'translations' and boundary objects: Amateurs and professionals in Berkeley's Museum of Vertebrate Zoology, 1907–39." *Social Studies of Science* 19 (3):387–420.

Stark, Laura. 2012. *Behind closed doors: IRBs and the making of ethical research*. Chicago: University of Chicago Press.

Stark, Laura. 2018. "Contracting health: Procurement contracts, total institutions, and the problem of virtuous suffering in post-war human experiment." *Social History of Medicine* 31 (4):818-846.

Stark, Laura. Forthcoming. *The normals: A people's history*. Chicago: University of Chicago Press.

Stein, C. Michael. 2003. "Managing risk in healthy subjects participating in clinical research." *Clinical Pharmacology and Therapeutics* 74 (6):511–512.

Strom, Brian L. 2006. "How the US drug safety system should be changed." *JAMA* 295 (17):2072–2075.

Suls, Jerry, and Ladd Wheeler, eds. 2000. *Handbook of social comparison: Theory and research*. New York: Kluwer Academic/Plenum Publishers.

Thernstrom, Stephan, and Abigail Thernstrom. 2009. *America in black and white: One nation, indivisible*. New York: Simon and Schuster.

Thorne, Deborah, and Leon Anderson. 2006. "Managing the stigma of personal bankruptcy." *Sociological Focus* 39 (2):77–97.

Timmermans, Stefan, and Tara McKay. 2009. "Clinical trials as treatment option: Bioethics and health care disparities in substance dependency." *Social Science and Medicine* 69 (12):1784–90.

Tishler, Carl L., and Suzanne Bartholomae. 2002. "The recruitment of normal healthy volunteers: A review of the literature on the use of financial incentives." *Journal of Clinical Pharmacology* 42:365–375.

Tishler, Carl L., and Suzanne Bartholomae. 2003. "Repeat participation among normal healthy research volunteers: Professional guinea pigs in clinical trials?" *Perspectives in Biology and Medicine* 46 (4):508–520.

Tolich, Martin. 2010. "What if institutional review boards (IRBs) treated healthy volunteers in clinical trials as their clients?" *Australasian Medical Journal* 3 (12):767–771.

Traweek, Sharon. 1988. *Beamtimes and lifetimes: The world of high energy physicists*. Cambridge, MA: Harvard University Press.

True, Gala, Leslie B. Alexander, and Kenneth A. Richman. 2011. "Misbehaviors of front-line research personnel and the integrity of community-based research." *Journal of Empirical Research on Human Research Ethics* 6 (2):3–12.

Tunis, Sean R., Daniel B. Stryer, and Carolyn M. Clancy. 2003. "Practical clinical trials: Increasing the value of clinical research for decision making in clinical and health policy." *JAMA* 290 (12):1624–1632.

Turner, Patricia A. 1993. *I heard it through the grapevine: Rumor in African-American culture*. Berkeley: University of California Press.

Twitchell, James B. 2012. *Living it up: Our love affair with luxury*. New York: Columbia University Press.

US Food and Drug Administration (FDA). 1998. "Information sheet guidance for institutional review boards (IRBs), clinical investigators, and sponsors: Payment to research subjects." http://www.fda.gov/.

US General Accounting Office (GAO). 2001. "Drug safety: Most drugs withdrawn in recent years had greater health risks for women." Washington, DC.

US National Institutes of Health (NIH). 2005. "NIH policy manual chapter 3014—Human research protection program." http://oma1.od.nih.gov.

Upadhyay, Ravi Kant. 2014. "Drug delivery systems, CNS protection, and the blood brain barrier." *BioMed Research International*, Article ID 869269.

Valdez, Zulema. 2011. *The new entrepreneurs: How race, class, and gender shape American enterprise*. Stanford, CA: Stanford University Press.

Van Gerven, Joop, and Milton Bonelli. 2018. "Commentary on the EMA guideline on strategies to identify and mitigate risks for first-in-human and early clinical trials with investigational medicinal products." *British Journal of Clinical Pharmacology* 84 (7):1401–1409.

VanderWalde, Ari, and Seth Kurzban. 2011. "Paying human subjects in research: Where are we, how did we get here, and now what?" *Journal of Law, Medicine and Ethics* 39 (3):543–558.

Vaughan, Diane. 1996. *The Challenger launch decision: Risky technology, culture and deviance at NASA*. Chicago: University of Chicago Press.

Wadmann, Sarah, and Klaus Hoeyer. 2014. "Beyond the 'therapeutic misconception': Research, care and moral friction." *BioSocieties* 9 (1):3–23.

Walker, Rebecca L. 2006. "Human and animal subjects of research: The moral significance of respect versus welfare." *Theoretical Medicine and Bioethics* 27 (4):305–331.

Walker, Rebecca L. 2007. "The good life for non-human animals: What virtue requires of humans." In *Working virtue: Virtue ethics and contemporary moral problems*, edited by Rebecca L. Walker and Philip J. Ivanhoe, 173–189. New York: Oxford University Press.

Walker, Rebecca L. 2016. "Beyond primates: Research protections and animal moral value." *Hastings Center Report* 46 (4):28–30.

Ward, Jamie. 2016. *Veteran friendships across lifetimes: Brothers and sisters in arms*. New York: Rowman and Littlefield.

Weil, Kari. 2012. *Thinking animals: Why animal studies now?* New York: Columbia University Press.

Weinstein, Matthew. 2010. *Bodies out of control: Rethinking science texts*. New York: Peter Lang.

Wentzell, Emily A. 2013. *Maturing masculinities: Aging, chronic illness, and Viagra in Mexico*. Durham, NC: Duke University Press.

Wertheimer, Alan. 1999. *Exploitation*. Princeton, NJ: Princeton University Press.

White, Naomi Rosh, and Peter B. White. 2009. "The comfort of strangers: Tourists in the Australian Outback." *International Journal of Tourism Research* 11 (2):143–153.

Whitmarsh, Ian. 2008. *Biomedical ambiguity: Race, asthma, and the contested meaning of genetic research in the Caribbean*. Ithaca, NY: Cornell University Press.

Whitmarsh, Ian, and David S. Jones. 2010. *What's the use of race?: Modern governance and the biology of difference*. Cambridge, MA: MIT Press.

Wilkinson, Martin, and Andrew Moore. 1997. "Inducement in research." *Bioethics* 11 (5):373–389.

Will, Catherine, and Tiago Moreira. 2016. *Medical proofs, social experiments: Clinical trials in shifting contexts*. New York: Routledge.

Williams, Quintin, and Jill A. Fisher. 2018. "Captive to the clinic: Phase I clinical trials as temporal total institutions." *Sociological Inquiry* 88 (4):724–748.

Williams, Simon J., Paul Martin, and Jonathan Gabe. 2011. "The pharmaceuticalisation of society? A framework for analysis." *Sociology of Health and Illness* 33 (5):710–725.

Wilson, William Julius. 2010. *More than just race: Being black and poor in the inner city*. New York: W. W. Norton.

Won, Christina S., Nicholas H. Oberlies, and Mary F. Paine. 2012. "Mechanisms underlying food-drug interactions: Inhibition of intestinal metabolism and transport." *Pharmacology and Therapeutics* 136 (2):186–201.

Wood, Alastair J. J., and Janet Darbyshire. 2006. "Injury to research volunteers: The clinical-research nightmare." *New England Journal of Medicine* 354 (18):1869–1871.

INDEX

Abadie, Roberto, 264n9

Academic Phase I: AE reporting issues at, 175–76; amenities lacking at, 110; building characteristics and location of, *103*, 104–5; demographics, *34*; hepatitis C study at, 230–34; interpersonal relationships valued at, 110–11; postponement of study at, 282n2; sleep paralysis experienced at, 179–80; time-points at, 149; training mission of, 109–10, 126; views of, 109–11. *See also* East Coast participants

addiction, 270n9

ADHD study. *See* attention deficit hyperactivity disorder study

adverse events (AEs): during Alzheimer's disease study, 123–24, 197–98; coding, 280n14; counter-narratives to, 197–98; death from, 182–83; from drug dose size, 211–13; ethics in relation to, 183; in everyday lives, 5; experiential information on, 195–97; financial compensation correlation with, 213–16; goal of generating, 135; healthy volunteers informed on risk of, 183–87; from HIV/AIDS medications, 216–17; information shared on, 8; language surrounding, 139; from lumbar punctures, 208, 220–21; meta-analysis on, 181–82; from nocebo effect, 160; Phase I trials for measuring, 2–3; protective power of health against, 225–28; from psychotropic medications, 217–19;

rarity of serious, 136; self-reporting of, 275n9; serious, 137–39; sleep paralysis as, 179–80; spinal headaches as, 220–21, 281n4; as trade-off, 254; validity concerns with reporting, 170–77

advocacy, registry, 264n8

AEs. *See* adverse events

affected patients, 2, 15, 132

alternates, 27–28, 142

altruism, 74, 271n11

Alzheimer's disease study, 281n1; AEs during, 123–24, 197–98; lumbar punctures for, 206–10

anarchist group, 264n9

Angell, Marcia, 267n25

anti-immigration narratives, 91–92

anxiety: physical manifestations of, 245–46; qualification, 234–35; risk of disqualification causing, 24–25; of women research staff, 276n16

Arizona Senate Bill 1070, 91

attention deficit hyperactivity disorder (ADHD) study, 218

bag checks procedure, 22–24

behavior: comparisons of gender, 269n14; deceptive, 18, 166; health, 7, 225–28, 238, 244–47, 248–50; inappropriate, 45–46; incentives for good, 40–41; serial participants on peers, 279n10

Berger, Michele, 264n10

stigma (*cont.*)
    264n10; locating and theorizing, 10–14;
    power of, 12; reinforcement of, 127;
    rejection of, 65; social relations,
    42–47; unemployment, 60. *See also*
    imbricated stigma
strategic ignorance, 277n2
structural coercion, 266n13
STS. *See* science and technology studies
student loans, 62–63, 67
student participation, 4
study design. *See* research participation
    criteria; research protocols
study fatigue, 40
study inputs, 132, 135
study outputs, 132, 134–35
subversive subjects, 18, 267n24
suicide, 182
survival-strategy entrepreneurs, 53

therapeutic misconceptions, 267n19
time-points, 149
total institution concept, 264n7
tourism studies, 269n11
training mission, 109–10, 126
transgendered people, 46–47
transparency, 22
transposition concept, 266n17
travel: by East Coast participants, 78;
    financial compensation for, 65–66;
    reflection on, 49–51; research clinic
    closures causing, 116–17
trust: in drug development safeguards,
    201–2; in IRB research oversight, 202–
    3; physician-investigators on, 167; in
    PK data, 172–74; of repeat participants,
    145, 150; in research enterprise, 200–
    203; in research staff, 201
t-shirt study color, 27, 140, 147
Tuskegee Syphilis Study, 11, 268n4, 273n5

undone science, 277n2
unemployment stigma, 60

vaccine studies, 242–43
Valdez, Zulema, 53, 269n1
validity problems: with AE report-
    ing, 170–77; criteria-based, 153–54,
    157–58; downplaying, 177–78; in
    later-phase trials, 279n8; masking,
    151–52; as organizational devi-
    ance, 277n1; protocol-based, 158–61;
    from protocol inflexibility, 163–66;
    race/ethnicity-based, 155–57; from
    rule-breaking model, 166–70; serial
    participants as, 161–62; sex-based,
    153–55
value: appreciation of consent form,
    192–94; of health, 248–50; of healthy
    volunteers in drug development, 15; of
    interpersonal relationships, 110–11; of
    repeat participants, 132; underestima-
    tion of consent form, 191
value extraction, 271n4
veins: criteria for, 143; ideal, 275n14; over-
    use of, 243–44; women disadvantages
    regarding, 275n12
venipuncture marks, 68
vital signs: fluctuations in, 163; manipula-
    tion of, 165–66
vulnerability: of immigrants, 95–96; of
    sexual minorities, 46–47; of women,
    44–46

war stories, 210–11. *See also* risk filters
washout period: definition of, 7; disregard
    for, 7, 166–68; lying about, 272n6; as
    recruitment obstacle, 151
wealth, 1, 7
welfare queen, 264n10
Wertheimer, Alan, 271n3
West Coast participants: anger of, 92;
    clinical-trial culture comparisons
    to, 97–99; clinical-trial culture of,
    90–97; demographics of, 35–36; fear
    from, 94; on financial compensa-
    tion, 93–95; gratitude of, 95; on Great

Jill A. Fisher, PhD, is Associate Professor in the Department of Social Medicine and Center for Bioethics at the University of North Carolina at Chapel Hill. She has published more than 50 articles and book chapters, is the author of *Medical Research for Hire: The Political Economy of Pharmaceutical Clinical Trials,* and is the editor of *Gender and the Science of Difference: Cultural Politics of Contemporary Science and Medicine.*